ALL THE SWEETER

ALL THE SWEETER

Families Share
Their Stories of
Adopting from
Foster Care

SHE WRITES PRESS

Published May 2019
Printed in the United States of America
Print ISBN: 978-1-63152-495-0
E-ISBN: 978-1-63152-496-7
Library of Congress Control Number: 2018967213

For information, address:
She Writes Press
1569 Solano Ave #546
Berkeley, CA 94707

Interior design by Tabitha Lahr

She Writes Press is a division of SparkPoint Studio, LLC.

Names and identifying characteristics have been changed to protect the
privacy of certain individuals.

To the families who shared their stories.
Thank you.

CONTENTS

INTRODUCTION

....

In the early 2000s, as a Peace Corps health volunteer in Malawi, I witnessed many children lose their parents to AIDS. Seeing the overwhelming need for families to care for these children opened my eyes to the possibility of adopting. Living in San Francisco a decade later, I volunteered on the board of directors for AASK (Adopt a Special Kid), a fost-adopt agency started in 1972 by Bob and Dorothy DeBolt, who pioneered the idea that a family didn't need to be a man and a woman parenting children who resembled them. AASK supported LGBTQ parents, single parents, and transracial adoptions and fought for all children in the US foster care system, especially those with disabilities. AASK's mission quickly captured my heart and cemented my desire to one day create my own forever family with the help of the foster-to-adopt process.

As I began to consider starting a family, I sought out resources to help me understand the foster-to-adopt system. I wanted to hear families' stories, understand whether any fears I had were valid, and, if so, how families managed through their challenges. While there are many valuable resources available, I didn't find any quite like what I wanted. So, when I had an opportunity to spend a year abroad, I paused my career and wrote *All the Sweeter*.

Researching this project, I read more than thirty insightful books and a much larger number of blog posts and websites on adoption-related subjects: transracial adoption, adoption of older children, adoption of traumatized children, how to talk to adopted children about adoption, foster care, and child development. I reference and recommend many of these in this book. I hope that the forever-family stories contained herein will complement these other resources and will ultimately inspire parents to consider building their families by adopting through the US foster care system.

My greatest hope for this book is that potential parents read these family stories and become inspired to fost-adopt. The families in these stories exhibit endless tenacity, love, and selflessness. As a result of caring for their children, one family received hundreds of support letters from colleagues, teachers, and friends and discovered a new depth of compassion in their community. One mom, after a tough parenting moment, became emotional when she overheard her older adopted son lovingly explain to his adopted sister her adoption story. Another family, who didn't think twice about receiving affection from their four biological daughters, experienced surprise and hard-earned joy when their adopted daughter returned a hug.

Stories like these are inspiring, but raising children (adopted from foster care or not) can also push parents to their limits. My greatest fear is that potential parents will read these family stories and find one that scares them out of taking their next step to adopt children from foster care. In her book, *Instant Mom*, actress and adoptive mom Nia Vardalos underscored this fear for me when she described her thoughts as she considered adoption. She wrote, "I was surrounded by positive stories of adoption, but of course the scary ones kept me up at night. . . . It's just human nature to pick up on the things that cause us anxiety. I could hear a hundred fantastic adoption stories in a row and then be stopped in my tracks by the negative one."[1]

While some aspects of these stories might be scary and initially discouraging, they reflect a real potential situation. Including these difficult realities allows families to learn from them. Families can then choose to either develop boundaries to avoid such situations or develop strategies for addressing these situations head-on. Throughout these stories, families emphasize that either of these choices is okay. Thankfully, Vardalos overcame her anxieties, adopted a daughter from foster care, and wrote a *New York Times* best-selling book about her experience.

All the Sweeter tells the stories of families who have adopted one or more children from the US foster care system. Each of the families interviewed has a dedicated chapter in which at least one representative tells his or her family's adoption story—highs, lows, and everything in between. *All the Sweeter* provides the reader with information through its subjects' actual firsthand experiences. During one of the family interviews, the mom, who is a reporter, said that the highlight of her foster care training was when adoptive parents came in to tell their stories. She said, "We all love hearing stories; it's part of being human. . . . The names have been changed, and maybe some of the details, but these are real stories and that's why it's powerful."

Families who read *All the Sweeter* will receive information regarding the potentially complicated adoption process and an intimate glance into the lives of families raising these children. The families interviewed understand that professionals do their absolute best in a very complicated system. However, if professionals are eager and able to improve the system, *All the Sweeter* will shed light on areas where families desperately need assistance.

Woven through these stories are topical chapters that take a deeper dive into the common challenges in which these families find themselves. These five chapters weave together families' experiences with information from literature related to foster care and adoption. The topics include helping children understand foster care and adoption, diverse families changing what we consider "normal" family structure, transracial adoption, raising a child with a history of trauma, and relationships between birth and adoptive families. These chapters scratch the surface of summarizing research, experience, and literature on these topics. Their purpose is to serve as a starting point for continued research, should families want to learn more about navigating these subjects. They also reference additional sources that I encourage readers to explore.

All the Sweeter provides a resource to families considering adoption, families in the process of adoption, and families postadoption of children from foster care. Each year, more than fifty thousand children are adopted from the US foster care system.[2] My interviews intentionally include families from diverse backgrounds in such areas as religion, sexual orientation, marital status, race, number of biological and adopted children in their families, child age, and parent age. Any family considering adoption will find more than one family situation in this book with similarities to their own. Those considering adoption from foster care will have many of their questions answered, those in the process of adoption will be better able to prepare for their future family, and those post adoption will learn from others' experiences. My ultimate goal with this book is to facilitate a better life for foster children.

Process

I interviewed the majority of the families in person. They come from four different US states; if an in-person interview wasn't possible, we spoke over the phone or via Skype or FaceTime. I found the families through personal networks, including friends, my board service, websites for parents, foster care classes, and work. I had a long list of questions for the families, which they reviewed ahead of our interview. However, I often started by asking the families to tell me their story and needed to ask only clarifying questions afterward.

In an effort to present the families' chapters in an oral-history style, I recorded and then transcribed each interview. Once I drafted a chapter, I sent it to the family to check it for accuracy and to reaffirm their willingness to share their story. Few families removed any information. Those who did usually did so in an effort to protect their anonymity.

I've kept the families anonymous to protect the identities of the children in the stories and have used pseudonyms throughout, as well as removed other identifying details. Each chapter includes a diagram intended to clarify the relationships between the people mentioned in that chapter. The diagram does not necessarily include the many people who have been involved in, have supported, or are considered family by these families.

Why Now?

Since 2000, the number of children adopted from the US foster care system has hovered between 50,000 and 60,000.[3] In 2017, the latest year for which published data exist (as of 2019), 59,430 foster children found their forever families. As the number of children available for adoption hovered consistently over 100,000 between 2000 and 2016,[4] the number of children adopted would ideally increase—a possibility, given the potential increased interest of many families in the United States.

Specifically, women continue to put off childbearing until later ages. In 2015, 11 births of every 1,000 were to women between the ages of 40 and 44.[5] This number has doubled since 1990, when it was 5.5. When some women find they are not able to bear children (fertility decreases after age 30 and declines rapidly around age 37–38),[6] adoption becomes a popular option for fulfilling their dream of parenthood. In addition, according to several researchers, "interest in adoption by sexual minorities has grown rapidly over the years, especially as policies, regulations, and laws preventing or discouraging them from adopting have been overturned."[7]

However, as interest in adopting children increases, so do the barriers to private domestic adoptions and intercountry adoptions. According to a 2009 Centers for Disease Control and Prevention Study, fewer than 7,000 infants (1 percent of those born between 1996 and 2002) are placed for adoption by never-married mothers in the United States each year. This is down from 9 percent of infants born prior to 1973.[8] Furthermore, intercountry adoptions have dropped drastically since 1999, from a high of 22,989 in 2004 to a low of 5,647 in 2015.[9] According to the 2007 National Survey of Adoptive Parents, there are many causes of this decline, including China's imposition of restrictions on those allowed to adopt (including age, income, and weight restrictions), Russian criticism of cross-border adoption and promotion of domestic adoption (no adoptions in 2015, compared with a high of 5,862 in 2004),[10] and cross-country adoptions all but halted from Guatemala in 2007, due to concerns that the country was not abiding by Hague Convention guidelines.[11]

Finally, the cost of private domestic and international adoption continues to rise. The latest range, listed by Child-Welfare.gov, of $15,000–$50,000, places these adoption options out of financial reach for many. Costs for adopting from the US foster care system are minimal, and states can provide a one-time subsidy for nonrecurring costs, as well as, for eligible children, monthly payments to help cover their costs until they reach 18 (and sometimes 21).[12]

Therefore, as more people seek to adopt, as the barriers

to other types of adoption increase, and as the desire to adopt children from the US foster care system grows, I intend for *All the Sweeter* to be a resource to both potential adoptive families and the professionals who assist them.

Joys and Challenges

For many, adopting a child from foster care may not be the least complicated path to the joys of parenthood. When faced with the choice of a natural pregnancy or fost-adopt, the Boltons (chapter 17) chose to have biological children before adopting their daughter. Laura Bolton jokingly commented, "Ten bucks for a co-pay, and I could be pregnant in two weeks." Whether or not they can have biological children, many families, including the Boltons, feel drawn to adopt children from foster care. For others who have struggled through years of infertility treatments, like several families featured in this book, adopting a child through the US foster care system provides long-awaited fulfillment of their dreams of parenthood.

Adopting through foster care presents families with many types of challenges, from complicated interactions with overburdened social workers to the possibility of adopting a child with special needs. However, while meeting, interviewing, and sharing meals with the families featured in this book, I witnessed parents successfully navigate situations I wouldn't have dreamed possible. These parents established boundaries during their journey to ensure their own health, created unbreakable family bonds with foster parents, found unexpected empathy for and relationships with birth parents, partnered with schools and doctors to wean their children off harmful medications, strengthened relationships with their spouses and biological children, and served as examples to friends and neighbors of the many ways to define a family.

People seek and find growth through challenges in many aspects of life—the extreme athlete who summits the world's tallest peaks comes to mind. For parents who adopt foster children, the sometimes painful challenges of their journey not only result in the joy of a forever family but also unexpectedly make their lives and the lives of those around them all the sweeter.

CHAPTER 1:

THREE LANGUAGES, TWO RELIGIONS, ONE FAMILY: THE FLETCHER FAMILY

....

A fter ten years of marriage, Daniel and Mariana chose to adopt two sisters from the foster care system. Several years later, they had their biological son. All three children are learning Spanish, English, and Hebrew. They live near Mariana's parents and spend time with both extended families, who support them in numerous ways.

Daniel tells their family's story.

Adoption Story

Mariana and I married in the late '90s, a few years out of law school for me, a few years out of undergrad for her. We thought about having a family. In high school, my wife volunteered at an orphanage in her hometown. From day one, whether we could have children biologically or not, we knew we would adopt.

People in the Fletcher Family's Story

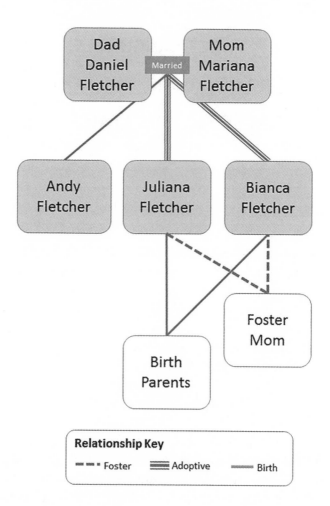

Just like everybody else, we didn't know if we'd ever be ready to have children. I worked for a legal nonprofit, making a ridiculously low salary, and my wife worked as a coordinator for a disease research and charity association, also not making much money. We pushed off children until our financial situation improved. If we conceived, great, but we weren't financially ready to adopt.

My wife had a condition that made it difficult for us to conceive. After about ten years of marriage, we considered fertility treatment. My wife said if it was really important to me, she would go through with it, but I'm cheap, and neither of us wanted chemicals in Mariana's body, and even if we did conceive, her extended family has a history of dying in childbirth. It was important to us to have children, but I didn't want to risk her health.

We also looked into adoption. We thought about Catholic charities and other private adoption agencies. Again my cheapness came out, and we also heard horror stories about bait and switches—you want a Chinese baby, and the next thing you know, you have a Laotian baby. There are companies that take your money and drag their feet and don't do anything. In the fost-adopt system, not only were costs extremely minimal, but there was so much support. The commitment to go through foster care licensing wasn't that bad—classes one night a week, and this kind of thing. We said, "Let's go for it." We entered the program and chose the "adoption" route, rather than doing "foster care and adoption."

We ruled out a lot of things right off the bat. We were not gung ho about an infant. We also knew we couldn't care for a child with certain characteristics, like fetal alcohol syndrome. However, because we couldn't conceive, we said, "Hey, let's do this all in one fell swoop." We checked the box to say we were fine and dandy with sibling groups.

We also learned that in our state, sibling groups are considered "special needs." Even if your kids are healthy, you still get the benefits that special needs children receive. The adoption assistance program provides a stipend per month, per child, to offset the cost of day care, as well as health insurance until the children turn eighteen.

After we applied for a sibling group, our county case-worker stayed on top of things and really looked out for us. She turned away several opportunities to place kids with us. She read the reports and knew, *There is a sexual abuse component to this. I don't think Daniel and Mariana can deal with that.* For a short period of time, there weren't any potential matches.

She suggested we attend an annual mini-carnival held by the county. They bring parents and foster kids to a park where families get to interact with the kids. Mariana said to me, "This feels really wrong, like we're at the pet store, looking at puppies," but we went anyway and my wife found a sibling group: two young boys, five and two, and a twelve-year-old girl.

My wife is Catholic. I'm Jewish. These kids had been raised Catholic in the foster care system. My wife had agreed that we would raise our kids Jewish. A five-year-old and a two-year-old, okay, but I saw too many problems for a twelve-year-old. At the risk of hurting our relationship, I said, "We can't do it."

A month after the fair, we received a call from our social worker about two girls, fourteen months apart; Juliana was almost two, Bianca nine months. There wasn't much health history or other documentation, just some drug exposure from the mother, but we said, "Let's make this happen!"

The foster mom didn't speak a word of English. Fortunately, I spoke enough Spanish to get through the initial meeting with her. We visited with the kids at her house. We'd take them down the street to the park or to a McDonald's PlayPlace. We tried to see the kids as much as possible. They were very wide-eyed and happy.

We knew the foster mom was in contact with the biological mother. We didn't know that she was working with the biological mother in an unrealistic attempt to reunite them. We found out that if the girls weren't reunited with their biological mom, the foster mom wanted the girls to go to a family down the street that hadn't gone through the foster system. It was crazy. The foster mom had a lot of issues. I think she had an issue with my being white.

Juliana, our older daughter, has Mongolian spots, a condition that causes skin spots that resemble bruises. The spots come and go and may last for six months to a year. The spots she had around this time were well documented. But one day, after a visit to the park, we returned the girls to their foster mom and she called Child Protective Services (CPS), claiming that she suspected I had hit Juliana. CPS stopped our visits immediately after that, even though our social worker and the girls' social worker worked feverishly to have the allegation dropped.

The CPS caseworker came out to our house and interviewed us. As it happened, because I work in juvenile law, I knew the caseworker. I worry that had this not been the situation, we would have had much more trouble. After eight or nine days, the kids' social worker called to say CPS had closed the investigation as unsubstantiated.

I picked up the girls, brought them to our condo for a visit, and received a call from the social worker telling us not to return the kids. She told us, "Keep them. We're going to expedite your request for an adoption." They had opened an investigation on the foster mother after her allegation.

The girls showed up with the clothes they had on. That was it. Imagine—we had no amount of preparation time; we had seen them only a few times. We hadn't painted their rooms. We didn't have a crib. We didn't have anything. We didn't even do a typical baby shower or anything like that, though a few friends gave us gift cards. And the foster mom refused to turn over anything. I had just left a law firm and was unemployed before I started my own practice, so I didn't have an income coming in. I had money going out. We had nothing. But the girls warmed up to us quickly; Juliana even started saying "Dada" to me.

From there, it was a whirlwind. We ended up with temporary foster care placement of the kids. The county filed the petition and submitted all of the paperwork. We're talking about a span of only a few months total. I didn't have to handle anything except for signing paperwork and making it to court. In November 2007, one of my favorite judges presided over juvenile court and granted the adoption.

All in all, this has been a great experience. I won't say it was a walk in the park or anything like that, especially the "hurry up" at the end. But there isn't anything in my life or in my wife's life that has been 100 percent easy, so we see the adoption process the same way. It could have been unbelievably worse.

Relationship with Biological Family

They didn't give us much information about the biological parents. We know they have the same mother and same father and that neither made it past a high school equivalent. I believe Juliana ended up in foster care because the mother was found under the influence of drugs. A little while later, Bianca was born and was immediately put into foster care with her sister. Apparently, there are three other kids, two living with extended family of the mother, and a little boy born after the adoption. We put ourselves on a list for additional siblings but didn't hear anything.

The system gave the girls' mom every opportunity to turn her life around, but she refused. We believe it took nine months for the courts to terminate her reunification rights.

Once the courts removed the rights, Bianca and Juliana became available for adoption.

We heard very little of the girls' dad. He was in jail and not in the kids' lives.

Shortly after the adoption, one of my wife's cousins told Mariana that she saw an interview on her local news where the birth mom was screaming at the camera that our county took away her babies. The report showed pictures of the girls.

It was horrible; we felt like we had to go into hiding to keep the girls safe.

It's the one unfortunate thing in our adoption. We won't sign a photo release at the kids' camp or school. There are certain places I don't take the girls. The biological mother caused so many issues in the beginning, and even though we finalized the adoption nine years ago, she's still out there.

Originally, we agreed to have a relatively open adoption. As soon as this happened, we notified the county not to release any information. Fortunately, it boiled over quickly; it was just those first six months that we were worried.

We have been totally up front with the kids about what happened. We don't say, "Your mom was a drug user." But we do say, "While your mom loved you, she was unable to continue to take care of you."

Juliana has asked, "When I am old enough, what if I want to go try to find my mom?" She sees programs on TV.

I say to her, "Juliana, you will have every opportunity if you really want to."

When she's more mature, we will give her a little bit more information about her mother. And when she's eighteen, she can do whatever she wants. She'll be an adult; she can tell me to go take a flying leap off a bridge. I would just encourage her, as with any potentially hostile or adversarial situation, "Make sure that you have somebody there with you—whether it's me, your mom, a friend—as a third party. You don't know how she'll react if you're able to find her."

With her dad, if she really wanted to, I would say, "Do your research before you hit the road." If she finds out that her dad is still in prison, it might discourage her or it might encourage her. We just want her to be safe.

Everyday Life

The kids' doctors always ask, "What do you know about their health history?" Not much.

Everything is a surprise. Juliana's got an orthopedic condition. We don't know if it was genetic or a result of the care that she had early on. Both girls are allergic to any contact with metal, unless it's twenty-four-karat gold or more. One of our kids is allergic to erythromycin.

The biggest concern that I had was that there wouldn't be that attachment. Were we setting ourselves up for raising two kids who didn't want anything to do with us? But I swiftly set all that aside, because the kids immediately took to us and were very happy. Honestly, they are as well adjusted as any kids could be, I hope in part because of what my wife and I have done.

Bianca has always been small. I think she has a Napoleonic complex. She loves gymnastics and horseback riding. She's the star of her school basketball team and extremely intelligent. Juliana is only in fifth grade but already reading at the college level. I'm pretty sure there's a component of what we've been doing that has promoted their athletic and academic endeavors. Giving them opportunities to do these activities has been successful. It seems like every week, they blossom in some way.

Our Family

You hear it often: parents adopt because they can't conceive, and then the wife gets pregnant. We adopted in '07. Mariana gave birth to our son in 2012. The girls not only get their own sibling rivalry between each other but also now have a little boy to compete with. It's been one lovefest. Bianca has middle-child syndrome from time to time; she gets a little jealous when Andy gets to take trips with Daddy because the girls are in school and my son is not.

The girls look a little different from each other but physically look like my wife. Juliana's toddler pictures were the spitting image of Mariana when she was that age. Andy looks just like me.

My brothers and I celebrated both Christmas and Hanukkah, so we've carried on that tradition with the girls. They're in synagogue and Hebrew school. They learn Hebrew, Spanish, and English. At my in-laws' house, they primarily speak Spanish.

My in-laws are enamored with the girls. They're very beautiful. Their parents are from the area where all of the Mexican beauty pageant winners and Mexican supermodels come from. That wasn't a factor in why we were excited to have these girls, though—especially now. It's an ordeal with them going into their preteens and dating and all that stuff that we've got to deal with.

One of the things that they tell you is, you're not supposed to bring anyone else to the visits—no extended family. Well, my in-laws, who live close by, don't listen to rules. On one of our first visits, they came to the same park and sat a little ways away at a picnic table. I don't remember exactly what happened, but my mother-in-law squealed with excitement, and Bianca saw her and started crawling toward her.

We are totally open with the adoption. Every year, my girls introduce themselves to their teacher and say, "I am adopted." In third grade, the teacher assigned a family tree to Juliana's class. That got a little complicated. Since then, we've always told people. It's part of our history.

Advice

With the exception of actually going through the foster-to-adopt process, I don't consider it any different than normal parenthood.

Ask about available resources. When you're going through the foster care licensing process, you get told about resources, but you think, *Oh, well, I'll never use that.* Keep those in mind. For example, our county has a program for families with children they've adopted from foster care where you can drop your kids off at day care on Friday nights. The kids get movies and popcorn, and we get a couple of hours for date night or whatever.

Finally, be assertive. If you have questions or concerns, ask your social worker. Don't fall into a sense of helplessness.

CHAPTER 2:

ALL OF THE KIDS RIGHT HERE:
THE TREVINO FAMILY

D ebbie and Jason Trevino adopted two children from foster care. Marco was three years old when he was adopted in 2004. At fifteen, in ninth grade, he dreams of becoming a baseball player. Emma was three months old when she joined the Trevino family. At ten years old, in fifth grade, she loves American Girl Dolls.

Debbie and Jason tell their family's story.

Adoption Story

DEBBIE: We had done some research and read about our agency. I was driving by where the agency used to be and was like, "I'm just going to stop." I pulled over, it was lunchtime, and there was only one social worker there. He got out his lunch, and we sat and talked for an hour.

At that point, we knew that fost-adopt was going to be right for us. We had read about all the different kinds of adoption: private adoptions, international adoptions, and

People in the Trevino Family's Story

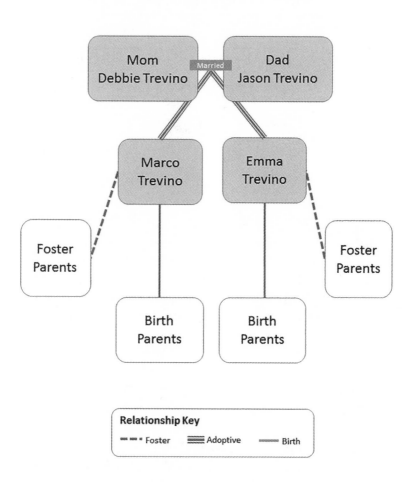

then fost-adopt. For us, the whole fost-adopt thing was the one that made sense. Yeah, you can do private adoption, and international adoption is great because there are many children in the world who need forever families, but we started thinking about all of the kids who are right here and chose fost-adopt.

JASON: The classes themselves were only six to eight weeks. It wasn't that long.

DEBBIE: We had classes and home study; we put together a family book. It's mainly for the children, but also so social workers can look at it. We did all of that and got our home study signed off on.

We went to our agency's October picnic for foster kids and prospective parents. They do it two or three times per year. The time we went, everyone brought a pumpkin to carve. We showed up at this huge park. There were just oodles of kids, social workers, and people who wanted to be parents.

One of the things that you're told is not to spend all your time with one child, even if you think that's the kid for you. You're supposed to mix and mingle and play with all the kids. Just as we were walking up, we saw this little boy. We all thought that he was two because he was so little. We were like, "That's the one for us." Everyone was probably doing the same thing. Our social worker sought out his social worker, and we spent well over an hour just chatting with her. We didn't even say "boo" to Marco, which was apparently the right thing to do. Many families were interested in him.

JASON: The kids don't decide. The social workers decide. It's like sports and an agent: you don't negotiate with the player; you negotiate with the agent. We didn't really know this until after the fact. We spent our time talking to the social worker, getting to know each other. When decision time came, she was like, "Well, I know them because I talked to them." They look in your file; all the other factors being equal, they go with "I know these people. I spent time with them." Shortly thereafter, we got a phone call saying we'd been chosen.

We were supposed to go for a disclosure meeting at the county office with the child's social worker and our social worker. They give you information, but you're kind of on a need-to-know basis. It ended up being the day before Thanksgiving. Marco's social worker left us saying, "I want you to spend this weekend thinking about it. We feel that you're the right people for Marco, but we want to make sure that you're making the right decision for you."

Of course, when we left, I was like, "I've already made my decision!" and Jason was like, "We're waiting until Monday. We're not making any phone calls until Monday." He wanted to make sure that we were not rushing into anything. I knew the moment that I set my eyes on Marco. Monday, we called and said yes.

Then we had to start setting up visits back and forth. One weekend, before we were getting ready to leave, we had been sitting on the floor playing, and Marco was sitting in my lap. He wouldn't let go of me and began crying. He wasn't very verbal at the time, so he wasn't able to put into words what he was feeling. The foster mom gently pulled him away and held him as we said our goodbyes and got into the car. They waved from the driveway as we pulled away. We were all in tears.

His foster mom—the whole family, actually—did a great job. Before us, he was calling her Mom. As soon as we knew that it was going to be us, she sat him down and explained to him, "I'm not your forever mom. Jason and Debbie are going to be your forever parents. I want you to start calling me Katherine, and when you see them, you're going to call them Mom and Dad."

JASON: Marco was in a fost-adopt placement that was disrupted. He was in the process of being adopted, but it fell apart for various reasons. Parental rights had already been terminated. His biological father was deported and wasn't really in his life after the first year and a half. It was one of the least complex cases, as there was no risk for reunification, because that had already been decided. The agency teaches you about things like attachment disorder and what might happen, and concurrent planning. We went to a meeting where a family came in, a young couple who told this heartbreaking story. After eighteen months with a child they had to let go. Everyone walked out of that going, "Uh, we don't want that to happen." They were simply trying to prepare everyone for what could be the case. That's a rare example, though. We had the other rare example, at the easy end of the spectrum, which no one ever talked about because it is so uncommon that it's not the kind of thing they want to prepare you for. We didn't know. We just knew "Okay, when we go into this process, there may be this period of time where we are waiting for the courts to do their thing, and there may still be contact with the biological family, and we'll just go with it." We didn't have to deal with that at all.

DEBBIE: Well, we brought Marco home, and we thought that was it. Then we got a phone call from our social worker saying, "We told you this wasn't going to happen, but it needs to happen: the judge decided that the birth mom needs to have one last visit."

JASON: And that's all it was.

DEBBIE: It was just a visit. However, we weren't told that that was going to happen and that it needed to take place within a certain amount of time. The visit was within the first month.

The beginning was not easy with Marco. He's not as articulate as an average kid. He certainly wasn't at three. He had a very hard time talking about how hard this was for him. He would do all kinds of nasty stuff: he kicked me, he spit at me once. In the evenings after he went to bed, we would go outside and I would say, "I can't do this!"

I wasn't working. I didn't want to be working. I wanted to be home. It was really hard. But our social worker was amazing. She came over every week, more if we needed her to. Marco's social worker visited, but I think that she realized early on that she didn't really have to be there. Each day was getting better, and then the day that we had to go visit the birth mom was like going back to square one, because he was confused. She had been told specifically not to call herself Mom, but she did.

It's suspected that she has Down syndrome. I feel for her—she doesn't understand—so I couldn't get too terribly upset. But it was really, really hard.

JASON: Another challenge was that Marco is a shaken baby [a baby shaken by an angry parent or caregiver], so there are issues there.

DEBBIE: He's got lingering effects from that. He's had all sorts of different tests and things. He has a hearing loss in one ear. It's not definitive whether it's biological or environmental.

You get certified as a foster parent the day you bring your child home. It's good for one year. Shortly before the end of that year, our social worker called and said, "I know you aren't sure about number two, but you might want to just do your recertification; it's easier to do it now than to have it expire and have to do additional classes." I was like, "I'm good. One's good." That was in my mind, not Jason's mind.

No sooner did we recertify than we started getting calls about the second child. We were pretty clear that if we were going to adopt a second, it would be a girl. It was almost like every single month we were getting a call, because our social worker worked hard for us and had us in the back of her head whenever a child became available.

First, we met a baby girl named Cara. I will never forget her. We got a phone call about this nine-month-old baby. We said, "Sure." Little did we know that we were actually going to the foster family's house. The foster family was there, the baby was there, the social workers were there. It was really uncomfortable because it felt to me like a full-court press: "This is the baby for you. You need to take this baby because we're leaving." The foster family was moving.

We met the baby and had a disclosure meeting the same day. Some of the stuff they told us was really troubling. I didn't sleep that night. I knew that I couldn't say yes, but I was so bothered by some of the stuff that they told us. The parents were both in prison because they murdered Cara's brother.

They found cigarette burns on Cara. One of the social workers mentioned that they thought she might have fragile X, a chromosomal disorder. I did not sleep that night because I was up doing research on fragile X. I would not have been able to tell that poor baby what had happened in her life, and the whole fragile X thing made me nervous.

The very next morning, we called our social worker and Cara's social worker to say no. I said, "I hope this doesn't mean that you'll never consider us again." I remember hysterically crying that day because I couldn't believe that I was going to say no to a baby, but I know in my heart it would not have been the right thing for us to do.

JASON: It's the hardest thing. You have to be prepared to say no. You want to say yes. You have to know your limitations.

They'll ask you. They give you a checklist, which is one of the oddest things that you will ever do. They tell you to check the things that you absolutely know you can't deal with, and those range from things like bed-wetting to animal cruelty to pyromania.

You get told all of these things, but when you actually see that list and you have to check boxes, it's like, *Oh my goodness!* I think that freaks a lot of people out.

DEBBIE: The next thing that we received from our social worker was an email with a picture of a three-month-old, Emma, with big, beautiful blue eyes, and a note saying, "This baby just became available, I submitted your home study. Please tell me now if you don't want me to pursue." I was like, "Holy crap! Jason! You will never believe this email."

He was like, "Yes, let's do it."

We went to Emma's foster parents' house. They are the most amazing foster parents. Their thing is that they only want newborns who are fragile: drug or alcohol addicted or something else wrong. That's what they feel they're best at—taking those babies in and being good to them until they can find a forever family. They are true advocates for the babies they foster. They go to every single court appearance, and they make sure that the judge knows that they need to find a placement before they are four months old. Four months old is when babies form a bond, and they want to make sure that when they hit that mark, the babies aren't with them, but with their forever families. Emma was the only healthy baby they had ever brought home, and they had had more than twenty babies.

We did the back-and-forth to their house over a two-week period and then brought Emma home in July. We thought we were heading for adoption finalization in January. We had expected to get a phone call from our social worker on January 6, the day the court expected to terminate parental rights.

Our social worker called and told me, "It didn't go like we thought it was going to go. There was a social worker error, and something that we thought had happened didn't happen."

Pause.

"You know how there isn't a father on the birth certificate?"

"Yeah."

"Nobody did the due diligence to make sure that he's not somewhere around, looking for his daughter."

So, they put an ad in the newspaper for forty-five days, and we had to wait. Basically, it said, "If you think you or someone you know fathered a child during this time frame, call X number."

There was never any response. After that, we scheduled the finalization.

There are some things that the kids are too young to know. Emma's birth mom has some mental problems, but nobody knows if they're biological or drug induced. A friend of the family reported the birth mom to CPS while she was pregnant. She had a social worker the entire time she was pregnant. She gave birth in the hospital with a social worker right next to her. Fortunately, Emma was born healthy. The birth mom visited a couple of times in the first month or so, but then nobody knows what happened.

Marco's birth father was deported for child and spousal abuse. That's one of the things that's not in any work that we have; it's just what we were told. He's gone, but Marco's uncle was very upset when he was taken away. He wrote letters. And Emma's family has an extensive CPS history, back two or three generations. There is no one in her family that would even be able to help. Always in the back of my mind I worry about somebody stalking us and snatching our kids, but I know that's never going to happen.

We got a court date near our home because the courts in Marco's birth county are very busy. Our judge was amazing. It was us and my sister-in-law and one of my nieces. The judge likes to do it all in her private chambers. It was just the five of us. It was really nice. We have pictures of us signing things.

Emma's was a little bit different. Her county did it as a big group, everybody at once. There is a woman who works at the courthouse who does handprints and footprints on tiles. Every time you walk into that courthouse, you see the entire front of the courthouse lined with these hands and feet. So we have Marco's and Emma's prints.

One of my favorite stories is of a day when I was in our old house on our main floor. I had had it and was like, "I am going to sit here and read, and you two are going to do art." I was sitting in the living room, reading, and all of a sudden, I heard Marco telling a story to Emma. I stopped reading and tried to listen to what he was saying, and he was telling her her story—how we chose her, when we brought her home. He was there, he was part of the whole thing, every single visit, everything. He drew a beautiful family picture: a house with a path leading up to it, a tree, smoke coming out of the chimney, all four of us, both cats—all of the things that point toward a happy kid. I framed it. In the middle of a rough parenting moment for me, there he was, telling his sister her story and drawing this beautiful family picture.

Biggest Fears

JASON: It's the fear of the unknown on a lot of fronts. The unknown in terms of the child's family history—not that I'm afraid that something is going to happen to them, but I can't answer questions. A fear of those awkward moments that are going to come up and how you deal with them. And that maybe the kids will have this thing in their mind about not knowing their birth parents, but eventually they can find out, they can try.

DEBBIE: One thing about that—I like to go to the same doctor. Every time you go to a new doctor, you have to go through "They are adopted," and the kids are right there. It's not like the children don't know they're adopted, but they have to hear you go through the whole thing.

JASON: People talk about nature versus nurture. When you decide to go into this process, you don't know about the nature part; you're basically erasing the nature part because you had nothing to do with it. It's funny because over time, after being together all the time, there are certain things that come from habit and repetition, and you think that's just part of your family, it's part of your history, but it's not. That's the weird thing, and it's hard to reconcile sometimes.

Overcoming Challenges

DEBBIE: A couple of years ago, when we went down this path of trying to figure out why Marco has hearing loss, the ear, nose, and throat doctor suggested we see a geneticist. At that appointment, we realized that Marco, at the tender age of nine, was almost full blown into puberty.

JASON: Precocious puberty.

DEBBIE: We ended up going to an endocrinologist. Marco started getting these injections monthly to stop puberty. If boys go into puberty too early, they grow too fast too soon and don't reach their full height potential. As soon as Marco heard that, even at nine, he was like, "I want to be tall." His bones in the very beginning were two years older than his actual age. But by the time he was done getting these injections, his bones had stopped growing and had come into line with his actual age. He was able to gain an inch or two in his height potential.

One comment that this doctor made was, "I see lots of adopted kids with precocious puberty, but there's never been a study on it. I'd really like to be part of a study on it because it's almost like it's a fight-or-flight thing. Even if they were adopted at a young age, it's almost like their body knows that something's not quite right and they try to grow up too early."

JASON: He was nine, and his voice dropped! The other thing is that his physical and emotional states were way out of whack. Your mind is still like, *I want to play with action figures,* but your body's like, "Oh, look at those girls." Precocious puberty. I'd never heard of such a thing.

Advice

DEBBIE: You just can't have any expectations.

JASON: You have to lower your expectations early on. I was the worst about this: "Is this because she's adopted? Is this because he's adopted? Is this because we aren't their biological parents?" Trying to blame . . . No, that's not the right word—trying to *rationalize* things by the fact that they aren't your biological offspring. You can't do that. Everybody I've talked to who has biological kids, you don't know about them, either. It's a total roll of the dice. You just have to be flexible. Try not to beat yourself up too much or try to be a superparent. I think Debbie is subject to this. She always tries to be supermom.

Back to that checklist thing, you have to be honest with yourself. You have to really do some serious soul-searching in terms of *What is my capacity?* Sometimes it's a guess because you have no clue. That's probably the best advice I can give. If you decide to go down this path, you just have to be ready for anything. But I think that's true whether your kid is about to be born or you're adopting a baby or a sixteen-year-old. You just don't know. You just kinda go for it.

Lastly: I think people who go the international route, I would never say that's a bad thing or fault them, but I feel like there's so much you could be doing right here.

CHAPTER 3:

HELPING YOUR CHILDREN UNDERSTAND

FOSTER CARE AND ADOPTION

....

M ost adopted children, and likely most people, want to know and be able to tell their story. As author Joshua Gamson wrote, "Stories help make things make sense. They put things in an order. This is how it happened. They are also the stuff from which identities are built. Creation stories, in particular, are about selfhood. . . . This is how I happened."[1]

Children adopted from foster care have a special need to understand their history. Their parents have the unique challenge of helping the child understand adoption, and the possible added complexity of trauma in previous homes. This history and a child's complex feelings about it make adoption a potentially difficult subject. When children ask challenging questions about their past, the authors of *Adopting Older Children* suggest for parents to provide an "age appropriate response that doesn't overcomplicate the story" and does not vilify but is empathetic to biological family members. It must assure children that previous traumas were not the fault of the child.[2] While such a calculated response may seem impossible to deliver and the following conversation impossible to have, experts in the adoption field and parents with experience can offer advice and communication tools that help parents build and maintain healthy communication around the subjects of adoption and a child's past.

Adoption experts use the construct of developmental stages to guide parents with appropriate timing and content for conversations about adoption. In their book, *Telling the Truth to Your Adopted or Foster Child*, authors Betsy Keefer and Jayne E. Schooler lay out these stages with clear explanations and suggestions. They introduce the concept of developmental stages as applicable to adopted children by explaining, "The child is able to understand his life story in layers. What he is told at age three may be a simplified version of reality, with more information supplied when he is better able to understand. The child receives another layer of understanding as he matures, and so on until the child has all the information the parent has."[3]

Adoptee Timothy illustrates a child's potential to comprehend a portion of his parents' explanation regarding his birth. When he was twelve, he told interviewer Jill Krementz, "When I was three, my sister, Rebecca, was born, and that's when I realized where babies come from. My mom explained that being adopted meant that I grew in somebody else's tummy, so it was at this time that I started asking any woman who came into the house if I had grown inside *her* tummy."[4] At age three, Timothy grasped that he did not come from his adopted mother, but he would require further information as he grew older to understand all the implications of adoption.

In the first stage of development, from birth to age three, infants don't yet speak and toddlers begin to learn their first words. At this age, children can learn words, and that makes it a good time to teach positive adoption language ("tummy mommy," "birth father," "adoption," etc.), even though children may not fully understand their meaning.[5] In her book *Come Rain or Come Shine*, Rachel Garlinghouse explains, "Your child is never too young to hear his or her adoption story; children this young can be told simplified versions. At this point in a child's life, sharing the story with him or her mainly benefits the adoptive parent: it is an opportunity for practice." This is an excellent time to begin reading stories about adoption to children.[6]

In his article "Children's Understanding of Adoption: Developmental and Clinical Implications," developmental psychologist David Brodzinsky also provides recommendations to parents for each stage of their adopted child's development. He describes the next important stage for adopted children as the preschool years, ages three to five. Brodzinsky cautions parents not to assume that children clearly understand their adoption when they use the aforementioned adoption language they learned as toddlers. He advises parents, especially those apprehensive about having adoption conversations, not to "curtail discussions about adoption prematurely" but to "remain attuned to their children's needs for additional information . . . [and create] a family atmosphere that makes it comfortable for children to ask relevant questions about their backgrounds and current family status."[7]

Keefer and Schooler add that preschool-age children will repeatedly ask to hear their adoption story.[8] Nia Vardalos's experience supports this observation. She explains her response when her daughter asked why God didn't give her a baby: "There was another plan for me: I was supposed to wait for her. I tell her it was hard to wait but she is worth it. I say, 'I used to look up at heaven and say, "When, when will I be a mother?" And you were on a cloud looking down at me, saying, "Wait for me, I'm coming."' She likes this story and asks for it a lot."[9]

As children leave the preschool years and move into middle childhood (up to age twelve), their ability to problem-solve expands, they start thinking logically, and they begin to empathize and understand others' perspectives. Brodzinsky writes that these developments can lead children to question whether their birth parents wanted them, to deeply feel adoption-related loss, and to have anxiety or sadness resulting from thoughts about their birth parents.[10] The Butlers (chapter 11) have three children in the early part of this stage. Lori, the mother, says, "We've been really open with the kids. We never want to badmouth their mom. They all know that their mom couldn't take care of them. They know that she loved them. I know she did. She just didn't know how to keep them safe—that's what I tell them. They tell everyone they're adopted, and we keep it really open. When Libby gets out of the car at school to say goodbye, she constantly says, not just to me but to Dad, too, 'You're the best mom I've ever had.' Some people laugh—'Oh that's so cute'—and they don't even know the story."

Sometimes, feelings of adoption-related loss, such as separation from birth parents, express themselves later in this stage.[11] Author and adoptee Sherrie Eldridge, in her book *Twenty Things Adopted Kids Wish Their Adoptive Parents Knew*, describes the effects of these feelings of loss:

> *Grief is the natural response to loss and those touched by adoption must be given permission to revisit emotionally the place of loss, feel the pain, scream the anger, cry the tears, and then allow themselves to be loved by others. If left unresolved, this grief can and often does sabotage the strongest of families and the deepest potential within the adopted child. It can undermine the most sincere parental commitment and force adoptees to suffer in private, choosing either rebellion or conformity as a mode of relating.[12]*

During this time, experts emphasize that while children may not talk about adoption, they are likely thinking about it.[13] Eldridge confirms this: "Many adoptees, no matter how positive their adoptive home, live with this unspoken fear of rejection. . . . Adoptees not only need to be given permission to talk about their uncomfortable feelings, they need to be openly invited and encouraged to do so."[14]

Throughout these developmental stages, Keefer and Schooler reiterate the need to initiate conversations with children about adoption. They advise parents never to lie to children and say that by age twelve, any information previously omitted must be shared. For children with a traumatic history, some of this information may be negative, in which case parents are encouraged to enlist an objective person, such as a therapist, to help share potentially painful details.[15]

All children establish their identity during their teenage years. Adopted teens have the added complexity of incorporating both their birth and their adoptive families into their sense of self. For some teens, this may include feelings of inferiority, as well as an interest in contacting birth-family members. Brodzinsky advocates, "Parents who are more open, supportive, and empathetic in their communication about adoption are more likely to have children who are able to integrate [the adoption] aspect of their lives into a positive sense of self."[16]

Keefer and Schooler add that during adolescence, teens may express anger while beginning to assert their independence, making comments about wishing they'd never been adopted and saying that their adopted parents are not their "real" parents.[17] While a parent's natural response could be one of anger, consider a story from bioethicist Veerle Provoost in which she describes a sperm donor–conceived teenage boy arguing with his father. The son yells, "You're telling me what to do? You're not even my father!" thereby actualizing a fear of many parents not genetically related to their children. Provoost described the father's reaction to his son's harsh words:

He said, "This outburst had nothing to do with the lack of a genetic link; it was about puberty, being difficult. It's what they do at that age. It will pass." What this man shows us is that when something goes wrong, we should not immediately think it is because the family is a little different. These things happen in all families. And every now and then, all parents may wonder, *Am I a good enough parent?*[18]

As Jason Trevino (chapter 2) mentioned in his advice to parents, he learned not to attribute his children's behaviors to their being adopted. Keefer and Schooler refer to this thought process as "insistence upon difference." Parents fall into this without realizing it causes a "subtle slide into disharmony and blame."[19] They recommend not responding to anger with anger. "If parents can understand that much of their child's anger is generated by his 'rejection' by the birth parent, and not aimed at them, they might not over-respond to angry outbursts."[20]

In addition to providing detailed descriptions of developmental stages and advice on communicating with adopted children throughout these stages, Keefer and Schooler give readers many suggestions for tools to use to communicate with adoptive children.[21] These tools include life books, life maps, doll and puppet play, family trees, writing letters, journaling, and collages. Many of the adoptive families I interviewed for *All the Sweeter* created some form of a life book for their children. Adoptive parents and adoption experts agree on this commonly used tool as a helpful method to communicate a child's adoption story.

In her book *Successful Foster Care Adoption*, author and adoptive mom Deborah A. Beasley emphasizes the importance and urgency of creating such a book. She says, "From their stark reality of loss and disconnection and often being too little to remember what happened to them, your efforts

may hold the sum of their young lives and become a pre-
cious link with their past."[22] Parents use pictures; birth
certificates; letters from social workers, teachers, and foster
parents; the child's drawings; and other mementos to follow
their child's path from birth to adoption. Because children
adopted from foster care often do not enter their adoptive
parents' home just after birth, a lack of information may
cause creating a life book to seem like a fruitless effort.
However, even without baby pictures, parents can search
the Internet for a picture of the hospital where their child
was born. If the child was born in a different town or state,
then stayed with another family, a parent can use Google
Maps to trace the child's journey. Parents can look up facts
about the year the child was born—for example, the pres-
ident of the United States at the time, as well as popular
movies and songs.

If the child's life before adoption seems too fraught
with unpleasant memories and trauma, similar to the Allen
Pierce family (chapter 4), parents and their children can
work with therapists to create a life book, allowing for conversations about difficult topics as they arise.

A life book has the ability to turn these unpleasant
memories into feelings of pride. Author Adam Pertman
described an adoptive family's life book experience: "As they
were growing up in Vermont . . . Kathryn's children were
asked to bring their life books to school every November
(National Adoption Awareness Month) as part of a lesson
on various kinds of families. Fellow students flocked around
to look at the pictures, listen to the stories, and sometimes
they expressed a little envy."[23] The life book then serves as
a tool not only to tell the child his or her adoption story,
but also for the child to share this same story with others.

In addition to life books, parents have a wealth of age-
appropriate adoption-themed children's books available to
them. Reading a book with a child of any age can be an

easy way to introduce and normalize important foster- and adoption-related concepts, and to help initiate what may feel like a difficult conversation. A simple online search for "adoption-themed children's books" reveals books on a wide range of topics: relationships with birth mothers, navigating good and bad memories, meeting a child for the first time, birth stories, an adoptee wondering what it would be like to live with his birth parents, family members not looking alike, adopting from foster care, and transracial adoptions.[24] The list seems endless and even includes books to prepare children already in the home for the adoption of a sibling.[25]

Often, families who choose to fost-adopt do so after having biological children or other adopted children. It is important to have conversations about adoption with children living at home, biological or adopted, because siblings influence an adopted child's sense of belonging and comfort.[26] The McPhersons (chapter 16) had a young daughter, Amelia, when they started the process to fost-adopt their son, Christian. Leah, now a mother of two, shared this story:

> When we first considered foster adopting, I was very concerned with how that process would affect Amelia. When we first told her what our plan was, she was six. I'm pretty sure all she gathered from that conversation was that she would possibly be getting a brother or sister. We were always very open and honest with her. We told her that we might have a child in our house for a few weeks, months, or years, and they might or might not stay with us. But we always told her that it is always important for us to love and take care of others when they are in a time of need, no matter what the outcome is. As young as she was, she was so emotionally intelligent that I think she grasped the concept.

We also talked constantly about family. What exactly did that word mean? We always would point out different scenarios of how family meant different things to different people. Amelia has a lot of "uncles" and "aunts" who are not blood, just close friends. We would talk about how family just means people you love, take care of, and put first.

When we brought Christian home, Amelia had the biggest smile on her face I had ever seen. The next weeks consisted of her doting on him, reading to him, holding him. She never once appeared as though our time had been taken from her and given to him. I knew then that no matter how long he stayed with us, the experience would be amazing for all of us. I never once questioned what we were doing. All we could do, even if we tried to do otherwise, was to love him 200 percent, and if he only stayed a few weeks, months, or years, he deserved every single thing we had to give him and we would have to pick ourselves up off the ground if he left. We would love him and show him as much love and sense of family as we could in the time we had.

Amelia got that 100 percent. It was amazing to see. One of my favorite moments ever of Amelia and Christian, I have on video. December 17, one day after he came home, Amelia, a first grader, wanted to hold him on the couch and read him a book. It melted my heart. My mom always says she was in awe of me, bringing a baby into the house that I didn't give birth to and never missing a beat, caring for him as my own. I was in awe of Amelia's immediately adapting to being a big sister without a hiccup, as if she had been prepared for his arrival for a year.

Each family's composition of children prior to fostering and adoption has unique characteristics that require careful consideration. The authors of *Adopting Older Children* advise, "Being aware of what to expect and planning ahead can make all the difference in how everyone responds to and experiences the change." They go on to suggest that children may have uncertainty about a new sibling, and that parents must empathize with this apprehension and find opportunities for children to attend preadoptive agency trainings or webinars.[27]

While it is certainly true that direct communication with your child and his or her siblings is very important, of equal importance is the communication that your child has with others, whether it is listening to conversations or engaging with friends or strangers. In their interviews, several families described unpleasant, unsolicited comments that come from strangers in public, sometimes after a child misbehaves. Lori Butler (chapter 11), who adopted three children after raising four biological girls, said, "I've had people in the grocery store tell me, 'You have too many kids—you can't even handle them.' Very hurtful stuff. I used to come home in tears all the time. I did not get my iron panties until two years ago."

Other times, feedback from strangers comes in the form of innocent or uninformed comments or questions that may be unintentionally hurtful and uncomfortable for a family.

In her book *Come Rain or Come Shine*, Rachel Garlinghouse gives this piece of advice:

> *I always respond to open adoption and birth parent assumptions with education. If someone asks, "Are her birth parents young?" I say, "My adoption agency shared with me that most birth parents they serve are in their twenties." If a person asks, "Aren't you scared that your daughter's birth parents will show up on your front doorstep?" my response is, "I would let them into my house if they came to my front door. In fact, they*

know they have an open invitation to visit us at any time." Turning a potentially negative conversation into something productive and educational demonstrates to your child that you respect his or her privacy (by not disclosing specifics) and are not embarrassed that your family is part of an open adoption. Of course, you always have the option to simply say, "That's not up for discussion" or "We don't share that information outside of our immediate family."[28]

Here, Garlinghouse provides possible responses to uncomfortable questions but also introduces the option not to share information, thereby keeping certain matters confidential. Different than secrets, which, according to Keefer and Schooler, "create exclusion, destroy authenticity, produce fantasies, evoke fear, and kindle shame," confidentiality "allows for appropriate communication within healthy boundaries by those directly touched by the event of circumstances or with those who can act within the arena of support."[29] Confidentiality gives parents and children the ability to discuss sensitive topics without the fear that others unnecessarily have knowledge of a child's private information.

A parent's response won't always be perfect the first time, and the importance of talking about fostering and adoption may seem overwhelming. However, working toward healthy communication, in which all family members can raise their questions and express their emotions about adoption, will create a safe environment for discussions. Beyond the scope of this chapter, but also very worthy of consideration, are conversations that parents will want to have with family members not living with them, as well as important community members, such as schoolteachers and religious leaders. Many families who participated in *All the Sweeter* said that communication was of primary importance in making the fost-adopt experience successful and subsequent child rearing rewarding.

The most essential, and sometimes most difficult, line of communication is that between parent and child. As Heidi Schneider and her sons Vance and Trevor (chapter 8) agree, "Communication is key." While conversations about adoption are difficult at times, a loving, understanding, and honest approach to them will normalize adoption for adoptees, help children make sense of their life's path, and strengthen relationships between family members.

CHAPTER 4:

AN INSPIRING TOOLBOX, RITUALS INCLUDED: THE ALLEN PIERCE FAMILY

....

After trying to conceive for eight years, Susanna and Trisha decided to fost-adopt. They met their daughter, Celeste, when Celeste was six years old and officially adopted her at age seven. Trisha shared that she feels the most love for her daughter when she sees "her nurture someone more vulnerable than herself. My girl is deeply sweet and empathetic to her core. I am moved to tears when I see her read books to a tiny cousin, whisper sweet words into our puppy's ear, or cheer on a friend who is afraid. She never wants anyone to feel bad or be left out—even a tiny bug she finds on the sidewalk and tries desperately to bring inside!"

Adoption Story

Four years ago, my wife, Susanna, and I did a one-hour orientation for bringing foster children into our home. We

People in the Allen Pierce Family's Story

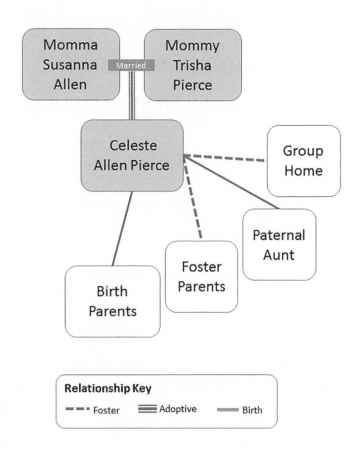

Momma Susanna Allen — Married — Mommy Trisha Pierce

Celeste Allen Pierce

Group Home

Paternal Aunt

Foster Parents

Birth Parents

Relationship Key

- – – Foster
- ▤▤ Adoptive
- ▬ Birth

pictured it to be a sibling set under the age of five. I have an early-education background. I tried to get pregnant for years. I wanted a chance to have a little kid and multiple kids.

What we pictured happening totally didn't happen.

After the training, about a year in, before we even were through with our home study, we went to a disclosure meeting[1] about a couple of kids whose birth family was still really involved. It felt more like taking kids from a family trying to keep them, versus giving a home to a kid who didn't have another choice. We said no to the first sibling set.

Not long after that, we got a call about this little girl and we knew right away that we wanted to have a disclosure meeting about her. She was mixed race, which was important to us. Susanna felt strongly that, as a black woman, she be able to provide that identity support to a child of color. And because we'd be a multicultural family, we felt particularly equipped to support the needs of a biracial child. We get help from adoption resources for multiracial families and are committed to parenting with intention around identity formation and self-acceptance. In our life book, we wrote to our daughter that we wanted a mixed-race child, so she could have another reminder that she was wanted and just right exactly as she is.

She had just turned six, so she was slightly out of our age group. We'd tried to get pregnant for eight years. So, after a year of the trainings and the meetings and the visits and the stuff, there is this sort of desperation. There is this really heightened, nonlogical, super-emotional thing that happens when you sit down at a disclosure meeting. It's happened to all of my friends who have done it and definitely to us, this excitement and eagerness to find your child and to start your family. We heard all about her, saw her picture, and I had this feeling, *This is it!*

That desperation clouded everything that happened in the really short, kind of manic, next few days. We had the disclosure meeting, but our home certification wasn't done. We rushed home and worked really hard and really fast to get our home certification together. This meant running out and finding a kid's bed and hanging stuff and locking the knives away—pages and pages of checklists.

We'd been told that when we met the child, we would have twenty-four hours to decide if we wanted to do an overnight. After the overnight, the assumption was that we'd bring her home. They were really clear: "Don't meet her, don't spend any time with her, if you don't think it's going to be a good fit."

We started by taking her out for a playdate. It was heartbreaking. We picked her up at this group home with high security. She was a tiny, underweight, six-year-old girl who looked absolutely terrified. We brought art supplies and sat down with her social worker. She was very social and very eager. Clearly, I now realize, her attachment was so scattered that even though we were complete strangers, she climbed all over me and sat in my lap. Meanwhile, she rejected Susanna completely. She wouldn't even look at her. She didn't want anything to do with her.

That was a tricky part of our early time with her, negotiating how normal it is for a child in this situation to attach to one person but not the other. How long do you give grace to that, versus not allowing it to happen?

It took months for Celeste to move beyond that first impression and her fear of Susanna. Fortunately, we came to realize that we were not seeing Celeste's real personality, we were seeing all of her defenses, and under that was this super-vulnerable child who felt like she had to act tough and put on all of this to make her way in the world.

We were also fortunate to have a social worker whose strengths were parent coaching, child development, and off-age parenting kids in the foster care system. She helped us understand it's likely a racially charged dynamic. In Celeste's life with us, she is going to go back and forth between favoring one of us. When you have two mothers, there are a lot of projections that happen. Celeste had two moms before; one was white and one was black. We re-create that dynamic for her. I look like her birth mom. Susanna looks like her auntie who raised her as a foster mom. We get all kinds of stuff projected onto us that has nothing to do with us.

After our first visit when we did the art project with her, we took her on an outing. She was swearing and littering and showing us how tough she could be and that she could handle herself. She didn't need anybody. We decided that, despite the challenges, we really wanted to continue getting to know her.

We got a hotel for a night in her town and, together with her social worker, gave her the choice to come and stay with us.

She was really excited to come to our hotel and have a sleepover.

There was a "that's where it all began" type of feeling to that night. We ate spaghetti that we ordered from a restaurant poolside. She wanted to put hot sauce on it. It's really common for foster kids to put hot sauce on everything because they're so sensory-seeking.

We let her jump on the bed, and we did each other's hair, and we stayed up and read books. We wanted to be able to show her pictures of our house, so we made a photo album, easy for her to flip through, that showed every room in our home and our backyard. I bought a little Hello Kitty stuffed animal—that was her favorite—and I put Hello Kitty in the corner of every shot. She would look through it and find it. Of course, we brought her the kitty so she could see that transitional object in each room, even silly ones, like "Hello Kitty's using the toilet."

I have a really sweet picture of this night with her. She loved this book. As we read it, I said, "This is our house. Do you want to come with us and be there?"

She gave us a resounding "Yes!"

It killed me how untethered she was, how this little child would see some pictures of a house and be like, "Let's go move there," but that's how it is with these little kids.

After the sleepover, we signed all of the paperwork and stopped to see her therapist, who she'd been seeing weekly and had a good relationship with. The therapist spent two hours with us, playing with Celeste, coaching us in therapeutic play. She gave us a bunch of resources. I remember being so wide-eyed, so excited, but also having this mania of, "We don't know what we're doing or what's going to happen." The therapist asked, "What is your discipline style? What is your plan?"

"Logical consequences. A lot of love and clear boundaries and expectations."

The therapist was like, "Uh-huh. What are you going to do when she kicks your dogs?"

I was like [takes a deep breath in], "What do you mean?!"

She tried to wake us out of that. "Do you realize who you are bringing home and what is going to happen?"

We had no idea.

The therapist helped us come up with three house rules that were going to be important, and we shared them together with Celeste. "In our home we are safe, we use kind words and kind voices," and "Listen to your mamas"—that "obey" piece that she was going to have so much trouble with. The idea that adults are there to help you and protect you and keep you listening to them is part of what happens in safe families.

The day we picked her up, she had all of her stuff in a black trash bag. We loaded her into the backseat and took her home.

A really wise social worker had given us this idea that I would recommend to all families, even if you are bringing home a teeny baby. She said, "Kids are so visceral, you want to give them opportunities to associate your home with comfort and sweetness." We'd given a friend a key and asked him to sneak into our house and bake chocolate chip cookies. We texted him thirty minutes out so that the first thing that she smelled, the primal response she had at the moment of walking into our house, was cookies. I will never forget, we opened the door, like, "Welcome to your new home," and she went [draws in a breath], *"Cookies!"*

We pulled them out of the oven and had cookies and milk. That was our first moment together in our home.

Pressed for Time

We did so much preparation in twenty-four hours. Now I know. If I had to do it again, I would say, "No, we need more time. This is a life decision." I get social workers' urgency. I have a lot of empathy and respect for them. It's really complicated. They didn't want her to be in a group home under emergency placement any longer than she had to be. She had only a certain amount of days that she was allowed to be in the group home, and they didn't want to have to move her again before she came to our home.

They have deadlines around paperwork that make them push really hard with a family. But sometimes they lose the paperwork or don't show up when they're supposed to. They're overworked and overtaxed. It's maddening.

This urgency that gets created is for a lot of different reasons. I wish that I had known to have more agency about our rhythm and our self-care and from the very beginning had trusted that I could be in charge of the way our family got made. It doesn't have to be from a manic, desperate place. I could have set some boundaries there. It wasn't helpful that I was up for twenty-four hours and didn't sleep the night before we got our daughter. I get that when people give birth, there's some of that, too. But the level of challenges we were going to face is very different from what other types of families go through.

The First Year

We focused our first year with Celeste on creating family rituals and getting to know her. We got really clear about our boundaries and made them part of our family system. We came up with lots of ways to find a balance between grace and understanding but also didn't allow her to control our home and our dynamic that way.

We were brand-new parents. Most people have a newborn who doesn't speak, much less project racially charged love-hate stuff onto you the first days of your parenthood. That's intense.

To complicate matters, we had one week to keep her at home, and then we had to put her in school. I wish I could have pushed back on this. I get it, you need to be in school, but the shift that she was going through . . . We had seven days to bond with her, acclimate her to our house, find the right school (they'd already started), get her in, and start a school routine.

She was not in her body. There were no tantrums. In the very beginning, there were some night fears and screaming, but we just held her tight until she fell asleep.

That first part, she was in total shock. We threw a big "welcome Celeste" party where all of our community came and brought gifts and she flitted around and didn't know anybody and didn't know what was going on. Two years later, she knows all of those people and she has the gifts that they brought and it makes sense. At the time, it was for us. It was our baby shower.

That period taught us that we needed to be really focused on helping her get all the things that she missed out on at each different age and stage, which is enormous when you bring in a neglected child. She was highly stressed and malnourished and needed so much. She ate four scrambled eggs for breakfast and slept twelve hours a night for months. She slept hard and in altered states, some sleepwalking, some talking in her sleep, some night terrors.

Everything took longer than we imagined, which felt really frustrating. Being part of the system, we didn't feel in control. We had to check first before cutting her hair. Meanwhile, there are all these visits that sometimes feel supportive and a lot of times just feel really invasive while we're constantly checking and waiting on them to move forward.

Once Celeste's shock wore off, we started to see lots and lots and lots of tantrums that would last for hours. As we tried to learn how to navigate that with her, how to help her feel safe in our home, we relied on a lot of really good advice. Our social worker gave us some input that has stuck with me almost more than the millions of other things: "Your daughter is treating you with contempt, and no one wants to attach to someone who is contemptuous. You cannot allow her to treat you as though you are stupid and incapable."

That was Celeste's tactic: *These adults are so dumb. They don't know how to take care of me. They don't know how to be trusted.* She used her super-primal adaptive strategies or manipulation and being rude and throwing epic tantrums to divide us and to push us away. It's been really important to be stronger than that.

We had to say, "No, no, that's not how we do it. If you won't let Momma Susanna help you get ready for bed, then you have to do it on your own."

Twice per week, I left the house in the evenings, I physically wouldn't be there, so she had no choice but to let Susanna take care of her. If Susanna offered to do something and she said no, I wouldn't then allow her to come to me to do it. Including affection—even if Susanna tried to give her a hug and she made an awful noise and ran to me and tried to climb into my lap.

This was a tricky one, because she needed that affection. I would say to her, "You have two mommies, we both love you, we're both right here. You don't get to be rude to one of us and loving to the other." At one point, I remember saying to her, "Honey, I've been married to your mom for thirteen years. You don't get to come in and try to push us apart. You are not that powerful. You just don't get to do it."

As she got a little older, my feedback got more nuanced: "It's okay to have preferences, of course—all kids do. You can say, 'I really want Momma Trisha to help me with such-and-such.' If you can ask for it calmly and nicely, then you can have it, but you can't be awful to one of us. We just won't tolerate it."

I got that she was regressing to being a one-year-old. But she wasn't one; she was six. For our own sanity, we couldn't allow that. We learned about the Holly Van Gulden parenting style, which requires a lot of skill as your child is going through different ages in a given day, and tuning in to where she is developmentally and what she actually needs right then, but still helping her match her peers and behave as appropriately as possible out in the world. It's a way to help kids master self-regulation. We all have lots of ages inside.

We did baby time, where we let her curl up in a rocking chair in my lap and I fed her a bottle. We did all that early-attachment, off-age parenting stuff. We contained it to nighttime, before bed, and in our house. We gave her space to be born into our family as a tiny baby but expected her to act more age appropriate when we were out in the world. That all helped her to feel the control and capacity to navigate all that.

We also did something called funneling, which is a controversial practice. The way we were coached in it worked for our family. It helped her to know that we were going to be the ones to help her and provide. She sees lots of adults, and she would jump into the laps of strangers. We worked with that indiscriminate stuff by letting her know that if she needs anything—permission, food, affection—she comes to us. Whenever we were with other families, we coached them to say, "Go ask your moms" or, "I'm sure your moms will help you" or, "Check first." She kept getting redirected back to us until we had it.

She didn't call us Mom until she was with us for a while.

I remember we were on this zoo roller coaster when she said to me, "Are you my mom?"

I said, "Well, I don't know. What do you think?"

She said, "I want you to be."

I said, "Okay, I will be, then." That sort of casual. Then she wanted to start calling me Mom but call my wife Susanna, or not refer to her at all.

I said, "Well, here's the thing, I only get to be your mom if Susanna's your mom, too, because we go together—we're married. You can't have me without her. We're a team."

"Oh, okay."

We just kept sticking with that. She started calling me Mommy and Susanna Momma.

She cast Susanna in a Dad role. In those early months, Susanna wrote a blog post about Celeste's projecting. "You are the one I am going to be really playful with and go out and do things with, but I don't want you to do the nurturing stuff." As long as Celeste was being respectful, we were fine with those kinds of preferences.

In that first year, a big part of the lead-up to the adoption court date was working with a very skilled therapist to create a life book. We worked on it weekly, and the last chapter was adoption day. For the first time, Celeste had the narrative of her whole story. She had not been filled in on these pieces of her history. That was sad, but it was also happy that we could give her this gift of the narrative.

It was a way to document her new cousins and all of the new family that she was getting. As we headed into the adoption, it felt really important to her to share about her birth family in her class for show-and-tell. We rehearsed it in therapy and gave her choices about how involved in it I would be. I sat and watched, and she asked me for help once. She didn't want to talk about adoption or say the word *adoption*. She had a lot of shame attached to it.

So, Susanna and I were thrilled—"Our dreams are coming true!"—and we had a kid who felt really worried and angry and anxious and sad. In her mind, it meant saying goodbye and leaving all the people she hadn't had contact with for a year. She had a lot of grief and anger about that. We set a date, we planned, my mom came out from Arizona, and mostly we chose to invite our adoptive family friends to come.

We have these three little candle eggs that we got as a gift at the "welcome Celeste" party. We saved them for a year for the adoption day. That morning, we woke up, we had a special breakfast, and we lit the candles for the first time, one for each of us. Celeste said that was her favorite part of the whole day. I lit a tall candle, and then she used it to light the other three. We also bought special dresses.

We went to the courthouse, and poor Celeste had to wait over an hour before we could go in.

We brought toys and we had friends. We hired a photographer so that we could document it for our own adoption book, but she hated having her picture taken. There are these gorgeous pictures of the judge and everybody, and Celeste is like this [frowns] in the middle. It's heartbreaking, but it's real. The judge was really sweet with her. She let Celeste sign the paperwork. She signed her name with hearts and Christmas trees all over it.

We went to lunch and had a little get-together at our house afterward. She wanted a friend from school to come with her family. We just played and had cake and let everybody run around. The day definitely ended with big tears and a huge meltdown. It was really stimulating. The next day we asked, "What were the hard parts? What were the good parts?" to help her hold flexibility around adoption.

We said, "Adoption is happy and sad at the same time, and all of that is okay." We could normalize it: "Yesterday was overwhelming for me, too, it was hard to wait in the courthouse for a long time, but I sure did love getting to be there with the whole family, and having everybody celebrating becoming a family together, that felt really good."

She was able to get there eventually but just needed a lot of help.

Birth Family

Susanna and I are respectful of Celeste's story as hers. At the same time, there are pieces that she was willing to share for first-grade show-and-tell, so that helps me know those are pieces that I can share. She is always going to be integrating what she wants to talk about and how.

She tends to share that she had birth parents who were too young and too unskilled to take care of her as a medically fragile, four-months-early preemie. The nurses in the hospital took really good care of her for those four months. We say in her life book that she was so resilient, so lovable, and so strong that even being on oxygen and fighting to breathe, she lived and survived and thrived as this teeny-tiny baby. She had one foster mom who took care of her until they could find birth-family members. She was placed with her paternal auntie and had her paternal grandma around as a featured caregiver. The social workers worked with that family for three years. She also lived with two cousins who were like sisters to her. When she shared in her class, she said, "The grown-ups couldn't stop fighting and hitting each other." She "doesn't know why they were fighting." That is the language that she holds and that we hold.

What is very confusing and is a huge source of her trauma and her heartbreak is that social workers put her in an emergency group home for ten days, but her cousins stayed home. She was the only one who left, and she doesn't know why. The social workers decided to protect her in this way.

What we know and what we hope for is that she is doing a lot of healing in our home. She's much less stressed, and she's growing, thriving, and developing.

After the heartbreak of losing her neighborhood, her school, her stuff, and all of the people who look like her, there's no visitation unless we choose to set it up down the road with a mediator. Our social workers felt strongly that it was a safety problem even for us to disclose who we are and where we live. It's tender—we're just opening family communication once per year through the social worker—but they don't know what town she is in; it's confidential.

To her, it's like everything that she ever had and knew burned down in a fire. Now she's about to get this correspondence where she sees how they've grown and what they've done, how much they miss her and love her. Wrapping her brain around how and why she's here with us is going to be a lifelong struggle for her, and it's a big factor in our parenting and in our lives.

Because of the system, contact with the birth family has not been in our control. We were told we would receive post-adoption services. I was given a phone number and a worker's name in Celeste's birth county. A month after the adoption, I started calling and didn't hear anything back. Part of the life-book process was writing a letter to the birth family. We'd gotten therapeutic support for her to put together all of these pictures and say, "I'm in ballet, and I do this, and I miss you, and I love you. Don't forget me, and I'm happy and I'm doing great."

We'd worked on this and gave it to her social worker at the adoption. We said, "Please make sure that her birth family gets this." I would then work with postadoption services to get correspondence back.

I was calling and calling and calling this office. We were having our therapist call and call and call this office. At some point, months later, someone finally told me that no one was currently hired in the postadoption worker position, and there was no one to help me, but try this number. There was a three-month period where I called every week because my daughter was in crisis and missing her family and she'd written that letter and knew we'd sent it off and hadn't heard back.

We were coached to hire a private investigator to find them. It's very confusing. Nobody was clear. I had a major meltdown myself about having adopted this kid and not having the services provided that were promised to me.

Because it was a cross-county adoption, we had our agency, but there's nothing they can do. The postadoption worker had to be from Celeste's side. Someone from the county finally contacted me out of the blue a year later with an apology, saying, "I'm a new hire in this position. Here's what I can do to help."

Only because help had been promised to us, we promised it to our daughter. It put us in the position where we were not following through on our promises. At one point, I let her see me cry so that she could see the level of frustration that I felt about not being able to help her with this.

We spent six months making the life book leading up to the adoption day and sending this letter off to the birth family. We knew that it would take a couple of months but that we would hear back. Instead, two full years have gone by and she hasn't had any contact with them. When that worker called me, she told me that she found a file with the letter sitting in it, *for a year*. They never even gave the family the letter. The birth family also hadn't heard from Celeste for two years.

The social worker finally sent it off, and the birth family just got it. They very quickly sent a pile of stuff back, and we're going to work with that same therapist to share it with Celeste. It's encouraging but also scary. Now the understanding is that once per year we can pass correspondence through in a way that is regulated and timed, and we can count on it. In fact, her family is desperate to be in touch with her. It really was just this bureaucratic system in the way.

In summary, they reached out to the birth family, shared our letter, received correspondence, got it back to us, and will hold and be this go-between for a few years until we decide that we are ready as a family to meet them in person.

The system has this support that is sometimes helpful, but the point of post adoption services is that someone who is skilled in birth family–adoptive family communication is holding all of those interactions. I'm not going to do that. I don't know how to do that. It puts us in too vulnerable a situation.

We can hire a service that does mediation where we might all get together and meet face-to-face at some point when we feel like Celeste is mature enough to handle something of that nature. In the meantime, this solution is working. The timing is frustrating because, on the one hand, so much time passing has created anxiety in her that she has been forgotten. On the other hand, it's allowed her to really bond and attach with us without being kicked up into longing for her birth family in a way that she now will get to feel when she gets these letters.

School and Reading

We had a really great opportunity to go to our local public elementary school. It happens to be a solid, well-run, well-loved, positive place. I couldn't be more grateful for that. It's a big deal for Celeste. Because she struggles socially, is academically delayed in math and in writing, and has a fine-motor-skills delay and a processing disorder, she needs a lot of added support, and we get it all free.

When we had our recent meeting with the school, it was Team Celeste. There were nine people in the room, and we called her in at the end. She was just beaming. We went around and all cheered her on in a little celebration. She's getting the academic support she needs. We'll be starting occupational therapy. She's getting social skills support through a friendship group that happens. Her principal is really tracking her, is really on board. And her teacher happens to have been adopted, had a positive experience, really gets and sees our little girl, and is in great communication with us.

One of the most wonderful joys is that her learning to read has been incredible. She had a lot of shame and "I'll never learn to read; I don't know how to read," and wouldn't even try when she was younger, but she was obsessed with books.

We noticed bedtime was hard, and I asked her, "Baby, what do you need for bedtime to go better? I really want to help you."

That's what's worked the best: identifying a challenge we see her having and asking, "What can I do for you to make that go better?" but then make her come up with a solution, because she rejects anything we suggest.

Her solution was, "Please read me five books." *Five*. For almost a year, we read her five books every night at bedtime and our bedtime ritual was an hour long. It was important nurturing, bonding time as a family, and now her reading has clicked and skyrocketed, so she is above grade level and reads to herself thirty to thirty-five minutes per day, quietly, in bed before bedtime. Reading has been this doorway to grounding and to peace and for her to feel really confident. She's good at it.

Rituals

Rituals have been a way to bring joy to our family. For all people, trying to hold on to pleasure and the sensory experiences, just tiny everyday things, that help us when we might be struggling with trauma is really difficult. I say "we" because, especially since Celeste's arrival, I have struggled with not knowing how to find day-to-day moments of joy as the stress overtakes our bodies in a visceral way.

We noticed that transitions are really hard for Celeste. So we created what we call the "family breath." When we come home, we stand in our doorway and hold hands in a circle and take three deep breaths and say, "Welcome home."

Or she has a little alarm clock that goes off every morning. She is responsible for jumping up and turning it off; then she can climb into bed with us. We have fifteen minutes of snuggle time in bed where we talk about how we slept and have a sweet family bonding moment, and then we all get up and move on.

At dinnertime, either we go around and say five things we are grateful for or we do, "High, low, Momma go." We share highs and lows from our day and make sure everybody gets a turn so that we're practicing sharing about ourselves and our different feelings.

The ritual of using words and art to process is another big one for our family. We had an artist friend doing an exhibit featuring multiracial families. She bought a big antique chest of drawers, and each family she interviewed got a drawer and a big beautiful photo of them. Our drawer had layered images of all of our artwork and our posters, including a family photo that Celeste had drawn.

Celeste's therapist does a lot of sticker charts. Celeste is really achievement focused, so tracking her progress with stickers gives her a sense of competency. To build on our attachment, her therapist suggested creating a sticker chart around love words, loving things that we say to one another in our family. Celeste writes the words and gets a sticker, and when we fill up a page with stickers for love words, we have a family dance party. That's our process. She loves it.

All this really did change the dynamic of our home. All of a sudden, there's a lot of this super-sweet language. She was a kid who was shut down and didn't trust adults and wouldn't speak up to say, "Can I have orange juice?" She would just throw a fit. Helping her communicate was a process. Now, it's like, "Wow, thank you, Mommy. That was so kind! I'm so glad you did that for me! Thanks for helping me," with hugs and kisses.

When you come to our house, there are lots of posters and stuff. She made a big one on her wall about friendship. It has stuff from her school, like, "I'm Celeste. I like Taylor Swift. What do you like?" All the stuff that she is learning about bridging interests. When kids get this level of help, at some point when it all sinks in, they have all these skills that typical kids don't have, or even adults don't have.

It's amazing, especially if they can use that competency to mentor younger ones. Celeste especially shines with coaching littler kids around social skills. It's an important way for her to take ownership of the things that she's learned. It feels like the challenges can be so big, it's important to focus on the sweet things and the day-to-day stuff that keeps us together.

Race

In a multiracial family, race is at the heart of things. Celeste has really made her need for addressing it in lots of ways ongoing. She has been clear from the very beginning. In her life book, the therapist who was working with us, in the first chapter, didn't include anything about racial identity, and Celeste was like, "Wait, what?"

We just did one chapter at a time. Her first response

was, "It doesn't make sense that we aren't talking about skin color."

For kids who are not white, race is always center stage. For me, having grown up white in a homogenous family who never talked about race, it seems unusual. It's actually not.

Celeste has been willing to articulate it right away, and we've adopted it as our ongoing family culture. Talking about race and talking about skin color are two different things for little kids. Celeste is so young that she'll show me a picture and say, "This is when I was white, but now I'm brown." Kids don't understand that skin color and race can't change over time. There's something about the way their minds are developing that prevents them from connecting language like "this is my whiteness, this is my brownness" to what their race is. Celeste has needed help with terminology like *biracial* and *mixed girl* and all of the race words. She would come home from kindergarten and say, "I get it, Mom—I'm Hispanic!" because someone in the girls' bathroom was. Not understanding that her body is different than somebody else's is perfectly normal.

No matter how many times we told her, it didn't sink in. She also couldn't understand what day of the week it was and what month of the year it was, or what holiday was coming up—it was all the same. Her brain couldn't hold things, much like the way a two-year-old's works.

We keep lots and lots and lots of books around. It's about narrating the media that we see. "I'm so curious why everyone in this cartoon has white skin. Hmm, what do you think about that? That doesn't match real life. In your classroom, what does it look like? Huh, okay." It's about responding to her questions about race with honest, age-appropriate answers, initiating conversations about race, and commenting just the same way I would when watching a cartoon where kids are being mean to each other: "Huh, I wonder why those girls are talking to one another like that."

If our family tracks kindness and respect and values around love, we're tracking race at that same level. It is as important. It's like any family value, especially during such a racially charged time in our county. We're holding the reality that she faces and will face, celebrating her for exactly who she is, and helping her find pride in that.

There are really beautiful resources, if you look for them, in literature, music, anything that celebrates diversity. We pay attention to the stuff that we buy her and that we allow other people to buy her. When we did our "welcome Celeste" party, we wanted to build a library that celebrates diversity. Books about girls of color and powerful girls were welcome. They all came in, so now we have fifty books like that.

She just got interviewed going into the diversity dinner at her school, and the woman facilitating said, "What is one thing that makes your family unique and special?"

She said, "We all have different skin colors."

Two Moms

Having two moms is another thing that is always there and will always evolve. She is in a school where other kids also have two moms or two dads. We could have chosen a school that had *many* more kids of color, and it was tempting to. Although this one was less diverse racially than we had hoped, we've chosen to prioritize the fact that there are gay families there. We have close gay friends who adopted their kids who we see regularly and spend holidays with. Celeste says, "I like hanging out with Jack—he has two dads just like I have two moms." Another time she said, "I wonder if this waitress thinks one of you is my auntie. Maybe she doesn't know about families with two moms."

It's also just so normalized. The other adults in our life call me "Momma T." and Susanna "Momma S." Celeste loves that.

Where it gets tricky is when a kid at school will say, "How many moms do you have?"

She'll say, "Two. Well, three. Well, four." She's tracking her birth family, too. Having four moms and a bio dad, that's the place where she is now in terms of navigating what feels comfortable to share.

The issue of having gay parents has never, as far as I know, been something that she has been teased about or feels insecure about. I suspect that will come at another time, but we have laid a really solid foundation for normalizing it and celebrating it.

We have a theater background, so drama therapy and role play are a big part of our family culture. We do actual role plays at the dinner table. We practice conversations. That's a big part of how we talk to her. We role-play through any interaction with friends that didn't go well to practice social skills, but we also role-play through challenging conversations.

Another way we role-play is by doing something we call a "do-over." When we have a tense moment as a family, whether it's because I've messed up or she has made an unwise choice, anybody can call for a do-over. If I snap at her, for example, two years in, it looks like, "Mommy, you had a mean tone of voice when you answered my question. I didn't like that."

"Thank you for telling me. Can we have a do-over?"

Then we'll pretend to rewind [shakes her head and moves her hands as if rewinding]—"*wooloowoo*"—and then we'll do it again.

I model that I am willing to do do-overs, and that way, when she does something rude or has a hard time, we can respond by saying, "Would you like a do-over?"

She doesn't have to do it, but if she doesn't take the do-over and try it again, then she has a consequence for whatever the behavior was.

The intention is to practice the things we want to see and want to hear and want to do. It takes a lot of learning and a therapist, but it's helped our family a lot.

Reactive Attachment

We got really good advice and support in our training about tracking the grief and loss that the kids have. For example, before Celeste, Christmas was this dreamy holiday. We were reminded that Christmas might mean crying and extra hugs and that your kid is too upset to leave the house. You might be a brand-new family in your first year and want to celebrate Christmas, but to them, it's their first year away from their family, who they love. I was prepared emotionally for that.

What I was not prepared for, and what caught me off guard in a way that has been almost more than I can handle, was the spectrum of reactive attachment and reactive behaviors and aggression. I was not prepared for rage and aggression directed at me.

Most older foster kids haven't had loving, positive experiences with adults where they learned that they could trust love. When they come to you, you can be in an intimate relationship with someone who feels like they have to fight for their life. They turn on you sometimes, in our experience, for months at a time, and you are so early in your relationship that you maybe haven't fully fallen in love with them yet. It's like bringing home a partner who you just met but who is abusive to you right away.

A lot of parents who bring home newborns who are colicky probably are like, "Oh my gosh, I'm a new parent, I'm struggling to attach to my kid and connect to her. They're screaming and crying all the time."

It's similar for us. "I've opened up my home to this child. She's rejecting my love in ways that are aggressive and hurtful and last for months on end."

They always tell you, "Make sure that you have your therapy, and make sure that you've worked on your own traumas." I did all that. I'm a very well-resourced person with a ton of tools. Falling in love with a person who is in that much pain and acting that way is not something that I was prepared to do. I felt so much guilt about not knowing how to do it and getting so triggered myself.

During stretches of this kind of thing, for days at a time, I have not been able to hold on to my compassion and hold on to my love for her. That has made me feel ashamed and terrible about myself.

You can have a kid who doesn't have a reactive attachment disorder who still has behaviors on the spectrum. In day-to-day life, those behaviors are very, very challenging in a marriage, especially if you are someone like me, who carries a lot of guilt from childhood trauma. To hold on to quality of life and joy and actual love for this person is super, super hard.

I wish I had been prepared.

We spent a year with therapists and social workers in our house. While writing a home study, you have all this buildup: "We're such good parents. Here's why you should place a kid with us. Come and observe us. Fill out all these reports." Then the child comes and is awful to you and hates on you.

It's important to remember that they are the vulnerable ones. They are hurting. The guilt that can come out of feeling overwhelmed and not being able to navigate very well is a recipe that resembles postpartum depression. I've had a huge spike of perfectionism, even though I've done a lot of work on that in myself. It got really turned up in the foster care process. Then my kid didn't know how to receive my love and I didn't know how to handle it and it was terrifying. It continues to be. Had I not been so surprised about that dynamic, it would have helped me.

Postadoption Depression

I didn't know there was such a thing as postadoption depression. I didn't know what that was and how it can happen. I want people to know how to hold themselves and their children with compassion, how not to go into shame about how awful the cycle can feel, and how not to resent her and blame her for it when she is a vulnerable kid who was hurt. If our kids have experienced violence, they may need to show us; they need to play it out. Trauma becomes like an active living family member in your home. Working with that in day-to-day life has taken me out of work for a year. I've been the primary caregiver to my daughter and to myself. I now feel ready, and she is independent enough, but I'm still struggling to find my way back into my career stuff because of how pulled into the undertow I have been.

I felt so guilty that I'm the adult and I should be able to hold it all together that I haven't been able to own how scary and hard it's been for me. I would want other parents to have permission, if it could be normalized a little bit, that this piece is almost harder than you can manage. Find support; don't be surprised by it. Maybe there wouldn't have to be so much shame about it for somebody else.

I cannot describe the exhaustion. I was a teacher for many years before bringing this kid in. I did social-emotional coaching as a consultant to schools. I taught violence prevention through role play all over the state of California. I have all of these skills, and I am telling you that I needed meds to leave the bed.

People who have fewer skills than my wife and I have, I don't know how they do it. Really. Sometimes I think that having all of the skills and having all of the language makes it feel like I should be able to control this, so that makes it harder. There is that perfectionism, so I own that. I think that I should be able to love and heal and cure this little girl. Sometimes my codependency kicks up in a way that isn't helpful.

I want to save her, but there is only so much that I can do, and in year two of parenting, I am getting much clearer and much better because we are not in that newborn phase anymore.

All that merging was important. Now, pulling back and boundaries feel appropriate and feel good. It's helping me release the fantasy that I have the superpower to undo this child's trauma and heal her up and love her into a high-functioning, safe, and happy life.

I will do my part, but she has to participate fully. A lot of times she rejects my help and needs to go into her own stuff in her own way, and there really is just nothing that I can do except work on myself. I say to Celeste a lot, "I'm just not going to fight with you about this. If you want to speak to me respectfully, you can find me in this room. But otherwise, you can feel all of your feelings. Bye."

Moving Through Rough Patches

One of the big shifts that we had to make was to spend less time with our daughter. When she came to us, she needed so much. My wife and I have a lot of skills and a lot of capacity. We were present and we wanted her to attach to us, so we gave and gave and gave and gave and gave.

Then we tried an after-school program. She went into fight-or-flight mode and beat up all of the kids in her program. We were like, "She's not ready for that." She started beating up everybody at school in kindergarten, so I started picking her up after a half day.

We had a year under our belts when I was home with her every day after school. I was not working, and I managed the therapeutic team to work to give her what she needed. That also meant that I was the primary target for her rage. I had to be willing to say, "It's more than I can handle. I am going to trust skilled community members to take care of my kiddo, and if she beats everyone up in the program, then they're going to have to help her through that. Meanwhile, I get to protect my heart and get back into my life. Two years is enough of this."

We even asked the school for added support with her. I went to the after-school program and said, "We had a six-hour tantrum about homework over the weekend. She's in second grade. I am not going to help my daughter with homework because it becomes about our attachment relationship, where she's just picking fights with me and she doesn't want to do what I tell her. I need you, as the school, to hold the container of why homework is important."

We worked it out. She does her homework in aftercare; those teachers help her. We still have a family rule, "You don't have to do your homework—of course not. You don't get to watch TV if you don't, but you're welcome to go right ahead, do it or not. We don't care. Totally up to you. We don't mind either way." It's on her to do it or not, to turn it in or not. But if she doesn't turn it in, there is whatever stuff at school that she doesn't get to have. So, while I haven't disappeared, I have been delegating some of the responsibility.

Now that I am no longer engaged in the homework or other big triggers, I'm really focused on my wellness. My own trauma was activated, so I have done things for myself like get on antianxiety medication and antidepressants for the first time ever. Our social worker once joked that they should hand you a prescription with the kid.

I also do neuromuscular reprogramming, a kind of somatic body work that really helps me redirect my fight-or-flight response. I have a therapist who specializes in PTSD and mindfulness, and she works with me on mindfulness tools for busy parents.

We have a domestic-violence cycle in our home, which is very common for kids with a lot of trauma in their lives to play out but which is just an awful ride that we're trying to interrupt. She explodes and wants to trigger us; she's trying to be hit. We don't hit, we haven't hit, we won't hit. But she works really hard to get what she's used to.

A period of repair follows—that's part of the cycle. We are in a phase of repair, and so it feels very much like a honeymoon. Maybe eventually that stuff will die down, but she has a PTSD diagnosis and not all kids have that who have trauma history.

Because she was born preemie, her brain develops differently. She has PTSD, which means she feels things excruciatingly and reexperiences her trauma and the triggers are unpredictable.

We have a respite team in place. We have people who are on an agreed list. If she is in major episodes and tantrumming for days on end, we can do an SOS text. She won't do it with anyone but Susanna and I. We are her attachment figures, so she saves it for us. We can text for help, and somebody will come by and have a lovely afternoon with her while we go restabilize, although she might go right back into it when we come back.

Advice

Remember that you have agency. Keep your feet on the ground. Ask questions. Push back. Breathe. Set the self-care tone from the very beginning, even if you're getting a lot of pushback. I want to make sure that other foster parents know to research the reactive attachment spectrum.

Good therapists share a lot. I'm learning more and more that what feels the best is when I am really tuned in. My daughter didn't reveal herself to us for a very long time. But once your kid does reveal herself to you, then you start to understand her learning style and her interests and what lights her up and what she responds to, and then strategies become easier to think of because you are relating to her as an actual human, not just a packet of paperwork.

I've read a million books. A lot of them don't take, and some of them make things much worse, and a lot of them give contradictory information. It's a lot of trial and error. The best way I've found is when I'm able to feel like a curious scientist and not have emotional fallout when things don't work.

I've had to work with an absolute ton of grief about letting go of the family that I thought I was going to have, with babies and love and attachment with no reactivity. When I picture Celeste born premature in the hospital, and her resiliency, and the way she fought, and the way she can wake up with joy and be a goofy kid who saw her first rainbow and I got to be there for it, or ride the bike for the first time, or learn how to use her words, or read at night, I feel really privileged and really blessed to get to be one of her mothers.

CHAPTER 5:

UNINTENTIONAL FOST-ADOPT:
THE KELLER FAMILY

W hen he was in his early forties, Aaron explored several paths to adoption as a single man. Although he ultimately decided on a private agency, information regarding his son, Ethan, arrived at the private agency from a county fost-adopt program. Ethan's birth county then worked with Aaron to carry out Ethan's adoption through the county's fost-adopt process.

Aaron tells his family's story.

Adoption Story

My mother trusted us with responsibility to the point where she put my name on the family checking account at twelve years old so that I could help pay the bills. I am the older of two kids, and my sister is nearly three years younger than I am. My parents separated and divorced when I was ten.

I learned to drive before my friends. I drove my friends to events. I organized outings in the summer. I was a leader

People in the Keller Family's Story

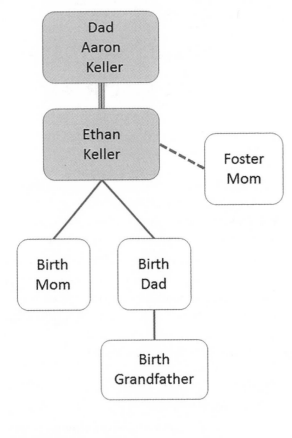

in school. I have a half brother who is fourteen years younger than I am, and as a high schooler, I often took care of him.

At age fifteen, I had a summer babysitting business. I had different clients, including a five-year-old girl and her twin brothers, three years old. There was a newborn. I even had two kids at once during the day sometimes, a four-year-old and a baby. I would go to the playground, and I would sit with the baby and then play with the four-year-old. I always wanted to be a parent.

I came to the realization that parenting, or having a child or children, was one of my major goals and desires. Thinking I had to be in a relationship first, I delayed my start to parenting.

During that time, I got my MBA, realized I liked marketing and business development, and got to a stable point in my career at a big company where my coworker helped us get an adoption benefit. I felt well cared for, in a very good atmosphere with people who were very supportive of me, and figured I should just do it. I started learning about the process.

First, I learned about fost-adopt through a local agency. I really thought that I would go that route. I did all of the training. Long story short, when I got done with everything, they asked what age child I wanted, and I said a baby or a toddler, maybe four at the oldest.

The agency social worker said, "It's really hard to place a younger child who isn't of school age with single parents, because studies show that whatever kind of couple it is, the kid is better off with two parents at home. It's so hard if you're working. Our goal is to put the kids in the most stable house."

That made sense. However, I felt a little duped because early in the process, I had filled out this form making it clear I preferred a younger child.

I then began working with an adoption attorney, who said, "You need to say this, and you need to say that." I printed a professionally designed, four-page color brochure all about me. That felt a little formulaic. Then I had to send it out to a million people I knew. I basically did all of the work, and the lawyer told me what to do. It was a tremendous undertaking; I must have sent out two hundred or three hundred mailings with brochures. I wanted open adoption, so that was the recommended approach. I had to convince the mother of a newborn child to choose me.

There are plenty of single dads, some of whom are doing it by adoption, some of whom are doing it because of divorce, or maybe the mother has died. Of course, I had to find the mother who wanted me to be the father.

Some women will choose a single father because in their mind, they aren't being replaced. I'm the husband they never had. If you think of all the options that a young woman would have if she says, "I can't take care of my baby, and I want to place the child in a great home," she would have married couples, gay couples, straight couples, lesbian couples. She would have single women, and then she would have single men. I fell to the bottom of the list.

Most successful adoptions are through word of mouth. Another friend at work went to her cousin's wedding in Ohio. A friend in the church had just gotten pregnant and didn't want to terminate her pregnancy. That child became my friend's son.

The lawyer introduced me to a member of the Academy of Adoption & Assisted Reproduction Attorneys, AAAA. These attorneys specialize in adoption and have a roster of all of their members. It's easy to see who's in good standing.

I wound up across the country for three weeks, exploring an adoption possibility with this AAAA lawyer that didn't work out. I had trouble getting my money back, researched whom to contact in his state, and reached the head of the ethics board at AAAA. Finally, we came to an agreement and the lawyer FedExed me a check for the $25,000 fee.

I had one other close experience before Ethan. I received a call at about one o'clock on a Tuesday from the attorney's office, telling me about an opportunity for a baby that might have a cleft lip or a cleft palate.

I said, "Well, okay."

"You have to go to the hospital; the mother's gone into labor."

I reviewed and signed all of these forms. I arrived at the hospital, checked in at the desk, and received a wristband like I was the father. I waited and waited and waited. I was by myself, no one else in the waiting room.

A nurse said, "Mr. Keller? It's a baby girl."

Oh my God! "How is she?"

Through a bit of a forced smile, she said, "Oh, she's great!"

We entered the recovery room, and the girl had a tremendous deformity, not just a cleft lip but a cleft palate. I had done research. It takes so many surgeries to correct a cleft palate, much more than for a cleft lip. I had said maybe a cleft lip, but no cleft palate. As a single parent, I couldn't deal with all of the surgeries.

The nurse even said, "You need to do what's right for you. Why don't you go home and sleep on it?"

Before I left the hospital, I met the birth mother's sister. The birth mother didn't speak any English, but the birth aunt had been in this country a long time. She translated and said that her sister, the birth mom, wanted to meet me. I hadn't really expected to meet her, but she was there in the recovery room, looking at me so adoringly and so appreciatively. This was after I had met the baby, so I knew that I probably wasn't going to be completing the process.

After I parted ways with the adoption attorney, I began to work with a nonsectarian private agency that was part of a larger community religious organization. It was not dissimilar to working with the attorney, but I paid more of a flat fee. Since I already had all of the documents and the completed home study and I knew what I wanted, the intake wasn't that difficult.

A mass email came in September 2008 to the private agency about a boy in the desert needing a permanent home.

I wrote back immediately, saying, "I am totally interested."

I didn't have a preference. Boy, girl, Hispanic, black, white, Asian, mixed race—I didn't really care. I threw my name in the ring. The adoption caseworker and the foster caseworker conducted a series of calls with the people who responded. They recorded the conversations and disclosed all of the details regarding the family. The situation didn't sound that bad to me. It sounded like a very conservative, family-first area where maybe the tolerance for difficulties in the home was lower than it would be elsewhere. The kid had been removed from the house and placed in foster care.

Ethan had almost finished the reunification process with his birth family and needed his forever family. The risk was quite low because he was at this last stage. So they told me all of the details and I told them I was still interested.

Ethan was born full term, normal weight; his mom did her prenatal appointments. There doesn't appear to have been any drug exposure. I really lucked out. His parents were seniors in high school and may not ever have really been together. The mother, a former foster youth herself, became pregnant while still in foster care. Apparently, when girls are about to age out at eighteen, they might have a child of their own, thinking somehow they will continue to be cared for. The birth mother did not have a stable home; I guess you can't necessarily bring your baby to foster care.

Ethan lived with his birth father and birth grandpa in the same home. The birth father was eighteen and had just finished high school. He still lived at home. It wasn't the most stable home in terms of an eighteen-year-old guy and his friends and whatever trouble they were getting into. The grandfather's job took him out of town for long periods of time, essentially leaving two kids at home.

The father's girlfriend got pregnant and moved in with them, and soon there was a half sibling, six months younger than Ethan. Then, along with the normal chaos I described, there was someone taking care of a child six months older than her own child, but it wasn't her child. Probably it evolved into the mother doing everything.

Ethan was removed from the home on his second birthday. What I have in my mind is, that was the last straw for the girlfriend—"Now we have to have a birthday party for this other kid?"—and there was some fight and the police were called. It was the most benign situation as these things go. It doesn't seem like there was any other abuse or mistreatment, just neglect. Does an eighteen-year-old boy know how to be a parent?

Ethan went from that chaos to his first foster home, which was very strict. I read in the case notes that it was a really tough match. He went from one extreme to the other. He was a little two-year-old; he wasn't adjusting well. They switched the assignment after a couple of months, to the foster care mother he had for the rest of the time, except for the reunification attempt. He lived with two different families after his removal from his birth family. But he had six moves between the ages of two and four (when he came home with me).

They narrowed it down to four families. They selected me and said, "Now you need to come to meet him."

Because I thought I had to be ready for a baby, I was that creepy guy who had a second room with a crib in it and a stroller and a car seat—a shrine to the baby I never had. When I found out about Ethan, of course, I didn't need any of those things. I went back to Target and returned everything. Then I went to the airport to fly to meet Ethan. When I got there, I saw him in the church schoolyard.

This little kid, same personality as now, was playing by himself outside, acting out some Power Rangers or some fantasy superheroes. He was karate kicking and jumping off the slide and running around.

I didn't go up to him because I didn't want to be the creepy guy. I introduced myself to the staff, and they introduced me to him. Three-year-olds are friendly, but they don't really care that much. *Another grown-up—whatever.*

The caseworker had to get Ethan into the car. She said, "Go ahead and get in. Go sit in the car seat."

"No."

I nicely got him to sit in the car seat. The caseworker later told me that was when she knew it was a match. I have a goddaughter, two nieces, I was in the Big Brothers program. I continued to demonstrate an interest and ability to parent, but when she saw that I got Ethan in the car nicely without yelling at him, she complimented me.

We chose to eat at Burger King, one of the five restaurants in town, because it had a play structure. After we ate, she came and checked the hotel and made sure there was a second bed and it was all suitable for him. Then she left us on our own. His foster mother had packed him a backpack, so he had a change of clothes and all the stuff he needed.

We went to the supermarket. There were some peaches in the produce department, and I asked, "Do you know what that is?"

"Apple!"

"No, that's a peach. Do you want to try it?"

"Okay."

We got peaches, strawberries. We bought yogurt, which he had never had before. These are very early experiences that he still remembers. He now jokes about calling a peach an apple.

They say that kids are like sponges. He has a great memory. Maybe with your own memory, you look back and think, *I don't really remember anything from when I was four.* But when they're eight, they still remember; when they're eleven, they still remember. That's part of growing up. Kids love talking about things that have happened.

We went back to the hotel. He took a bath. I read him a story, gave him a stuffed animal. It was all fine. He went to sleep, no problem.

We woke up in the morning, and he had wet the bed. Not uncommon, I didn't really think that much of it. I didn't really say anything. I mentioned it to the house cleaner, said "I'm sorry." She changed the sheets.

We went out and did stuff. There's not much to do there. We had a good time at a local ghost town, we had dinner, came home, he took a bath, went to sleep.

He wet the bed again.

I clued in: "Ethan, do you sometimes wear pull-ups?"

"Yeah."

His foster mom just didn't pack any pull-ups.

If you've not been around kids and you don't know what happens at what age, of course. I suddenly realized, *He's three. . . . Boys at night.*

I had to leave to finish the last part of all of my business trips. I took a red-eye to New York and the next day flew to Florida. During that time, I was approved. It all happened very fast. Day one, I got the email. Day seven, I got phone screened. Day ten, I found out I was first up. Day fifteen, I got to meet Ethan. Day eighteen, I left Ethan and went on this business trip. Day twenty-five, I picked him up and we went home. Boom, boom, boom. *He's not getting any younger. We found a placement—let's get him home.*

While I was away, he and I talked every day. I still have some of the voice mails, where he says, "Hi, Daddy. I'm hugging you. I love you. Bye." The cutest message, I'm sure his foster mom was telling him what to say. She knew about developing his relationship with me and vice versa.

I met his foster mom; she was awesome. He lived in a house with three other brothers—two foster, one her natural son. She was African American. There were two black boys and a white boy, and her son is mixed race. It was a typical house. They sat down to dinner every night. She was religious. She had a pretty good job. His foster mom played such an important role. She was so loving to him. He called her his mom; he was really into it. It was a great dynamic, and it set him up for success in his life, even though she always knew it might end.

She and I decided, because they had planned a birthday party for Ethan's upcoming birthday, I'd come the next day and pick him up. The day after his birthday, I showed up in my car. We spent some time together with his foster mom, played with the dog. Then we put his stuff in the car. I thought there would be more sadness when we left, but I don't think he really cried.

We drove home. His birthday falls right before Halloween, so we stopped at Target and got him a Halloween costume.

He has his own room at home. He had stuff there; he had the toys that he'd brought with him. We fell into a pattern very quickly. Since the school year had started, I took a few days off, but I wanted to get him around other kids. He went to pre-K every day until June, when he graduated.

We did all of the normal things. We went to the doctor, the dentist. We got him some more clothes, a lunch box. It was what you would expect if you had a four-year-old; it's just *suddenly* I had a four-year-old. But everything was pretty hunky-dory.

Foster parents get a bad rap sometimes, but most foster parents are just doing their best. They're working and trying to do something good, whether it is based on faith or their own beliefs, or for extra income.

On Adopting from Foster Care

One of the odd things about fost-adopt is that you continue to receive the monthly benefit as an adoptive parent. If I was a birth parent, I would have to pay for expenses. The adoption caseworker said, "I know that you don't need the money, per se, but it's for Ethan, too, so you may as well use it."

They do it so that people actually adopt, because otherwise there would be a financial disincentive to stop being a foster parent. I put $300 per month of that into a college fund for Ethan.

Until he's at least eighteen, he's going to have medical benefits. Good to have a backup, but I've had the medical benefits through work. Now that Ethan is going to therapy, coming out of some of the challenges from this school year, wow, it's adding up a lot. So I have started to use Ethan's government health care benefits for this reason.

Now, the county approved the same therapist, so, going forward, I won't be paying. Especially for a single person, even if my income is high, costs can add up very quickly, so it's nice that there is the government supplemental plan to go along with the benefits that I have from work.

What was weird about the experience was that it was fost-adopt, and I had a home study, but I was never an approved foster home. It wasn't set up that way with the private agency. In the audit process, two weeks later, the caseworker called me and said, "You're fine, but someone from the county is going to come to your house to make sure that it's suitable."

So, this woman flew up, came and checked the house, made sure there was nothing inappropriate, met Ethan. She said, "Oh, I think these windows can be pushed open; you need to put a lock on them. I need to see it fixed." So I went to the hardware store, got some dowels to put in the track.

Because they had kinda messed up, they were like, "We're just going to wrap this up quickly."

They had communicated the decision to the parents, and the only thing that could happen was that they could appeal it, but only if there was a factual error that wasn't considered. You don't just get to appeal to extend the process. They did file an appeal, but it didn't go anywhere.

Then we were done, it was final, and all we had to do was wait for the birth certificate. You think you've finished, but you can't do anything without a birth certificate. You don't have any proof. You worry about traveling because you don't have any documentation, especially as a single father. You get very anxious about these milestones because you think something could go wrong. But the document finally came and we were official. There's no birth mother on his certificate; it says that I am the only parent.

The higher meaning of fost-adopt is that you hear the personal anecdotes of these kids and see, "Wow, this really, really sucks." I appreciate that trying to place kids in permanent homes is a priority. It's like Maslow's hierarchy. At the bottom are food and shelter. If kids constantly worry about that, how can they do any schoolwork? How can they have normal relationships? How can they learn to navigate the world if there's this constant anxiety about where they live and whether they'll get to see their mom or not?

Ethan has had some challenges in the last year that may or may not harken back to all of these early transitions and some of the uncertainties, but it also is not abnormal for eleven-year-old boys to have trouble adjusting to being in school. In middle school, you change classrooms all the time. This is a brand-new school where a lot of teachers have quit and there are new teachers all the time.

It was a bad year for a lot of kids, but Ethan really did have a tough time, when he had had a great time in school the other seven years. I would say until last October, when we started seeing some of these issues, I didn't think anything was directly attributable to his earlier upbringing. But now, for the first time ever, I feel like there could be some aspects that are attributable to his early life, whether it's about attachment or separation or transitions.

My main fear was the age of the child. I thought I was good with babies and younger kids, but I didn't want an older kid. I had in my mind that the older the kid, the more the brain is developed and the more you can encounter something where the kid has some more profound challenges. I had friends with foster kids who had been placed when they were older, and they had a really tough time. One of the benefits of becoming a parent through adoption is that you get to make the choice. It's not your child until you choose that it *is* your child.

I thought, *I'm going to be a single dad, not just a single parent, and I don't want it to be even more challenging. It's going to be enough work to raise my child successfully, and, to the extent that I can minimize added challenges, I would like to do that, I think in part because I know I don't want a nine-year-old. If I can avoid that, I'd like to start with a younger child.*

I think fost-adopt is the easiest and the fastest path to adoption. There are tons of kids, it's an established system, and once you get in and are approved, it can happen quite quickly. The other paths take longer, for various reasons, and are more fraught with challenges.

Interaction with Birth Family

We don't have contact with either birth parent. They didn't even know who I was; they knew only my first name and my last initial. I really guarded Ethan's privacy. However, all foster children are entitled to visit with or communicate with their birth parents. Ethan's birth mother and birth father were entitled to get a bus ticket to come and visit us, but they didn't avail themselves of any of it.

She called one time, the day after Thanksgiving. That one phone call was pretty uneventful. I listened to it on speakerphone. Ethan doesn't like talking on the phone even now, much less at four. She said, "I miss you. I wish I could see you." She didn't ask questions: "How are you doing?" "What's your new house like?" Nothing. She called one time between October and May. Then I just turned the number off when Ethan's adoption was finalized in May. The birth father never called.

It's not so unknown that it's some kind of mystery who they are; I'm just trying not to make it a hot-button topic for Ethan. We talk about it happily and openly from time to time. We talk about it on Mother's Day. When he was little, I used to get a Mother's Day card because the teacher suggested it, or he thought of it—I don't know. On Mother's Day, I tell him, "I really love your mom because she brought you into the world."

As recently as a couple weeks ago, Ethan asked me some questions about his birth family. I said, "When you are old enough and ready for it, we can try to get in touch with them. It doesn't mean they want to get in touch with you. It's nothing personal; they may have moved on with their lives."

I used to hold a grudge, I used to be very judgmental, thinking, *How could you not have done right by this perfect child?* On the other hand, I wouldn't have been a parent had his birth mother been able to do it herself, so it's complicated.

The whole philosophy behind open adoption is that everyone says it's better for both the mother and the child to have as much of an ongoing relationship as they want to. It was hard for me to get my head around that. People have said to me, "How could you ever accommodate that?" The reality is, I'm the parent; I'm the one spending all the time with him. It's not like I would be replaced. I would be supplemented. I wasn't the birth father. He did come from somewhere, and it's healthy to want to know where that is. You can't pretend it didn't happen.

Single-Parent Logistics

For me, there was the philosophy of wanting to do it myself. It was a better way. It's just pragmatism. My closest relationship right now is with my child, which is great because I like being a parent. In terms of logistics, it's probably not that different from what any couple with two working parents would have to do. When Ethan was pre-K, he could be in day care from eight to six o'clock. If I had trips when he was younger, my mother would fly out. I think there were two or three trips in the first year that I went on. I wasn't traveling that much.

As he's gotten older, I've had sitters who can stay over-night with him when I travel. One of the greatest life lessons that's come out of this for me is that I've learned to ask for help. Because I was the responsible one growing up in my family, I wasn't in the habit of asking for help. Even when I would offer to help other people and they would take me up on it, it never occurred to me that in the grand scheme of things there should be reciprocity. Now I know that it's a natural give-and-take: if you are more collaborative, all the burden won't fall on you. That was a very important learning experience for me, and it helped me both professionally and personally.

Because I'm a single parent by choice, I have to find a way to fulfill my job duties. I like traveling—it's a nice way for me to have a forced break—but it also means that I have to spend a lot of money on overnight and childcare. People are like, "Oh my God, it's so expensive."

My standard, sexist joke back is, "It would be more expensive if I had a wife who stayed home."

People ask, "Do you turn that in on your expense report? Does the company pay when you have to travel?" and I say, "No, travel is part of the job, and I have to have childcare."

It's hard, especially for guys. They can't get their head around the whole thing because they aren't that involved, especially as parents. "Wait, *what* are you doing? That sounds crazy."

A support system is important in terms of seeking help but also talking about parenting. I talk a lot to other parents. So much comfort and learning comes out of those ongoing discussions.

Advice

There are different levels of risk, and they always warn you about this. The earlier you take the child in the foster care process (while birth parents are still trying to reunite successfully with the child), the more risk there is that the parents could get themselves back on track in such a way that they will be able to keep the child. The fewer of those milestone hearings that have happened, the more risk there is. On the other hand, the earlier you can get the kid, the better you'll be as a family, both the kids and the parents. I think that for some people, the uncertainty, the irregularity, the unpredictability of the process is very off-putting.

People also think a lot about the time that it takes. A couple says, "We can have a baby in nine months." Sometimes the length of time it takes can be discouraging. But the more restrictions on the type of kid that you are willing to take, the longer it will take.

The other aspect is there is a lot of prework to do. People think once they say, "I want to have a foster child" or, "I want to fost-adopt," the needs must be so profound, they'll get set up with a child right away. The reality is, there are always processes and it always takes longer than you think. That said, there are always things you can do to get yourself ready. A lot of the delays are caused by things that you yourself can manage. The home study is a big one.

You have to have your fingerprints taken. Get on it. Do the stuff that needs to be done. Once your mind is ready, you'll be anxious to become a parent as quickly as possible. They are happy to place a child with you as quickly as possible; the timing just depends on what the needs are and how fast you do your part.

For the home study, the reference checking, and the fingerprints, you have to open yourself up a bit. For some people, that's odd. People say, "You had a harder time having a kid than I did; I just had to have sex. Ha ha ha." I get that a lot. Look at it as a positive thing. I've really been scrutinized and probably will do a good job.

The invasiveness that some people might find in the process of the home visits isn't for everyone. It does take a village, and the village is still going to be involved in making sure that the kid is in a good situation and you are getting the resources you need to be a good parent.

CHAPTER 6:

DIVERSE FAMILIES
REFORM THE NORM

....

In her book *The Way We Never Were*, Sandra Coontz reminds her readers, "Contrary to popular opinion, *Leave It to Beaver* was not a documentary."[1] Many people in America continue to embrace a nostalgia for what is often referred to as the "traditional family," commonly defined as a heterosexual couple with biological children. However, as exemplified by the stories in *All the Sweeter*, shifting attitudes, policy changes, and the reality of people's lives have allowed for greater diversity in family formation, including a growing acceptance of adoption from foster care in the United States.

In her 1997 follow-up book, *The Way We Really Are*, Coontz elaborates, "People didn't watch [*Leave It to Beaver* and *Ozzie and Harriet*] to see their own lives reflected back at them. They watched to see how families were supposed to live—and also to get a little reassurance that they were headed in the right direction."[2] However, Coontz points out, these shows may not have accurately portrayed reality; if we concede that TV families provide a reflection of our culture, we see an evolution of families since the days of Ward and June and Ozzie and Harriet. In 1969, *The Brady Brunch* gave viewers the blended family of three girls belonging to Carol Brady and three boys belonging to Mike Brady. In 1978, on *Diff'rent Strokes*, a single white father with one biological daughter adopted two black sons. In 1990, Will Smith moved in with his aunt and uncle in *The Fresh Prince of Bel-Air*, and in 2000, a single mom raised her daughter on *Gilmore Girls*. Finally, in 2009, *Modern Family* introduced the Pritchetts, who combine biological, step, same-sex, multicultural, and adoptive families into one.[3]

As modern media have evolved, so too have America's policies, paving the way for family diversification and adoption from foster care for many families. In June 2015, the US Supreme Court legalized same-sex marriage across the country. Now that the freedom to marry is nationwide, same-sex married couples are allowed to jointly foster and adopt in nearly every state.[4] In her book *Single by Chance, Mothers by Choice*, Rosanna Hertz suggests that legal enactments of the civil rights era erased the "legal stigma of illegitimacy" by "redefining parental responsibility to children as no longer dependent upon marital status." In addition to birth control legalization that gave women control over when they became pregnant and thereby reduced the social stigma of single motherhood, these changes granted women an increased legal ability to have children outside marriage.[5]

And older parents? While minimum age requirements vary by state, most states do not list a maximum age requirement for fostering and adopting. Some states require additional review or waivers at age sixty-five (Arkansas, Delaware, West Virginia) and others at age sixty (Maryland); only Louisiana requires foster parents to be under age sixty-five with no exceptions.[6]

While the majority of states' policies and modern media portray an America recognizing and supporting diverse family structures, the public's acceptance may not be as clear. In his book *Modern Families*, Joshua Gamson notes that there remain some states that permit "state-licensed child welfare agencies to refuse to place and provide services to children and families, including LGBT people and same-sex couples, if doing so conflicts with their religious beliefs." Furthermore, Gamson references a 2010 study by Brian Powell and colleagues in which "100 percent of respondents agreed that 'husband, wife, children,' counted as a family, and a single man or a single woman with children counted for around 94 percent; the percentage saying that two women or two men with children counted as a family hovered around 55 percent."[7]

In addition, according to Susan Golombok, "It is commonly assumed that the more a family deviates from the norm of the traditional two-parent heterosexual family, the greater the risks to the psychological well-being of the children." However, in her book, also titled *Modern Families*, Golombok reviews countless studies to conclude that "the growing body of research on new family forms leads to the conclusion that family structure—including the number, gender, sexual orientation, and genetic relatedness of parents, as well as their method of conception—does not play a fundamental role in children's psychological adjustment or gender development."[8] The public's lack of recognition, as well as judgments based on assumptions, rather than on research, that children raised in nontraditional families will grow up with disadvantages can lead parents to question their family's identity as normal. Gamson cautions against this:

> *The goal of a life others recognize as "normal" seems at best a modest one. In fact, the pursuit of normalcy, which has a long history in lesbian and gay politics, has been roundly, and I think soundly, criticized. The idea that our worth is contingent on others' perception of us*

as normal is dangerous—for people who are deemed abnormal and absorb the conclusion that this makes them unworthy, it can be lethal. That idea needs to be challenged.[9]

A Pew Research Center study published in 2012 found gay marriage acceptance growing over time: 47 percent of respondents supported it, compared with 39 percent and 31 percent in similar studies in 2008 and 2004, respectively.[10] Subsequently, in 2015, just prior to the Supreme Court ruling, Andrew Flores published a study concluding that the majority of the public supports same-sex marriage and that differences in the framing of poll questions explain inconsistencies in results from polls that claim otherwise.[11] Although these studies show that recognition and support of diverse family structures may not be universal, they do show it as expanding. As Gamson reminds his readers, the aforementioned show, *Modern Family*, "was nominated for over a hundred major awards, including fifty-seven Emmy Awards, and won 'Best Comedy' Emmys five years in a row. Family diversity is not just visible; it gets awards."[12]

With this increased visibility and acceptance comes acceptance and recognition of adoption and, more specifically, adoption from foster care. Although parents adopting from foster care recognize and can celebrate the diversity of families, Debbie Trevino (chapter 2) pointed out that even in her family, which appears traditional and in which heterosexual parents and all family members share similar physical characteristics, society's difficulty recognizing diverse families can be as subtle as a lack of realization that a child can be adopted:

There have been instances during Emma's school life when she's gotten a little bit upset because not everybody thinks about how different families might be. Not all families are built the same way, especially now. There are so many different ways that you can be a family. Teachers don't always think about that. It's a challenge of being in a Catholic school. The thought is always, You have a dad, you have a mom, everything is this perfect little family. *I was born and raised Catholic, they are being raised Catholic, and sometimes there is a lack of open-mindedness about things. Our previous pastor, who recently retired, has an open mind. He fostered kids as a priest, and he still calls two of the boys his sons. He helps them financially and emotionally. He was better about having an open mind about how different families can be.*

Experts in the adoption field also recognize the potential for adoptive families to be viewed as different. The authors of *Adopting Older Children* reflect, "Some people continue to hold deep cultural or religious beliefs that family can only be formed through birth or marriage. Inflexible notions of family can make adoptive families feel marginalized in certain cultures or communities. But adoptive families have a unique opportunity to prove through their lived experiences that love, not blood, defines family."[13] This opportunity exists for all types of parents: older, single, gay, and lesbian included.

Since the turn of the millennium, as laws have opened up opportunities for gay and lesbian parents to adopt from foster care, these parents and their families have solidified their part in normalizing diverse family structures. While sources agree that the number of gay and lesbian parents adopting from foster care continues to grow, up-to-date national statistics exemplifying this trend, if they exist, are not easily found.[14]

In his article "Where She Comes From: Locating Queer Transracial Adoption," Don Romesburg explains the reason for this growth from the perspective of gay men:

For gay men, paths to biological reproduction require costly surrogacy or complex coparenting arrangements. Institutional and birth parent bias and expense make private adoption difficult. . . . Transnational adoption . . . is harder for gay men due to greater scrutiny of men and country policies banning same-sex adoption. Perhaps most significant, many gay men arrive at foster-adoption as a first choice rather than a fallback after failed reproduction, which is often the case for heterosexual and lesbian couples.[15]

Similarly, one of the adoptive moms from Rosanna Hertz's study describes how growing cultural acceptance of diverse families affected her perspective as a lesbian woman considering adoption. She said, "It just wasn't part of the culture, and I just have a lot of concerns about raising a child where other people would see our family as not healthy, and I didn't want to raise a child in that kind of environment. But as it became more and more of a popular thing to do within the gay and lesbian community, it just seemed like it was an okay option."[16]

Both parents and children play a role in helping neighbors, friends, classmates, and family understand their families. In his interview, Hugh Booker (chapter 7) described an interaction his son had with friends. He said, "We really do try to give our children positive language. From the time they were little, we had to give them language about having two dads. Rafael was teased about not having a mother, and I knew that would come up. He said to the person, 'Of course I have a mother. We all have a mother. That's who we grow inside of. I just don't live with my mother.' I was so proud of him."

As gay parents shed the assumption that only heterosexual partners can be parents, single parents, gay and straight, also work to discard the assumption that one must be coupled to have children. If they marry at all, men and women are pushing back their age at first marriage. In 1955, the median age at first marriage was 22.6 for men, 20.2 for women. By 2016, the age increased by about seven years for both sexes, to 29.5 and 27.4 for men and women, respectively.[17] In her 1997 book, Sandra Coontz describes marriage as "an option rather than a necessity for men and women, even during the child-raising years," and noted that 3.8 million single parents in 1970 grew to 12.2 by 1996.[18]

In 2000, KIDS COUNT Data Center began tracking the number of children living with single parents. The number stood at 20.7 million in 2000, or 31 percent of children in the United States, and grew to 24.4 million, or 35 percent of US children, in 2015.[19] In 2017, single parents adopted almost a third of children adopted from foster care. Single females adopted 14,811 children, and single males adopted 1,983.[20]

While there may not be quite as many single fathers as single mothers adopting from foster care, their numbers are slowly and steadily increasing, up from 669 in 1998.[21] Unfortunately, resources for single dads remain minimal. Hugh Booker commented on the lack of information specific to dads. He said that when his kids first moved in, he "had subscriptions to three magazines. Most of it is geared toward moms. I always thought that if I had the time and money, I would do one for dads. So much doesn't apply to us."

Brian Tessier, a single adoptive parent of two boys from foster care, had similar feelings and wrote *The Intentional Father: Adventures in Adoptive Single Parenting.* Tessier echoes the sentiments of many single parents when he says, "I decided to become a father, as becoming a husband was proving much more difficult. I was beginning to think I had a better chance at pregnancy."[22]

Similar to Tessier, as they pass through childbearing ages, many single women decide not to wait any longer to find a partner and move forward with having a child. Rosanna Hertz, who interviewed sixty-five single moms for her book *Single by Chance, Mothers by Choice*, describes how single women today make the decision to become a parent on their own:

> *As they believed marriage to be slipping further and further out of their reach, motherhood, on the other hand, moved closer, drawn in by their desire for children. As Claudia put it, women were "running two races and losing at both." Faced with the decision to choose one or the other in order to win, women found themselves making a difficult life decision. While social norms would dictate throwing the baby out with the bathwater—that is, discarding motherhood because marriage seemed unattainable—women salvaged the baby [and] shed the burden of marriage, determined to win the race to motherhood alone. Taking stock of the road ahead, women saw a course very different from that of women in generations before.* [23]

Although men and women may often arrive at the decision to have children on their own for similar reasons, women uniquely possess the option of bearing their own child. Some women try to become pregnant and arrive at the decision to fost-adopt only after failed attempts at pregnancy. Others, like Anna Walters (chapter 13), know they would like to adopt and state financial support makes it possible. Still others, like Brooke Olson (chapter 14), explore additional options:

> *I thought of going the in vitro way; I even went to a sperm bank and found a donor. But I had the worst migraine of my life that night and decided that wasn't for me; I wasn't comfortable. I had a foster sister when*

I was young, for two years, and I think because of her, I was not uncomfortable with [the foster-to-adopt process] at all.

Once single men and women decide to adopt children from foster care, they must prepare for the challenges of raising children without a partner. Brooke Olson commented:

I have some friends who say, "Oh yeah, my husband is out of town, it's such a nightmare, I totally know how you feel." I think, No you don't, you don't. I don't mean that in a bad way, I don't say that to them, but it's very different because there's nobody coming home. I went into it with my eyes wide open. People say, "How do you do it?" and I say, "I don't know any different," right? Single mothers by choice.

Anna Walters found tremendous support in her son's first foster parents, who are now his godparents. Brooke also has a strong support system in her family and neighbors. Aaron Keller (chapter 5) adds that the financial support from the state helps. He says that, in addition to using state assistance funding to add money to Ethan's college fund, "We have a housekeeper come the second day of every week. I use the [state support] for something that helps me. As a single parent, I could spend all of my time cooking and cleaning and shopping. I try to find ways to use the money to offset that a little bit." He added that he likes being the only parent. "I think it's actually easier. I can seek advice, but what I say goes; there is no court of higher appeal."

Older parents, single or partnered, also can fost-adopt. Similar to the growing number of gay, lesbian, and single parents, older parents are breaking the traditional family mold. Assisting to normalize the older parents' role in society is the statistic that one in ten children live with a grandparent. In about one-third of these homes, the grandparent(s) have primary responsibility for the children.[24] In 2007, the National Survey of Adoptive Parents found 38 percent of children age zero to seventeen adopted from foster care live with a parent between the ages of fifty and sixty, and 16 percent have parents over the age of sixty.[25]

Laura Bolton (chapter 17) described a fellow fost-adopt parent in her county:

> One woman, probably in her late seventies now, has been a foster mom for a really long time and adopted a lot of kids. I remember telling someone else about her. They said, "Oh, that's too old." But there's nowhere else for these kids to go. It was a sibling set of three girls; no one else would take them. I remember seeing them at a foster party; these three little girls were all around her, touching her. They were this beautiful little family. Who's to say that's wrong—a seventy-three-year-old woman with three children of a different race? It works. They're a family. I just love that about adoption—a family can be anything.

Truly. As Adam Pertman said in his book, *Adoption Nation*, "Our collective definition of 'normal' is evolving every day, and yet, in many ways, we cling to the concept of the biologically formed nuclear family. Our perceptions will catch up to reality only when everyone faces up to the fact that a huge percentage of our children are adopted, or have divorced or single or gay or foster parents, or have a skin color different from that of other members of their families."[26]

Supporting Pertman's comment, in 2014, Pew Research found that more than half of American children live in a "non-traditional" family. Specifically, 46 percent "of US kids younger than eighteen years of age are living in a home with

two married heterosexual parents in their first marriage."
This is a decrease from 73 percent in 1960 and 61 percent
in 1980.[27] In his interview, Aaron Keller emphasized the
foster parent trainings reflecting this shift in our society:

> *You see who is in the class with you. There are empty
> nesters, religious people, infertile people. There was a
> lesbian couple. There were second families who wanted
> to have a kid together, but they weren't going to have
> one naturally. There was a single guy, me. It was liter-
> ally every family type. Then you do all of these exercises
> with each other and realize that there are different
> motivations but we're all doing the same thing. . . .
> Everyone comes to be a parent differently. Even people
> who have children on their own, that happens in so
> many different ways. The whole white-picket-fence-
> and-everyone-is-married thing, that's really just not
> the norm.*

Whether parents find themselves beginning the foster-
to-adopt process or are in the middle of raising children
adopted from foster care, they will find themselves in a
growing number of families that also do not fit the "traditional
family mold." These families will devise creative strategies,
similar to those of Hugh Booker and Celeste's moms, that
help their children and families navigate potentially difficult
situations in their communities. In doing so, these families
exercise their opportunity to define their unique family and
potentially help others understand and accept the many
diverse forms of families in America today.

CHAPTER 7:

COME AND MEET MY CHILDREN:
THE BOOKER FAMILY

Hugh and his then husband, Mark, adopted siblings, three boys, ages seven, four, and three. When I interviewed the Bookers in the spring of 2016, Rickey, the oldest, was sixteen. He was in eleventh grade, played baseball, and had worked as a camp counselor the previous summer. Troy, thirteen, played the trombone, practiced parkour, and worked as a camp counselor in training. He started high school that year. The youngest, Rafael, twelve, liked art and archery, played tennis, and was studying the clarinet and the flute. He was in eighth grade and excelled in school. All three boys would be in high school together in the fall. When Hugh and Mark divorced in 2013, they agreed that Hugh would have custody of the children. Hugh tells his family's story, and the boys participate at several points.

Adoption Story

RAFAEL: I was three, Troy was four, and Rickey was seven.

People in the Booker Family's Story

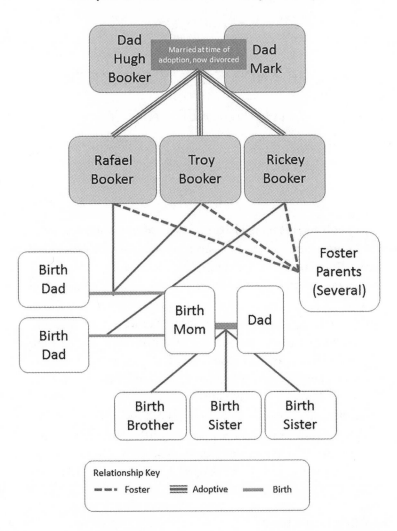

RICKEY: I remember going to at least two foster homes. In one, I remember watching a lot of TV and going to parks with them. They were nice. They invited a lot of friends over all the time, and they'd have parties and we'd play in the backyard. That was a couple of months.

HUGH: That was your last placement before you guys moved in with us. There were a lot. Michelle and Jack was one, and I'll share that story so that you guys don't have to talk about that. September will be our ten-year anniversary since they moved in. I will have three teenagers, thirteen, fourteen, and seventeen. Aaah!

Do you guys remember the first day we met?

TROY: No, but supposedly I knocked down Daddy.

RICKEY: I remember being a little bit shy, and then I felt really comfortable because they were happy to see us.

HUGH: Legally we were not able to apply for permanent adoption or permanent placement until they had lived with us for six months. At six months and a day, we had the adoption agency fill out the paperwork. We were sure. The parental rights had been terminated already, though the biological parents were still notified, and there was a waiting period. We set our court date as soon as we could after that. It was right before Mother's Day weekend ten years ago. Do you remember going to court?

RAFAEL: I do. I remember getting out of the car and going in, and I remember sitting in front of the judge and him talking to us. Aunt Kathy and Uncle Rob went with us.

HUGH: At court, we had friends around us. Vicky and Sarah were there. Mark and I are both emotional people and we knew we would cry. There were a lot of happy tears. Mark and I had to sign a thousand things.

RAFAEL: In the first picture they sent to Daddy and Papi of us, we had all been sleeping. They woke me up from my nap, and I was crying in the photo. Rickey was smiling, and Troy was just staring off.

HUGH: When you go through the process and you get to the point where you're ready to be matched, you sit at the agency and you go through binders. You put a Post-it note on the pages of the children you're interested in. It's awful. It's like catalog shopping. There's a boys section, a girls section, and a siblings section. Every Tuesday or every other Tuesday, it was updated, and we were there every time.

We did a family book because we had to sell ourselves to the children's social workers. We were not considered for any of the sibling groups that we were interested in. Their social worker saw our profile and said, "Hey, how about these three boys?"

Papi [Hugh's ex] and I were in Seattle on vacation with some friends. We were on the ferry going to Bainbridge Island when we got a call that said they would email us a picture. The social worker lined them up against the wall to take a picture of them, and Rafael was crying because they had woken him up from a nap. It was out of the blue. It was August 22 when we met them, and they moved in on September 6. We didn't even have the house ready.

They say there's a long process in foster care. You meet them, you meet them again, you possibly do an overnight with them. Because Rickey was starting first grade, they asked us, "Are you willing to take him as soon as possible so that he isn't put into a school and then pulled out again?"

That Labor Day weekend, we went to IKEA to buy

furniture. We moved our house around and put together furniture. I don't think we slept. [Laughs.]

RICKEY: I kind of remember the first day. I remember trying to arrange our rooms. That took a long time. And I remember I didn't want Troy and Rafael to be far from me, but Troy wanted to be far. I got mad at him for that.

HUGH: Do you remember on the ride home how I got you guys to take a nap in the car?

RAFAEL: He said the first one to take a nap would get to pick which bed they had.

RICKEY: That's right! I got the worst one.

HUGH: When I was younger, probably before I explored with our agency, I was going to have a child with a friend of mine. Ultimately, she wasn't ready, so it didn't happen. When we were exploring adoptions, I considered international adoptions. It didn't feel right to me because there were so many kids in our state. We considered surrogacy, and that didn't really feel right to me. So it was always, "Let's go through the county." While I would have loved to have an infant, I was older and knew I wouldn't have had the energy for one. That's another thing—everyone wants that little kid. When I've talked to friends of mine or acquaintances, friends of friends who are interested in adoption, they all want babies. I always invite them to come and meet my children.

If I had held out and just wanted an infant, I wouldn't have this family.

I felt like I was really prepared, I had gone through the adoption process as a single person with my agency. Then, when it got to the matching stage, I realized I couldn't do this by myself. However, even growing up as a gay man, I've always known that I wanted to be a parent. So I stopped the process, but when Mark and I got together, I let him know that I was interested in having a child. He never thought that he would be a parent growing up as a gay man, but he comes from a big family, so he was open to it.

I knew I wanted to adopt these boys the day I met them. We met them at a park. Their social worker brought them. I don't know how they were prepped for it. I remember Troy running up to me and literally knocking me down with a big hug. We had brought a picnic, so the five of us sat at the park and ate together. At the end of the day, Troy was like, "I don't want to leave."

When they first moved in, because most of his life was in foster care, Rafael really didn't talk. It may be that he didn't know how long he would be in this situation, so he just didn't bother. Rickey would talk for him or translate for him because we couldn't really understand him. Well, now he's the talker. He's the one who advocates for himself the most.

They get along well. They bicker, but they don't really fight. I'm very lucky.

Overcoming Challenges

The boys were in the adoption process with another family. Before they can get to that point, parental rights have to be terminated. The family petitioned the court to move them out of state, which is rarely granted, but it was for work. They were days away from finalizing the adoption, and Rickey was taken to the emergency room. It had been an abusive household. They had never been caught. When they took him to the emergency room and he said that he fell down, the attending physician said, "No, you didn't" and called CPS. The parents went to jail. It was over something stupid. He ate one of her diet bars or something, and she picked him up and threw him against the wall. He lost consciousness. He was six at the time. We could see the trauma on the boys when they moved in with us.

There's no manual for parenting. When I used to wash Troy's hair, I washed his hair the way my mom washed my hair when I was young. I said, "Lean back into my hand," and I scooped water onto his head. He would freak out; he wouldn't let me put him down. He would say, "Daddy, Daddy, I love you, I love you."

I would be like, "I know you do, buddy. I'm just going to wash your hair." There was something around water and trauma.

There was also trauma surrounding air travel. They were removed from the abusive home, and they were brought back to California, which still had jurisdiction over them, since the adoption had not been finalized. The first time they were on a plane was under these circumstances, so it was really traumatic for them. Now they're great fliers, great travelers.

I googled [the foster parents] afterward and found the story. It was distributed by AP; it was a big story. Then the boys had a short-term foster family who actually didn't want them to be placed with Mark and me because we're gay. The agency really went to bat for us and let them know they couldn't make that choice. The agency and the social workers for the children make that choice.

The great thing about our agency, which I have found out through talking to other parents, is that the other adoption agencies aren't as realistic about what happens. I felt that our agency was very realistic and told us honestly, "This is what you might encounter, and this is what you can do, and this is what we support you with." I felt really prepared for what might be. We got really great support from the agency in finding mental health services. We went as a family. Because we were so overwhelmed going from zero to three and both working full-time, our action plan was family therapy and therapy on a who-needs-it-most basis. It was Rickey. Rickey has been in therapy probably eight of the ten years with different therapists. He exhibits the most trauma—even as a teenager, he's afraid to be alone. He has his own bedroom here, but he sleeps with his brothers. The way he sleeps, he wraps his legs up and curls around. He either dreamed it often or someone used to come into his room and pull at his legs to get him out of bed. He did it for a really long time; he just needed to tuck himself in and feel safe. Even now, his bed is up against the wall. He stuffs things between the wall and the bed. Fear is irrational. We don't make a big deal out of it.

We've had some great therapists. We get to a point where they say he's okay. But whenever a big change happens, such as when Mark and I made the decision to divorce, it's Rickey that we're most concerned about. Finally, a couple of years ago, he said, "Can I stop talking to people? I'm just sick and tired. Can I just talk to you about stuff?"

I said, "Yes, but know that those people and those resources are always available to you."

I think in our community, we are really fortunate because community members are a little more educated. Before we got here, there was a two-dad family, and then we joined and then they moved on and then another family came in. Because that family, our family, and this family were all very involved in school, people knew us. That was intentional on my part, for the teachers and the administration to know me. My kids tease me because they say I talk to people all the time. I say, "I do not want people having a preconception of me without knowing me."

There are also countless two-mommy families at that school, so same-sex parenting was never really too big of an issue. Rickey went to a private middle school, and again, because the parents there are a little more educated, it was never an issue, and the headmaster was also gay.

Rickey has always played sports, so he's around a lot of testosterone. But his teammates always know me. A couple of years ago when his team made it to state finals, the coach for that team asked me to be the team parent. Again, I'm lucky, I was born and raised in a city where it really was never an issue for me. I got teased about it at school, but not in a big way. I was out in high school. That long ago.

I don't know how my kids feel about it. It would be interesting to ask them. I do ask them when they start a new school, "Does anyone tease you about having two dads?"

"No, not really."

I check in with them whenever the environment is new for them. It's never really been an issue, or they're not sharing that it is.

Relationship with Biological Family

We knew when we saw the boys that they were good kids. Our one hesitation was that their social worker asked us to consider having a relationship with their birth family. We were really insecure about that. We had heard the stories of, "Oh, you get the birth families involved, and they try to take the kids back." Emotionally, we knew that we wouldn't be up for that battle.

The boys are the youngest of six. They have three older siblings who were separated from them. We keep in touch with the siblings. The siblings initiate contact with us all the time. They FaceTime and text the boys. We see them four or five times a year. They live ninety minutes away. They've come to the boys' sports games. You can tell that they were all brought up in the same way. They are all really nice, polite, good kids. Really, it was just a circumstance of the adult in their lives not knowing how to be an adult.

Their birth mother had the older three kids with one man and then had Rickey with a different man and then Troy and Rafael with a different man. The six of them have three different fathers. Apparently, those fathers all have other families. I wasn't so concerned about the birth mom. The social worker let us know that her parental rights had been terminated by the time we met her. However, we do keep in touch with her; she's seen them six times in the last ten years. But she doesn't seem very interested in them. She asks about them, but when we're together, she wants to talk to me. The boys don't really know her.

Talking About Adoption

We have open dialogue that the boys are adopted. You can see that they are. We talk about role models who are adopted adults. My dad is adopted. He grew up in China, where people want a son. His adoptive parents had a girl and physically weren't able to have more children. In those days, if you had money and wanted another child, you purchased another child—you know, an adoption fee.

My dad moved to Hong Kong, where he met my mom, and they emigrated to the US. His adoptive parents emigrated to Canada, and then my maternal grandparents emigrated here and sponsored my parents.

The boys and I want to be advocates. They like to share their stories.

Family Activities

RAFAEL: We go to camp down the street, at a recreation center.

HUGH: They grew up going to camp there. It will be Troy's first year volunteering, and Rickey has volunteered two summers, so this will be the first year that he gets paid. Our goal is to see different baseball stadiums every year. Last year we saw both of the New York stadiums, and this year, hopefully we will see both of the Chicago stadiums.

RAFAEL: We went at the beginning of last summer. We saw the two baseball teams, the Yankees and the Mets. We went to the Statue of Liberty and the Empire State building, and our hotel was very close to Times Square. We went to the Guggenheim museum and the Museum of Natural History.

TROY: We have family game night with five other families who went to our elementary school.

RICKEY: Whoever is hosting is supposed to have a board game ready. The older kids, like me, watch scary movies, or we go outside and just run around and yell and play. We also play video games together and go shopping for shoes together.

HUGH: One thing that my children unfortunately got from me is a love of shoes.

We like to scare one another. I love to scare my children.

RICKEY: One time we were outside and Rafael had gone in early. I went in after Rafael and saw that Troy was still outside. I hid in the garage in a really good hiding spot and waited for him to put away his bike. I scared him really bad, got him screaming really loud on video.

RICKEY: We like to prank each other. Rafael likes to whistle and sing.

RAFAEL: I don't sing!

ALL: Yes, you do.

RICKEY: He never talked when he was little. But then one day he went outside and started whistling, and a little bird just came up to him and landed on him, and he thought he was talking to the bird. You know how birds talk, like, every three seconds? They have a pattern that they tweet to. You whistled in between those tweets and thought they were talking to you.

RAFAEL: I did not.

RICKEY: Troy is a comedian. He makes us laugh a lot.

RAFAEL: Troy's the comedian, Rickey is the athletic one, and I'm the brains.

HUGH: I'm very lucky. I have really good boys.

Advice

RICKEY: Take it slow.

HUGH: Don't do it—they ruin everything! [Laughs.]

RAFAEL: I'd say that at first it seems a little scary, depending on how you process it, but then it turns out to be great because you get all these opportunities and you get to know new people. If we weren't adopted, we wouldn't know anyone that we know now in our lives. We wouldn't be living here; we wouldn't have any of the friends that we have now.

RICKEY: That's totally true.

RAFAEL: They should be prepared, because it's definitely a lot of responsibility.

RICKEY: Yeah, don't rush it. They let us have the option of where we wanted our beds. They asked us what we wanted. Make sure they are comfortable, too, before you start deciding what they want—until they're comfortable and you're comfortable with them. The kids should be open to new things and not scared of them, because the outcome could be better than they thought it would.

RAFAEL: Sometimes I assume the worst of things where they're really not that bad. You can't assume the worst of everything.

HUGH: My advice to potential parents: read a lot, really know what you're getting into, and don't stop. We read a boatload of books that people we knew who had adopted passed along to us. We didn't really identify with much of it, so really it was skimming. Then it was parenting magazines. I would say, do a lot of research and know what you're in for. Ask the questions of the adoption agency. I know it sounds awful, but I think, given the way that foster placements happen or concurrent planning happens, you can try it out. They can come live with you on a trial basis. There should be no guilt because you can't commit to it. Just because you started it, it has to be right.

Our parameters were to get a sibling pair under the age of three. I was older and did not want to have to repeat the process. I wanted my children to have blood relationships to one another because I'm older and thought, *What if I have a medical issue?*

Also, in my mind, under three was the age where I could still love them and hold them and they would let me hold them and love them. When we were presented with the boys at three, four, and seven, it was tough for me. I worried about a seven-year-old. But it turned out to be the best thing. He was their caretaker, and he had to be. So, my advice is, know what you want and start there, but leave your options open. And when you're presented with something that may not fit your parameters, really consider it.

CHAPTER 8:

PATCHWORK:

THE SCHNEIDER FAMILY

....

Heidi and Jeffrey met in Heidi's home country of Germany and moved together to Jeffrey's home country, the United States, in 2003. When they married, Jeffrey became a stepfather to Heidi's two children from a previous marriage. They then had two biological children, Stewart and Sacha. When Stewart and Sacha were in elementary school in 2012, the family adopted Vance and Trevor. Heidi and Jeffrey now have four children in high school. Vance, the oldest, is a senior, Trevor is a junior, Sacha is a sophomore, and Stewart, the youngest, is a freshman. Heidi says that Trevor makes her smile when he "comes into the living room and says, 'Did I already get my daily kiss?'" The whole family (except for Heidi's older kids, who have moved out of the house) tells their story.

People in the Schneider Family's Story

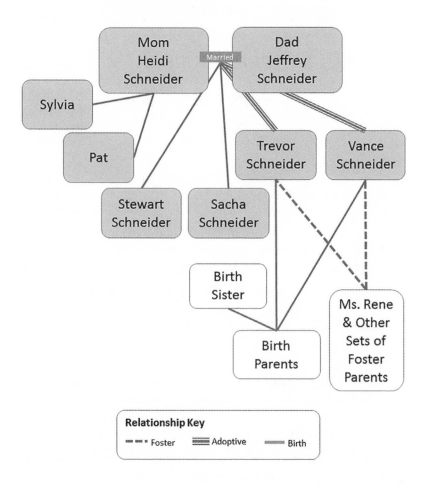

Introductions

HEIDI: I'm Heidi. I'm the mama. The patchwork starts with me because I am German. I have two older children from a previous marriage, and we have two biological children from our marriage together, and then Vance and Trevor as the additions. We are very happy and lucky that we found each other; it feels like a match made in heaven. We are really working well together. From my side, I always wanted to adopt children my whole life. I feel like every child should have the same opportunity to get the best out of life.

SACHA: I'm Sacha. I like music. I'm in a band; it is very important to me. I love my family, even with how crazy and mixed up it is.

TREVOR: I'm Trevor. I'm very outgoing and social. I love dancing. I play soccer. I love my family. We have our ups and downs like every other family.

STEWART: I'm Stewart. I like coding and making games. It's fun being in this family. We all have different dislikes and likes.

VANCE: I'm Vance, and I am the oldest of the little ones. I like playing football, and I love my family.

JEFFREY: I'm Jeffrey. I'm the dad. I went over to Germany to work on the German banking systems, and that's when I met Heidi. I played soccer in Germany. I am a computer executive right now for Vance Systems. Vance likes that because I work for him.

Basically, we just try to create paths for the kids. That's all that you can do as an adult: create paths for the children and try to show them the right direction, whether they are biological, adoptive, step, whatever. It's "Here is the path that you can take; if you make decisions to go on the wrong path, there's not a whole lot that we can do about it, but we can show you that that's not necessarily the best path to be taking."

Adoption Story

HEIDI: Jeffrey and I talked about adoption over and over again, but it never took shape. We went to a CPS meeting to get information about fostering and adoption and all that comes with it. There were a few people there from different adoption agencies, and there was one specific agency that felt right, their policies and the whole feeling about them. It was a match. We talked to them and decided to go on.

We talked with Stewart and Sacha before we got into the whole process. We asked them their opinion, and they said that they would be very happy to share what they have because they felt that other kids should have the opportunities they've had. They always looked at you guys as full siblings. They never said, "That's my mom" or, "This is actually mine." They 100 percent accepted the situation, and they were 100 percent brothers from day one.

The agency loved us from the first moment because many people say, "I want a white child, I want a Hispanic child, I want an African American child, this age, this gender," but we said, "We don't care. We are taking everything; we don't care if it is a two- or three-year-old. We don't care if it is an eighteen-year-old. We don't care about race. We don't care if it's a sibling group, if it's a single person. It doesn't matter as long as we can help a child or more than one child." They loved us.

Then CPS and the Rotary Club invited us to a Funfest. People looking for kids to adopt could go to the park, and social workers or foster families came with their kids.

Jeffrey immediately went to this bounce house. He didn't come back. He was watching Vance and Trevor in this bounce house: "Oh my God. Oh my God. Look at them. Aren't they cute?"

They must have felt there was this guy stalking them through the park the whole time.

TREVOR: I didn't even notice until Stewart and I were playing the Wii.

HEIDI: You didn't notice that he was following you guys around? It was hilarious. I said, "Oh my God, yeah, they are so cute."

It was time to have lunch, and we sat with a lady and her husband. He was in a wheelchair. We started chatting with them, and suddenly Vance and Trevor came to the table and sat down. We were like, "Oh my God." It was their foster parents.

Ms. Rene was their foster mom. She really liked us and pushed for us, too. She helped to convince CPS that we were the right fit.

We applied for a group of three. They have a sister, but at the time, she was not ready for adoption. We are going to visit her today. She was adopted by an amazing couple. We love them. We have aunties and uncles, too; our family just grew.

TREVOR: We see our biological sister once every other week. She likes to come over. Sometimes she comes here, or we go there and we go out. She lives ten minutes away. She is fifteen.

JEFFREY: It was right before Halloween. They came over to go trick-or-treating, and they spent the night. When we asked them, they said, "Yes," they wanted to come. They officially switched to us as foster parents right before Vance's birthday. Vance was twelve, and Trevor was eleven. Vance turned thirteen that year. That was our first teenager in a while. We'd just sent Sylvia off to college.

TREVOR: I remember at the festival after we got out of the bounce house, because I like video games as well, I went to the Wii. I didn't know it was Stewart who was playing with me the whole time.

VANCE: To me it was just like a party. Nobody told us what was going on. After that day, they told us, "You are going to have to go to a different family. This family that you are with is not going to be able to have all the things that you need, like a mom and dad." That's when I started noticing.

TREVOR: Kids in foster care get so used to a family; then they end up having to move to a new family and a new school and they have to adjust to a new climate. Adoption is good because it helps kids be able to get to know the family well. The kids know they could stay with this family for the rest of their lives and be happy with them and have things that they didn't have before. It's a good thing.

Being adopted made me feel more relaxed, more comfortable. As a kid, I'm still hyper, and I had to get used to waking up and thinking, *Oh my gosh, am I going to have to move?* It could be anytime; CPS would come and take you away. This time, I actually knew that it wasn't going to happen. It made me feel more loved, more wanted.

VANCE: I felt I had to get unattached to my last foster home. She was nice, and she did a lot of things for me, but she told me, "It's not going to stay like this forever."

HEIDI: For Vance, it was especially hard to leave the last foster family. We love Renee, and we loved her husband. Unfortunately, her husband died. Vance really wanted to stay with them. Renee was fair and always said, "I love you guys dearly. If I would adopt, I would adopt you, but I'm not going to." I think it was very nice that she was always open and honest.

TREVOR: I remember taking a road trip on adoption day. It was all of us: me, my mom, my sister, my brother, my dad and Vance, my grandma and grandpa—Oma and Opa, we called them. We all drove to the court, and I think we played auto bingo or something on the way there.

When we got to the court, we went through the security scan and waited until the judge was ready. We met with the judge. He knew our history, and he explained the process to us. He asked us, "Do you want this family to be your family for the rest of your life?"

I said, "Yes." After that, I was happy for the whole day. It was fun. I think afterward we celebrated.

JEFFREY: We asked you guys where you wanted to go, and you said Denny's.

VANCE: I remember it was the day of saying yes or no. They already prepared us for months to stay with them, and I already got used to the family, and all of this was to confirm it.

HEIDI: The most important part was that we were all happy to get rid of CPS. We never had to write reports anymore and never had to answer to them anymore. We could just do our thing.

JEFFREY: You can't understand how limiting CPS is. I understand why they have to do it, don't get me wrong. But when we have to ask whether or not we can take them on a family trip to Georgia to go to a wedding, that's kind of ridiculous; it doesn't make them feel like part of the family when every time that we want to go do something, or if they want to spend the night with a friend, we have to submit forms. We almost had to get a judge's approval to take them to Georgia. The point of a foster family is that it is a family.

It seems as if CPS is following a set of rules that were created by people who have no concept of what foster families are and what sorts of tensions and interactions and bonding are going on. They have to create a generic set of rules, but that generic set of rules becomes onerous. I remember when Trevor broke his thumb at basketball practice.

HEIDI: Oh, the forms we had to fill out—my God.

JEFFREY: All I wanted to do was make sure that he got the treatment that he needed. I spent a good ten days filling out forms. Again, I understand—there are people who do bad things—but it really is a deterrent for good people who want to do good things for the kids.

TREVOR: I played football, and I really liked it. One of the families let Vance play football and not me, and that felt unfair. We stayed in our room most of the day. The only time we came out of our room was to eat and watch TV for thirty minutes. It was pretty mortifying.

HEIDI: Unfortunately, there are families in the foster system that are just doing it for the money. It's horrible. On top of all the bad experiences that the kids have, they're sometimes coming into a foster family that's keeping them almost captured, locked up in the room. They were feeding you guys Tuna Helper, and they were eating steaks. There is a trauma on top of trauma.

JEFFREY: I remember in the paperwork that toward the end of their stay, they were apparently being sent to school in dirty clothes. That's what triggered the teachers to call CPS. We obviously weren't around at that point.

HEIDI: After the adoption, nobody came anymore.

JEFFREY: Preadoption, we had a visit once every six weeks.

HEIDI: The adoption agency required us to write weekly reports about medication and about everything that we did. "Today we went to the mall with them. Today we went to a movie." It was crazy. You don't feel like preparing for normal family life because you're so into your reports, you have to watch every step you make—*Is that allowed? Is that not allowed?*

JEFFREY: But if someone doesn't want to give you that information . . . I really suspect that foster family didn't write that they locked the kids in their room every day, or that they served Tuna Helper. I can almost guarantee that they talked about when they took Vance to football. You should know as a CPS worker that it wouldn't be difficult to go and visit them in school, take a look, and see what's going on. You don't even have to have an interview with the kids. You can just look and see: Do they look like they're adjusting? Do they look like they're getting the things they need in order to be kids? Ask Vance—he didn't feel like a kid for a long time.

VANCE: I guess I felt like I had to look out for Trevor, yeah.

TREVOR: I think I looked up to him when I was a kid. I was following him. That's how it usually goes—you look up to your older brother.

HEIDI: It's an automatic if you have a sibling group in foster care. They have each other, so they look out for each other. I think it's always a thing that the older one looks out for the younger ones. It's far too much pressure for a ten- or twelve-year-old to have the feeling that they need to protect their younger siblings. Whether they have to do it or not, they will do it.

Transitioning to a New Family

TREVOR: They gave us our first opportunities. Being in a family, we were able to do certain things for the first time. We could actually have stuff to do and have fun at the same time while adjusting to the process. For kids like us, just be patient. Like I said, there are ups and downs. *Patience* is a good word for it.

Adoption comes with a lot of things. Of course, you have problems and you have happy times and you have sad times, and there are usually things that you have to work through. I mean, that's basically the definition of family.

HEIDI: Cooking is a very important part of that for me, too. Feed them well, and they will be happy. There are a lot of little daily things to think about, especially when you have this mix of cultures and everything else. I cook a lot of German food, and at first my kids were like, "What is that?" Now we all know that Vance hates potato dumplings and Trevor loves them. They all like my red cabbage with bacon, and they like goulash. You just have to figure out the little things. You have to be very patient and chew through all of these ups and downs and get to know each other. You can't do this in a few months. They are kids or teenagers, and they develop in different directions because they have a background that plays a big role. We cannot expect that we are the only influence on them. We always have to consider that there is the past and there always will be the past and this is what made them who they are today. A little bit of this and a little bit of that.

School Life

JEFFREY: Stewart is a freshman in high school, Sacha's a sophomore in high school, Trevor's a junior in high school, and Vance is a senior in high school. They couldn't make it easy and attend the same school—that would have been way too simple. Vance and Sacha are both at one high school, Trevor's at a different high school, and Stewart is at a different high school. Stewart is in an international baccalaureate program, so he had to go to a different high school. Vance and Sacha said that they wanted to stay in the same school when we moved to a different house, and Trevor said he wanted to move away from the school because he wasn't happy with it.

TREVOR: It's nice to have changed schools, because you get to meet new people. At Brooks, my old school, you have to, like, fit into a clique. At my new school, it's more people all together; they all get along better.

SACHA: I have band at Brooks. I didn't really want to leave my band family. I'm happy that I stayed, because I really like the band there.

VANCE: I always played football. They asked me if I wanted to move, and I was like, "No, why would I?" I already had friends at Brooks since I was a freshman. Why would I move to a different school and meet new people and graduate with people that I don't even know?

Race and Religion

HEIDI: We have an atheist, we have two Baptists, we have a Methodist, we have kind of a Christian, and we have a freethinker all in one family. Try to find a church for that. You have to build a lot of tolerance about all of these things. We are not African American [like two of our sons are]. I don't have a lot of African American friends, so I cannot provide them with any of their heritage culture. They have a lot of African American friends, and when they go to their houses, they can experience a little bit more of it, like the soul food and all of this stuff. This is something that I am really sorry about but cannot provide.

But it's the same with all my kids. I don't want them to be typical Caucasian kids. I like multicultural. If one of them wants to be a Buddhist or a Hindu, I would support that. If they suddenly ran around in, I don't know, traditional Kenyan robes, I would be fine with that, too. Everybody should live their own unique culture, religion, whatever.

TREVOR: I really don't care. I have a lot of white friends and a lot of black friends. It's even. It's nothing different. When they come over here, some people are surprised because they don't know that I'm adopted. They're like, "Your parents are white?" I'm like, "Yeah, I'm adopted. I think it's cool; it's a special thing." If they're your friends, they should be okay with it, and if they're not okay with it, then I guess they shouldn't be your friends.

VANCE: I think the same. At first it was a little weird just to tell people, because they were kind of confused: "How are your parents white and you're black?" But I've gotten used to it. It just doesn't cross my mind now, because they're my family and they love me.

HEIDI: Just peel off the outer layer, and we're all red underneath anyway.

We try to talk about a lot of race-related subjects over family dinner. Let's say the stuff in the news, like kids [of color] being shot by white officers. We don't have any taboos. We are talking about religion, sex, and crime and everything—no taboos in our family. We have conversations about problems that black people in America have, like the Ku Klux Klan. We are walking toward a time where these people will be more accepted, and this is scary. I try to raise all of my kids with a backbone, and if they think there's something going on that's not right, they will speak up. They will defend their rights.

JEFFREY: One of the things that we have always done is try to say that there is no color. At the same time, not everyone believes that particular notion and so we've had some very frank conversations about the fact that they are young black males walking around the streets of the South and they are going to have a different set of standards applied to them. Even if we don't apply those standards, other people do. It's very concerning to me.

Let's say they're walking around with their black friends and they get picked up by police officers for some stupid reason. If I walk in there, I'll be able to take Vance out of there with no problem, whereas his friend may have to spend the night in jail because his parents are black. That is a conversation that we've had, because the injustice and the inequality are a fact. We try to tell them not to get themselves in that sort of situation.

In football this year, unfortunately, we believe very strongly that Vance got a racist coach. I think in the beginning, he didn't see that. When we pointed out the little things that closet racists do and things that people who have not been taught better do to cause that level of racism, you can't deny the fact that he's acted in a racist manner this year. Yeah, there will be some big things, but it's going to be the little things that they are going to have to work against and work with.

HEIDI: Our old town was so white. They were in middle school, and there was only one other black kid in the whole school.

TREVOR: We were popular because we were the only black kids. They knew who we were.

HEIDI: But they were totally accepted. People were very nice there.

JEFFREY: Even that little thing: you feel different; you are being treated differently. Okay, it was in a positive manner there, but you're still being treated differently from the person who is standing next to you who is doing the exact same things that you are.

As much as we want to give them the tools, I don't think anyone can prepare you for that. If I was a black man trying to give this information, I might be able to give more experiential information. That could also taint the way that I gave the information, because that experience might be awful. The main difference is the experiential information, historical information. We can't give them that.

Advice

VANCE: Like I said, communication. Just talk.

TREVOR: Open up. Communication is key. We learned that the hard way.

HEIDI: This is always the thing. I think it's very hard for them to open up. Of course, they cannot sit down and say, "You know what? I had a very bad experience with this and this, and if you please would not go there or whatever, it would make it easier." My advice to other parents is to wait, make nice conversation, and at one point, the kids will come and tell you stories. We've heard some shocking stories, and we've heard some nice stories. They will eventually open up and tell you about what they experienced. Right, guys?

Sometimes it needs to be a big fight where you just yell out what the problem is. Sometimes it takes these fights to get to know each other better and for our kids to finally say what they wanted to say for such a long time. They just never did because I felt that they were respecting us as authorities and parents. They tried to obey our house rules and everything else, so they did not say one or another thing. We needed to have the big fight to finally hear some stuff like that.

VANCE: My advice for the kids is to make sure that if you had a rough path, you fight past the path, are willing to learn different things, and live the path you are blessed with now.

TREVOR: Think about the pros and the cons of the situation. The good things are things like "Oh, I'll be able to do different stuff now that I wasn't able to do." Try to move on.

HEIDI: It is very sad that a lot of teenagers, older kids, never have a chance to be adopted, because they age out of the system. There are so many programs that prepare these children for living as they age out of the system. But there is something that the system cannot provide that they need to be able to have a nice family and a normal life themselves. This is why I would encourage everybody to go get the older children, too. If you want the baby, get the baby, and get the older one on top of it. It doesn't matter.

JEFFREY: My advice would be, if you have the heart, if you have the desire, you will overcome any sort of issue. If you are really thinking about taking the step to expand your family and that's what you feel in your heart you want to do, do it. You will have the resources, you will have the support, you will have what it takes. If you have it in your heart, you have what it takes to overcome issues. Not everything is easy, not everything is straightforward, not everything comes without struggle. That is true whether you are talking about an adoptive family or a biological family. But if you really feel like this is something that you want to do, do it. Then figure out how you are going to do it as you go along. If you think you've got a plan, trust me, there are things that are going to blow that plan to kingdom come. Like Trevor said, you have to have patience, you have to communicate, you have to be flexible.

HEIDI: Tolerant.

JEFFREY: You have to be tolerant, you have to know how to set boundaries, you have to know how to work to make everyone understand and respect those boundaries. At the same time, if you are tolerant, if you understand that this is one child and this is another child and this is another child and that's another child and each one of them is unique and has their own unique way of thinking about things, then it works. If you say, "I've got four children, and I am going to treat them all the same," one, it's just a fallacy because you are not going to do that, and two, you are probably going to wind up in a situation where you can't help.

Trevor needs a totally different level of communication than Vance. Sacha needs a totally different level of physical contact than Stewart. Each one of them has their own uniqueness about them, and you have to understand that.

You have to understand that not everyone is going to react in the same way. Not everyone is going to take advice and information in the same way. You've got to tailor your message based on who it is that you are talking to and how you are talking to them.

CHAPTER 9:

TRANSRACIAL ADOPTION

....

As the number of transracial adoptive families continues to grow, so does the attention to the unique character-istics of these families in American society. The writings of transracial adoptees and transracial parents, these family interviews, and experts in the adoption field all highlight the importance of recognizing and acknowledging the racial differences in transracial families. Recommendations common to those touched by transracial adoption include the need to expose children to the culture of their birth, to appreciate that racial differences do matter, and to speak openly, honestly, and often about race.

In the early 1950s, Americans began to question long-held beliefs that adopted children needed to resemble their adoptive parents.[1] The Doss family adopted twelve children from several cultural backgrounds, and the mother, Helen Doss, told her story in *The Family Nobody Wanted*.[2] Soon after, in 1955, the Holt family successfully lobbied to adopt eight children from South Korea after the Korean War. The Holts founded what is now Holt International and, as well as laying the foundation for international adoption to the

United States, "proved that a family's love is not limited by differences of race or nationality, that the true bonds of a family are love and commitment."[3] As international adoption began to grow in the United States, so did the adoption of black children by white parents, which further expanded the diversity potential of American families. According to author and transracial adoptee Rhonda Roorda, "During the civil rights movement of the 1960s, society became aware of the acute needs of parentless black children in America."[4] Between 1968 and 1975, white parents adopted more than eleven thousand black children.[5] The option for transracial placements was not without controversy, as exemplified by concerns about "white parents' ability to raise a child of color, specifically, their abilities to racially socialize that child,"[6] and the National Association of Black Social Workers' (NABSW's) often cited 1972 statement opposing placement of black children with white parents.[7]

As adopted children grow to be adults, even though they generally express love for their parents, they also have powerful stories to share about the challenges they faced as children. Author and adoptive parent Gregory Walters reflected on a video he watched during his foster care training:

> *It was incredibly eye-opening to watch interviews with children of Asian, Hispanic, and black ethnicities talk about their experiences in [largely] Caucasian households. How they worked through serious issues of self-identity, how they encountered other children who were merciless in their mockery of their situation, how they felt anger and resentment toward their adoptive parents. It was, frankly, a bit shocking. It was also honest, unvarnished, and very real.*
>
> *Now, I want to emphasize that not everyone in the video and training had a negative experience— some of the people interviewed led very normal lives,*

and most all of the children interviewed had a lot of love for their adoptive parents.[8]

While much of the adoption literature focuses on the adoption of black children by white parents and international adoptions, transracial adoptions from foster care have the potential to span all races and cultures. According to the AFCARS report, in 2017, 21 percent (12,621) of children adopted from the US foster care system were Hispanic, 17 percent (10,332) were black, and 49 percent (28,868) were white. The remaining 12 percent were American Indian/Alaskan Native, Asian, Native Hawaiian/other Pacific Islander, unknown, or two or more races.[9] While AFCARS does not track the race of parents adopting from foster care, the diversity of children available for adoption leaves a high probability for transracial adoptions from foster care and justifies the need to prepare families for how best to support children of a different race.

Each book referenced in this chapter emphasizes the need for what Elizabeth Vonk describes as multicultural planning, which she defines as "the creation of avenues for the transracially adopted child to learn about and participate in his or her culture of birth."[10] It is easy for parents to find themselves in neighborhoods and social circles whose members resemble them and not their transracially adopted children.[11] This can result in a child's being the only representative of his culture in his school, place of worship, or social activity, and that, Vonk's literature review suggests, makes "it difficult for some adoptees to identify with and develop pride in their race, ethnicity, or culture of birth."[12]

In his book *Black Baby White Hands*, author and transracial adoptee Jaiya John reflects on his lack of exposure to African American culture and remembers fondly the importance of one of his very few connections with it:

One of my few sources of racial pride growing up was the storybook I had, John Henry—*the folk tale of a strong Black baby who, legend had it, was born with a hammer in his hand. In the story, John Henry grew to be big and proud, and went off to become a steel-driving man for the railroads. I gazed in wonder at John Henry's Black image, feeling an admiration and intimacy. John Henry was my man.*

I didn't realize what John Henry *had done for me then until later, after college, when I saw the book in a bookstore and immediately broke into a grin.* John Henry, my man! *My memories flooded back, and I wondered what had ever become of my original book. Of course, I bought the copy I was looking at on the spot and promised myself to keep the book around for any children I might have. It was then that I began to fully realize the value of such* little things.[13]

Adoption experts now encourage parents to connect their children and their families to each culture represented in their family. Melinda, age ten, who was adopted by a Puerto Rican mother and a Greek father, told interviewer Jill Krementz, "My mom, the one who adopted me, is Puerto Rican, and so are both her parents. I'm especially happy about that, because Lauren and I are both Puerto Rican and it's fun to keep in touch with our real background. My grandma has taught us how to cook all different kinds of Spanish foods. Adam likes the tasting part."[14]

There are numerous ways to embrace a child's culture. Jaiya John recognized the importance of books; Melinda liked cooking Spanish foods. Of course, living in neighborhoods and attending religious services that include families from a child's culture, as well as having the child attend a school with a diverse student population, are obvious options. Hugh Booker (chapter 7) who is Chinese and adopted three Hispanic boys, said that he and his ex-hus-band "absolutely" considered race when choosing a place to live: "A diverse school was and continues to be important to me. For a while, [my ex-husband] wanted to move to [a less diverse area]. I wouldn't agree and told him that the families who live in those communities 'don't look like us.' I like [where we live] for its diversity. Our friends are from the full spectrum of race, gender, religion, and [sexual] orientation."

In her book *Come Rain or Come Shine*, Rachel Gar-linghouse offers additional suggestions, such as attending culture camps that ensure children are part of a majority, or visiting cultural hot spots (restaurants, shops, monuments, festivals, parades, etc.), to ensure children have racial role models.[15] In her interview with Rhonda Roorda, a tran-sracial adoptee and author of four books on transracial adoption (three coauthored with Rita Simon), Mahisha Delinger describes how she surrounded her daughter with positive role models:

> *I made sure first that she had a lot of images around her that looked like her. My daughter's pediatrician was African American. Her dentist was African American. The books that she had included black characters in them, and her baby dolls were also black. There was a preteen TV show called* That's So Raven, *which featured the little girl who was on* The Cosby Show. *I actually took my young daughter at the time to the taping of that show so that she could meet Raven (Raven-Symoné) and see someone who looked like her. I wanted her to see images of herself in all of these good places so that she could build a good sense of self. My daughter attended a mostly white private school so I had to bring all of these extra images to her of black people so that she could see like images of her. From that I constantly told her how beautiful she was: her*

character, her skin, her hair—even though she was different, she was also beautiful![16]

Hugh Booker also recognized the importance of ensuring that there are people of Hispanic origin in his sons' lives. He said they have a friend "who has watched over us since the boys were in elementary school. She is Hispanic and will include the boys in her family outings and celebrations. . . . We also encourage the boys to reach out to their older birth siblings, who are very involved with cultural celebrations."

It may be difficult for some parents to accept that they cannot provide everything that their child needs. Authors and transracial adoptive parents Beth Hall and Gail Steinberg comment, "You will not be able to provide directly for all of your child's needs, no matter how hard you try and no matter how much you want to. . . . You will always be acting beyond your own intuition and experience and can never be fully conscious of all the implications of your child's birth identity."[17] Transracial adoptive parents interviewed for this book recognize this need and provided numerous examples of how they've ensured their children have role models of their own race, including friends' parents (Schneider family, chapter 8), birth-family members (Booker family, chapter 7), and therapists (Watts family, chapter 10).

A second important aspect of transracial adoptions is the need for parents and family members to appreciate that racial differences do matter. Parents may innocently embrace an attitude of "color blindness." However, as authors Keefer and Schooler wrote, "While it can be tempting to announce, 'I don't see color, I only see the child,' parents must remember that everyone else in the community will see both. Ignoring racial and cultural issues, like the proverbial ostrich with its head in the sand, leaves children ill equipped to build a positive racial and cultural identity. It also leaves them without the survival skills necessary to be successful adults."[18]

Recognizing the importance of color includes understanding white privilege, which Hall and Steinberg explain in their book, *Inside Transracial Adoption*:

> *Privilege is a benefit we receive that is not earned but simply given to people of a particular race, class, or gender.* White people may be presumed by others to be smart, safe, or trustworthy not because they demonstrate those traits but simply based on racial stereotypes—this is the essence of white privilege . . . *It is presumptuous for white people who have not experienced racism to think that they are in a better position to decide how people of color should feel and/or respond to subtle or overt racial bias. . . . White privilege is believing that racism is being eradicated* because white people don't experience it or see it themselves. *It cannot become the "job" of adopted children of color to help their parents understand that racism exists—or to make the message of racism palatable so their parents won't feel too guilty.*[19]

According to Rhonda Roorda, if adoptive parents didn't recognize the importance of white privilege, adoptees often belatedly realized the importance of race and ethnicity when they "left their white adoptive homes and entered society as adults of color. They no longer were protected by the privileges of their white parents but rather were viewed by society based on the color of their skin. . . . Transracial adoptees find that race and ethnicity issues become a priority in their lives as they go on to higher education, marry (whether their spouse is black or white), parent children of color, and work in corporate America."[20]

In her 2015 book, *In Their Voices*, Roorda interviews black Americans to obtain their views on transracial adoption. Demetrius Walker, founder of dN|BE apparel and adoption heritage camp speaker, said:

> *One of the things that breaks my heart, that I hear from white folks that I know, even here in my neighborhood, is, "We don't see race. That does not matter to us." Whether you are black, Hispanic, or Asian, you don't see race? Really? Let's be realistic. If you try to pretend that race does not matter, therein lies the problem. I understand that many of these folks want to treat everybody equally. That is good. But it is also important to* respect *that there are going to be differences. We are also at a point in the United States where we have not progressed to be truly color blind. So I think, first and foremost, white adoptive parents should recognize that their child of color is going to have different experiences than them because of their different racial and ethnic background. Two, I think that it is important for transracial adoptive parents to understand that their children are going to be naturally curious about those differences and pretending that they don't exist is going to do a lot of damage to the child and to them.[21]*

Another interviewee, Tabitha, chief of the Child Welfare Bureau, concurred:

> *[It] is really important to accept that love is not enough. You cannot simply think that love is enough and that colorblindness is the way to go. Actually, the family that has that mind-set scares me more than a family that is really able to sit down and say that this will be different, this is another layer of parenting on top of the regular developmental things. This child will experience driving while black. This child will experience being called the*

"n-word." This child will have to deal with images of race and of skin color and the complexities of different textures of hair. A transracial adoptive parent needs to think, I need to be ten steps ahead in my level of awareness so that I can be of use to my child.[22]

In addition to emphasizing the need to see color, both of these interviewees touch on the importance of dialogue about race among family members. This dialogue can be difficult for parents; additionally, children may not feel comfortable raising, or have the skills to raise, the subject. Garlinghouse provides this observation:

Talking about race is much like talking about sex. It's inevitable that the topic will come up, but your child might bring it up only once or twice (or never!). It's up to you as parents to take initiative to discuss such crucial topics and to reintroduce and continue such discussions when necessary. Children shouldn't be burdened with the responsibility of initiating important discussions, because for one thing, they are children, and for another, depending on the child's personality and level of comfort, the discussion may never come about.[23]

Reflecting on his childhood, Jaiya John emphasizes the need a child may have to discuss race:

Maybe what I really wanted . . . was to have honest and explicit conversation with my parents—where I could ask questions and they could explain humanity, as they understood it. Conversation about why people are prejudiced; why so many White people have the kinds of feelings and ideas about Black people that they do; why Black people are not what those prejudices claim;

what was it about being Black that I should be feeling good about. I wanted us to walk verbally through that unfortunate valley together, turning over the rocks that revealed ugliness, kicking clutter from my path.[24]

He continues by offering some words he wished he heard from his parents:

I had no idea what those words would have been, not then. But now I know them, and they roll like this:

"You know, it must be a painful thing for you to look different than everyone around you, and to have those people with tainted hearts look at you through prejudiced eyes. It must be difficult having no one in your life who can relate to what it's like for you being Black in this White family; this White town; this White society. It must be hard to feel [bad] about what you know has happened to other Black people in this country, and not have people around with whom you feel comfortable sharing those feelings.

"We can relate to how it feels to stick out, but we can't assume what it must be like to be surrounded by the very groups of people [who have] done Black people the most harm. We respect that it is hurting you deeply, even if we don't fully understand the pain itself. There is nothing wrong with the fact that these things are hurting you. We will always grant you the right to struggle through this. This is the way we can be here for you, and we will."[25]

Authors Keefer and Schooler provide additional advice to parents on how to speak to their children about race. "Listen more, talk less," the authors state. "As the authorities in the family, parents often feel that they are appropriately providing guidance and instruction for their children only when they are doing the talking. Yet all effective leaders and teachers have learned the art of listening. Before teaching and guiding, parents must first understand where the child is in his experience, perception, and development."[26] They continue by encouraging parents, "Ask open-ended questions." In order "to understand the child's perceptions, parents should not ask questions that can be answered with a monosyllable."[27]

Dialogue about race must also include what Vonk refers to as "survival skills," or children's ability to effectively cope and respond to racism. While important for any child to learn, coping mechanisms may be more difficult to learn from white parents who have not been on the receiving end of racism. Vonk provides twelve suggestions for parents, including educating "children about the realities of racism and discrimination" and helping them recognize racism when it occurs, not tolerating racist remarks against any race or culture, and helping "children understand that being discriminated against does not reflect personal shortcomings."[28]

Garlinghouse concludes that while "adoptive parents do not want to overly emphasize race and racism . . . a parent's willingness to discuss difficult subjects demonstrates that when an incident does occur (as it will at some point), that the lines of communication are open, honesty is welcomed and encouraged, and the family will work together to face difficult situations."[29]

In summary, without too much effort, parents who wish to adopt transracially can find plenty of information from both parents and children of transracial families, as well as from adoption experts, to raise their racial consciousness and assist children in developing a positive racial identity.

At the end of *In Their Voices*, Roorda provides a seven-point succinct and detailed Multicultural Adoption Plan, which includes advice on such matters as how to "continuously build a reservoir of knowledge of your child's ethnic and/or cultural heritage and the subject of adoption" and how to "develop a smart support system for you and your family, and take steps to limit contact with anyone you suspect will be hurtful or less than accepting." [30]

Elizabeth Vonk provides cultural competency suggestions divided into three categories: Racial Awareness, Multicultural Planning, and Survival Skills. Together with colleagues, she also developed a Transracial Adoptive Parenting Scale that parents can use to measure their cultural competence. [31]

Finally, Rachel Garlinghouse (*Come Rain or Come Shine*) and Beth Hall and Gail Steinberg (*Inside Transracial Adoption*) all provide countless examples and strategies for parents, many of which they draw from personal experience.

Each of these sources, as well as families interviewed, echo the comments of transracial adoptive mom and author Deborah Beasley, who writes, "Parenting children of a race or culture not our own provides us with new possibilities for personal growth and expands the unlimited love and respect we impart in our relationships with our children. . . . By deciding to honor and respect the rich ethnic cultures of our children, we instill within them a growing pride of who they are and how well they are loved." [32]

CHAPTER 10:

IT'S HARD:

THE WATTS FAMILY

....

Charlotte and Greg Watts have two children. Their bio-logical son, Quinn, and their adopted daughter, Raquel, are both now fourteen. Raquel joined the Watts family at age two. She was diagnosed with reactive attachment disorder and PTSD and faces challenges at school, at home, and in extracurricular activities. Charlotte tells their family's story.

Adoption Story

I knew I wanted to adopt before I knew I wanted to have my own kids. I was fourteen when I made that decision. Initially, I wasn't going to have my own kids; I was just going to adopt. As I got older and with Greg and everything, my clock started ticking and I decided, *Okay, I want one of my own, at the very least, and I'll adopt another one.* We decided to start trying, and within five seconds I was pregnant. We had Quinn, and probably six months later, we decided to get licensed to be foster parents. Greg was a little on the

People in the Watts Family's Story

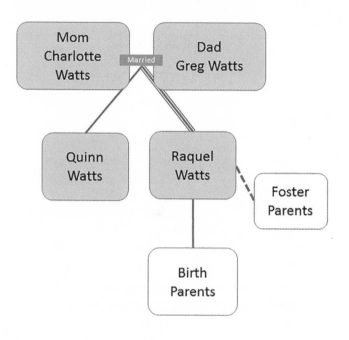

fence initially, but he was willing to give it a go. We did the course, and he knew it was the right decision. You see the videos of all these kids, you find out all of the statistics, and it's really daunting. There are so many children out there who don't have homes. Our philosophy, mine especially, was that every child is as lovable as your own and deserves a home. So we went through the foster program, we got licensed, and we put together a family book to show to the prospective kids or their social workers.

Our agency was recommended to us by someone Greg worked for who had adopted through them. That agency gave us the sugarcoated version of a lot of this. It didn't really spend a lot of time focusing on reactive attachment disorder. It ended up focusing a lot on the end result of how great these kids were. You see the videos of them in college, being thankful to their parents for x, y, and z. That's not reality. That's not preparing you for the reality of the struggles that you might have to go through. It was a classroom exercise; it wasn't a life exercise.

We wanted a girl younger than Quinn. We knew that we couldn't handle a lot of physical disability, but other than that, our box was quite large in terms of what we were willing to have. There were a couple of babies that came our way, but we weren't selected. Then Raquel came along. She was in emergency placement. She had lived with a family for quite some time that was connected to her biological family. A live-in boyfriend lied about some criminal record that he had. Although it wasn't a big deal overall, the fact that he lied disqualified them. Then, instead of saying, "We love her; take your time to find someone else," they basically said, "If we can't have her, then get her out of here."

When we met her, she lived with an older woman, very heavy, not very mobile, and Raquel was definitely neglected. When we met Raquel, she was playing with an office chair that swiveled in the corner of the room. We engaged with her as much as we could. Within a week, she was in our house.

You have to foster for six months before you can adopt, and during that six months, it was very, very, very difficult. I took three months off, as though I had just gotten a newborn. There were periods where I said to Greg, "I can't do this, this doesn't feel right, I can't do this." But for him, it was like, "I can't send her back." I understood. Ultimately, I didn't want to lose my marriage over it. That was it. We took her in and adopted her. That was almost twelve years ago.

Postadoption, our agency helped us with some of the stuff that we needed in terms of getting mental health support. They would check in. They did their reports. They were there because they had to be; that was part of the process, to stay in touch and make sure that we were doing okay. They wanted this kid adopted, so, even though they might have seen some of the negative stuff or the things that were hard, they just tried to provide support. That was it.

Challenges

It's hard. It's hard. It's hard. It just seems to be perpetually getting harder or just to a different level of difficult because she's bigger, stronger. She wants her independence. She's got no respect whatsoever, no fear whatsoever. Which is scary. She's got a real strong and stubborn personality. It's her way of not taking shit. But the problem is that she's doing it completely the wrong way and with the wrong people.

For example, I've been sick. When she found out about it, she said, "Dad told me you were sick. You're not sick. You're not coughing. You're walking around. You look fine to me. You must be lying yet again." That's her right now.

"Dad's late. How long does it take to do a massage? You know what he's doing, he's probably cheating on you. You don't even care? *Wow*." That's Raquel right now.

Sometimes you have to laugh. We just let it roll a lot of the times. But then again, there are those moments. We finally contacted the regional center for respite.

Greg and I try to give each other some breaks here and there just to be able to deal with the difficulty. It's our life. It is what it is.

Quinn is wonderful; he is absolutely brilliant. I don't know what I would do without him. He's very awake. He gets it, and he tries to help Raquel along. She bothers him as well. They have a typical sibling love-hate relationship, but he's definitely getting to that age where it's hard for him to have to deal with it. We talk about it a lot, because I feel bad and I don't want to fuck him up as well. He's like an old soul. You can have that conversation with him.

My parents are available; they'll take her. We went abroad for two weeks, and they had her and Quinn. For a long time, they didn't understand, because they aren't here day in and day out. They thought, *Oh my God, relax. Let her be. Let her live.* Then, eventually, as they had her for longer periods, they said they thought that she should go to boarding school.

Even Greg's parents aren't like my parents. They're very supportive. They've turned around and said they think we should send her away because it has impacted every aspect of our lives. Our marriage initially was stronger because we were on the same page with her. But the issue became that I was basically the only one working to find a solution. I got her the therapists, I scheduled everything, I read the books. He was there to take her to the appointments, but he never read the books with me, he never took a proactive role to really try to figure out how to make things better. So I became resentful.

As it got progressively worse, our marriage started to fall apart. He was absent emotionally, and I was angry. This led to my moving out for about four months a couple of years ago. He kept the kids. They would stay with me on the weekends. I picked them up three days a week and took them to school. It devastated my kids, but for me it was the last effort to see if the marriage could be repaired. We started therapy, he and I.

Then, during one of the therapy sessions, he confessed that really, he did not feel too much of a connection with Raquel from the beginning. He had never told me that. I was so angry that he had forced this decision, although he didn't want it either. For him, the guilt that he had of potentially putting her back in the system made it so he was willing to live like this and have his future be this difficult, when it didn't have to be and he didn't tell me. For me, the guilt of being the only one to feel like it was all me being this crazy, heartless bitch . . . It took me a long time to be able to let go of that and not feel angry as hell toward him.

Having some distance helped. It helped me for a while to appreciate my kids more and want to do some different things with them. Having the distance made it easier for me to deal with Raquel. Having the distance also allowed me to work with Greg on some of the shit that we were going through.

Eventually, I moved back in and we continued to go to therapy. We try to support each other more when it comes to Raquel. We're united and solid now, but our dynamic is still quite complicated and difficult and we still have our ups and downs.

Another challenge for us is that she really hasn't found or stuck to any activity or sport or anything. We've tried it *all*! We did say we were going to try again with tennis lessons, but the day of her first lesson she was a complete wench, wouldn't get ready, and I was like, "All right, canceling. We're done."

She did play soccer for her school. We bought her new shoes and a soccer bag and all that. But she ended up losing the privilege of playing because of her disrespectful attitude toward the teachers and coach. She made negative comments about her peers, like "They suck."

I will say, we make a little less effort on her behalf than we do for Quinn because Quinn puts the effort in. We've tried so many things with her, and it all goes by the wayside, so it's been hard to really put the effort out. When you're being treated like crap, it's hard to give.

Race

A couple of years ago, it was just Greg, Quinn, and Raquel out to dinner or something; I don't know where I was. She wanted to go to the bookstore by herself. Greg said, "You have to go with Quinn."

She said, "You're not letting me go because I'm black, and you think I'm just going to go play around in the streets."

He almost lunged across the table. "How dare you? Really?"

That's how she's thrown it at us. I think that she has identity issues, trying to figure it all out. She's around minorities all the time, so she knows what being black means, to a fourteen-year-old's extent. My sister-in-law, my husband's brother's wife, is African American. They've got mixed kids. My business partner is black, and her husband is white; they've got mixed kids. One of my best friends, he's black, his wife is white, they have mixed kids. There's a lot more black-white mix than anything else in the group. She has all kinds of role models. I get that we aren't black, so there's a certain aspect that we can't explain, or we can't be there in that way, but she's got people to turn to who are more than willing to chat. She's got her individual therapist, who she sees once per week, and she's black. She's been helping Raquel try to deal with and discuss race and identity issues. She knows about the Black Lives Matter movement and all of the police [brutality toward black people]. But I don't know that she processes it the right way or the way that someone without her disabilities would. Rather than realizing she is not getting TV because she yelled at me and cussed me out, she's got to find any reason why she is being treated that way, and race is the most obvious for her, because she's not able to see that she creates the majority of shit that happens through her behavior.

For example, she writes down insults:

"My mom's a bitch."

"I fucking can't stand her."

"I wish she would die in a car crash."

"Greg's a nigger."

Really? Okay.

"They're racist, they must be racist, because that is the only reason I can give for them treating me this way."

She literally wrote this all down on papers that she spread out and put on a tenderloin that I was seasoning. Really? Can you just leave it on the table if you're going to insult me?

My parents disowned me when we adopted Raquel. My father is a French Moroccan Jew; my mother is a Polish Jew. I was born in France, lived there for the first ten years of my life. Very different cultural mentality there. You stay home until you get married. It took years for girls to leave home and move into their own apartments and do their own thing before they got married, at least then.

Coming here from France, I definitely became a little different. My family and I have not seen eye to eye with respect to religion, with respect to men, with respect to my education in some ways, so it's always been an issue.

Initially, my father was like, "There are so many parents out there who want kids. You're taking kids away from people who need them, who can't have their own."

I said, "What world do you live in that you think the foster care system only has a couple of kids with a whole bunch of parents knocking down the door, trying to get them? Have you lost your fucking mind?"

He was trying it on. "She's not Jewish. She's black." They said, "If you take her, don't ever speak to us again."

We went six months. That was the longest that I was not in the relationship. I told them, "This is not me doing this; this is you doing this. You are missing out on your grandkids' lives. You are walking away from your daughter, and that's your choice, but my door will always be open."

After about six months, my mom contacted me. For her, her kids are everything. I know that it was really hard for her, and I would try to reach out here and there, but they wouldn't have it.

I said, "I will go to therapy with you guys, and we will try to figure out whether or not we can have a relationship." I went twice, for two-and-a-half-hour sessions.

In the end, it clicked, at least for my mom, and she said, "I don't think that we've ever allowed you to be an adult with your own views and with your own life, and we were wrong."

It helped change the direction of the conversation, and now we're good.

They see the struggles with Raquel. It breaks their heart because they know how exhausted I am and how hard it's been. But they're there.

Support for School and Therapy

Initially the therapy, the mental health benefits, were quite difficult to get because they were saying that I had to go all the way to the county where Raquel was adopted. I had to petition and file shit with the state to have it transferred to our county. It took almost a frickin' year before we got it sorted out.

School-wise, if the public system can't provide what a child with disabilities is in need of, then the school district that is responsible for the education of that kid needs to do whatever it can to provide the environment for them to get what they need.

She couldn't continue in public school, so we looked into a private school, where she ended up for a few years. We started making the requests to our school district. I had to get a lawyer involved, and she helped me negotiate and get a settlement, which included being reimbursed by our county for her tuition.

Our school district had not given her Speech and Language, and she was supposed to get a behavioral assessment at the beginning of the school year. They knew that they were in violation and I could sue them, so they were willing to negotiate. She gets transportation; the school bus picks her up every morning and drops her off every afternoon.

The school's team has been wonderful. It's so funny, because they're like, "She's lovely" and, "We love her." Then we get emails here and there from the teachers that say, "She is talking back a little bit" or, "She's trying to manipulate, but we can deal with this; this is fine."

She hated us for sending her there. She said, "I hate this school. I don't want to be here." She still kind of says that.

Grade-wise, she is starting to improve within the academics that they provide, which is good because it gives her confidence. We get it at home, though, which I guess is a good thing—she feels comfortable enough and safe enough—but it's exhausting.

So, we are now looking at special needs boarding schools that deal with kids with emotional behavioral issues, ADHD, depression, and mood issues. We can't afford it, and the school district won't pay for it because she is technically doing okay in school. Mind you, she is in a behaviorally based private school. It's her first year there. They're not as focused on grades as they are on behaviors. In some ways, it's childcare away from home.

The school district won't pay for a residential placement because she's got to show that she is a danger to herself or others, and it's got to be in a school setting, not just at home.

So, I'm trying to get the funding through the county. The county where Raquel was adopted from will look at the bigger picture and look at the home. The counties are more worried about the families than they are about the schools in that regard.

I don't know that it's going to work. I'm trying to figure out how to make an application, get the doctor stuff and the counselor information, to have them all fill out something to say that it might be healthier for everybody if she was at a facility that might be better able to handle her.

If we can't afford it, there is part of me that would be willing to take out a loan for at least one year to get something different for her.

The schools are mostly out of state. What I like about these programs is that they are very rigid and they really try to focus on the kids' needs and how to give them the skills that they need to be able to function and have relationships. It's a safer place for her to be able to analyze herself, see herself, without worrying that we're going to jump down her throat.

Advice

Learn about reactive attachment disorder. That is the biggest piece of advice that I could give anyone looking to the foster care system to adopt. She was diagnosed a long time ago with that and ADHD and PTSD, among other things. Learn techniques and tools, learn what you should expect, so that you can be prepared to deal with it, and if the match isn't right, don't do it. Don't do it.

I know it sounds horrible, but don't be afraid to put the kid back in the system. At the end of the day, I don't think it's the best thing. There are a lot of times where I feel like I have made Raquel's life worse, not better. Although she's got the house, she's got the shoes, she's got all these opportunities, emotionally, she's not happy. And emotionally, we're not happy. So, was it worth it? I'm not sure.

I've tried not to feel like this. It's because the relationship has been so difficult, because of this reactive attachment stuff, I've never been able to bond with her. I didn't know how to deal with it, so I just got frustrated.

You know, we're very similar personalities. She's stubborn, which is great; she needs to be a strong woman. The problem is, she doesn't quite know how to do it in a way that is constructive, not destructive. I think I'm part of the problem.

In the beginning, had I had a choice, I would have learned about reactive attachment disorder and hopefully prepared myself differently, and maybe I would have felt differently about Raquel had that been the case.

CHAPTER 11:

GIRLS: 6, BOYS: 1, GAME OVER: THE BUTLER FAMILY

··

The Butlers have seven children: four biological daughters, two adopted daughters, and one adopted son. The eldest, Livia, a triple-threat performer (actor, singer, dancer), lives with her husband and two sons. Lindsey, their second, lives near Livia and trains wild mustangs. Laurel, their third, currently serves as a missionary near the Butlers' hometown. Liesl, their fourth, lives with them and will graduate high school this year. After their fourth daughter started first grade, the Butlers explored adoption. They adopted two girls, now ages nine and eight, and a boy, now age seven.

Lori tells their family's story.

Adoption Story

We had our four girls. They were older. I always wanted a boy, but I couldn't have any more kids. Our youngest at this time was about six, and I just had the feeling that our family wasn't done.

People in the Butler Family's Story

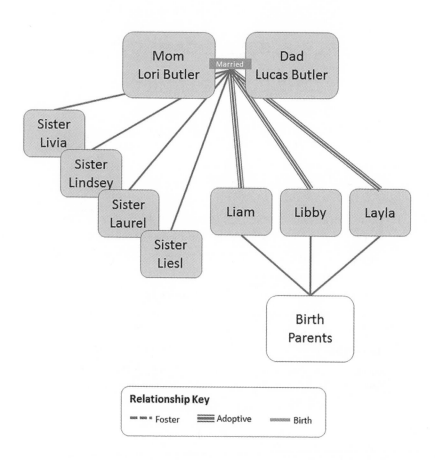

I'm adopted, so I always wanted to give back because I have the most incredible mother. I asked my husband one night, "Could you love another?"

He was like, "What?" We talked about adoption, and that night he said, "Yeah, I think that would be great."

We thought we wanted to adopt internationally and started our journey there. We completed our home study and got approved for two children. They started sending us profiles on kids, and my husband is such a softy, he would just look at them and cry.

"How do you choose a child? They all need homes," he said. "I don't think I can do this." We were over forty and too old to have an agency look at us for adoption,[1] so someone suggested we look at the foster system. We called them. We asked some questions. They sent an intake person out to our house to see if we understood all of the ramifications and whether we would be good candidates for foster parents. When they left, we decided it wasn't for us.

We didn't think we were emotionally stable enough to set ourselves up to bring a child in and then have to give it back if the child reunited with its parents. I don't remember what changed our mind, but three months later, we were sitting in our foster classes.

Finally, I think it was six months later, a social worker called us in January. They had an abused baby who needed a home. That's our Layla.

We got her a week later. She was in a shelter home. I tried to drive up to the shelter home and couldn't make it up the hill, because it was in the middle of a snowstorm. I just kept spinning out, so I had to have them bring her down to me. The sun had already set. It was almost dark. They just handed me this little girl with these big eyes. She literally had no emotion. She was almost eight months old, and she didn't sit up, she didn't roll over, the back of her head was flat—severely, severely neglected.

Three-plus months later, the bio mom delivered another girl. She was born with some medical problems and spent three weeks in the NICU. We [took in that child and] found ourselves with two infants eleven months apart.

We took them for visits with the bio mom for well over a year and a half before they terminated her rights. Though I was comfortable with the system, I often wondered, *Why do they try and reunite them? Why do they push for this when there's nothing but red flags on the other side?*

For example, bio mom chose to live out of the city, so I had to drive forty-five minutes each way to take the children for weekly supervised visits. One time after a visit, Layla became extremely ill and was taken to the hospital, where she stayed for four days. On many other occasions, Libby was hospitalized for respiratory failure because she was exposed to secondhand smoke on bio mom's clothes, something her fragile system could not take. But bio mom wouldn't listen to instructions to quit smoking or to change her clothes and wash before every visit.

Despite all the complications, and with no progress being made in the bio mom's behavior, each week, the visits continued.

Finally, a doctor got on the stand and testified. With Libby, there was a court order to keep her away from bio mom for at least a week to see if the child's respiratory health would improve. Every time Libby got out of the hospital, we had to take her back to see bio mom, whose clothes were full of smoke. It turned out Libby had pulmonary sling and had a form of tracheomalacia, laryngomalacia, and severe asthma. In court, they had people testify. They asked the mom, "How do you think you can take care of this baby?"

We had an oxygen tank at home. We had a one-hundred-foot cord. I had to give her breathing treatments around the clock, listen to her lungs with my stethoscope, and keep track of all of the hospital records. The mom's like, "I know a friend that will take care of her."

The doctor got on the stand and said, "This child will die if she is not in the care of [the Butler] family." They finally terminated her rights to the girls. We adopted them. Layla was two and a half, and Libby was one and a half. The mom was pregnant again.

We originally said no to more children. There was so much medically going on with Libby, she was just a full-time job. My husband was working in a different state, commuting back and forth. Then CPS called us. Liam was a week old. She goes, "We have a little baby boy down here." Even though we had our plates full with the little girls, we just had a hard time with the idea of not taking Liam. We wanted to keep the siblings together, and, after parenting six daughters, how could we say no to a son?

He will turn seven in a few months; the girls just turned eight and nine.

Overcoming Challenges

We constantly tell them that they are a gift and we are so lucky to have them. My older girls are really good about doing the same thing.

The seventeen-year-old has a hard time. She got displaced. She feels I don't have a lot of time for her, and we never go off anymore and go away. The younger kids have changed our life a lot that way. At night, same thing: it's like we have newborns because Layla and Libby have a hard time sleeping through the night, really bad dreams, especially Layla. She used to pull her hair out and eat it. A lot of traumatic stuff. I couldn't even go to the bathroom without her. She would cry and scream if she got separated from me.

Libby, even being autistic, does great playing by herself, but she has to be right there. The occupational therapist told us to get this cuddle swing where she can be enclosed. It does me no good to put it up in her room, because she won't use it unless I'm sitting there twenty-four-seven with her.

One of the ER docs at work looked at our Christmas picture, and I heard him say, "There's something wrong with that one." You could tell. Libby was on so many steroids and medications. I remember a doctor looked at her list and was like, "This looks like something a senior citizen with [chronic obstructive pulmonary disease] would be on."

We noticed Libby doing things differently and acting out something awful. She wouldn't get what is socially acceptable—I mean, at all. Out in public, something that you wouldn't think about doing doesn't bother her; she doesn't get it—running out into the street, or she started doing a little bit of violent stuff and screeching in public. We didn't know what to do.

We started seeing a psychiatrist who put her on Risperdal for a while. It's to help with anger in autistic kids, because Libby would go from zero to ten in the anger department in seconds flat, and it was hard to pinpoint triggers. She also has obsessive behaviors. She'll just keep on and keep on, just saying a word like *cars, cars* if she wants a car. Or, for a while, she just wanted to go to garage sales. She wanted to do that instead of going to Disneyland.

I had people at church tell me, "Just take her out." People don't understand; they get upset. If we're in the store, they think, *That's a bratty kid*. I've had people in the grocery store tell me, "You have too many kids. You can't even handle them." Very hurtful stuff. I used to come home in tears all the time. I didn't get my iron panties until two years ago. I would take it personally, and I wanted to say, "I'm a good mom. I really am. I've done this four times."

We raised four kids. We thought we knew what we were doing. My four girls are amazing women. We thought, *We've got this parenting thing down.*

With these guys, it's a whole other story. The oldest one, Layla, besides pulling her hair out and eating it, was doing self-soothing. She would food-stuff, too—she put food in her pockets. We'd constantly remind her there would always be food for her. We'd find food in her room.

As far as their connectedness goes, they love their older siblings so much. The interesting thing with Libby is, this just shows how [differently autism shows up on the spectrum]. Often, I think, *Oh, man, she is so sensory integrated.* Then there are times when I think, *Wow. She shouldn't really care so much about other people's feelings*, as a lot of times [autistic kids] don't.

If one of them loses an opportunity, that's what we have to do. We have to give them goals to work toward. They have little balls and a jar. We try different things because they always seem to buck the system. A system will work for so long. Then they find a way out of it and we start again.

Right now, our system is a ball. They need to obey what I ask, and if they don't obey the first time, they're not going to get that ball in the jar. Layla is very hard to keep focused.

Both Layla and Libby have been diagnosed with ADHD. I can put Layla and Libby in a room and say, "Get dressed for school." I help Libby brush her hair. I come back ten minutes later, Layla is sitting on the bed and her clothes are next to her. She needs constant direction.

Then they have a list of five things that in the summertime they have to do in order to have electronics (computer or the Wii). They have to read for twenty minutes, build something, play outside for thirty minutes, clean one room, and then do something nice for someone. They have their checklist.

If I know there's something that they're still lacking and I take something away from someone, Libby is there. She's like, "Just give her another chance!" They can fight like cats and dogs, but, man, when they pull together, they pull together. They want everyone to have the same opportunity. They don't want anyone to miss out.

I'll give you an example that happened yesterday that I marked off for their nice thing they did for another person. We went on a bike ride for their exercise, their thirty minutes outside. We found a park, we stopped, and they were playing. There were some little kids, like, two and four, and there was another one, who I think was about two or three. And my littles said, "Hi, do you want to be friends?"

They're really friendly kids. They were playing with this four-year-old, and when it was time to leave, Liam said, "Bye, my friend. Thank you very much. We'll be here every morning if you want to come and play with us again." They told the little boy how much fun it was to play with him. They actually told him thank you. As we were leaving, the two moms said to me, "Your kids are so sweet."

When we got home, I made sure that I told them, "You just did something really nice for someone." Every opportunity I get, I point it out. They've helped elderly people put groceries on the checkout belt. They love to help cook. Liam, because he has a texture aversion, wouldn't even touch food before. Now, he'll help cut strawberries or spread stuff even if he doesn't eat it.

I've found with these guys, my way of bucking their system is keeping them active. Just being really productive.

They have a list that I made for each of them. I put their picture on it, and I laminated it. I give it to them in the morning, and it says right on there what they need to do to get ready for school. They can look at their list and go, "Did I do that?" It has their evening routine on there as well.

It works, especially with Layla. I would be at her side all day long—"Do this, do this." She feels more grown-up if she can be responsible for herself.

Early on, we made a bead necklace for her, and I had one, too, and said, "I have to go to the bathroom. You can hold your necklace and think about me, and I will hold my necklace." I made them pillow beds last Christmas, so if they do wake up in the middle of the night, they'll lay them next to our bed. Sometimes they'll end up in our bed. I come home from work, they're in there and I have to go sleep in their bed. They still have sleeping problems at night.

We had a real scary thing happen with Libby. She was on a really high dosage of Risperdal for her size, and she was getting worse and worse. In January, she started doing this weird swallowing thing. I thought she picked it up from someone at school, just mimicking them. Then she started doing this pouty thing with her lower lip. All of a sudden, I realized she was having tardive dyskinesia, TD.

A lot of the psych drugs do that, the antipsychotics, if you're on them too long. They cause involuntary movement of the feet, the hands. Pretty soon she was sticking out her tongue involuntarily, it was just jutting out, and she was screeching every morning.

We withdrew from that medication. I was like, "No, she's not going to be on it anymore. We're going to figure something else out."

We started using essential oils. I got her a weighted vest and headphones. Any little thing to try and help her. I started giving her women's-strength gummy vitamins. We've been TD-free now for two months.

It turns out the psych drugs were causing half the problems, because she's a totally different girl now. She's manageable, whereas before, she would just constantly hit and kick the walls.

People would be like, "Put her in her room and give her a time-out."

You can't. She breaks doors. People don't understand that we cannot discipline these guys. They think of doing things that my other children would not think of. The stuff they take apart. Things that you think no one could destroy, they figure out.

Then, just after we moved, Lucas was out of town one day, when I tried to take Liam to Sunday school. He was being a little destructive, so they came and got me. I tried to keep him on my lap. He was twisting my arm, and he bit it. He had never done that. Here I was, trying to handle him, and people were watching me. It was my first Sunday there, and I just wanted my kids to make some friends and get to know other people.

This man came over in a flight suit. He was a pilot for the Air Force. He sat next to me, and he looked down and went, "Hey, buddy, you want to look at this?" The man pulled off his watch, and Liam kind of stopped for a moment. By now he was on the ground in between my legs. Then the man started ripping his patches off—I didn't even know that patches were Velcroed on; I would have thought they were sewn on—and having Liam feel them.

I leaned over and I said, "He's usually not like this, I'm so embarrassed." I said, "He has autism."

The pilot shook his head. He said, "Don't say anything. I've got two of my own. I recognized it right away."

He had one child with very mild autism and one who was moderate on the spectrum. It was the first time that someone in public, a total stranger, just knew it and got it. I learned a lot from that man, and I still do, watching him. We've become friends. My husband team-teaches with him in a younger Sunday-school class, and he's learned a lot of techniques that this man does with the little kids who start getting out of control.

The School Experience

Layla, the oldest, has had a very hard time with learning. She was having staring seizures. They sent her to a neurologist, and her first EEG said her brain seized all night long. This is why she can't sleep. This is why she's not learning. She's not storing what she learned during the day. She was on Depakote for a good year. I can't remember all the other meds they put her on. They repeated two EEGs, and now she's seizure-free, but the learning disabilities continue.

She was just put into special ed at the end of this year, which is good. They finally, just this year, did a full gamut of testing to figure out what's going on in her brain. If you just talk to her, she's a smart cookie, but there's some disconnect in her. She was the recipient of severe neglect and abuse for her first seven and a half months, as well as whatever happened in utero, so when you talk about environment versus biology, I think there's a lot that happened or that didn't happen for her early on.

They say that she's having a hard time decoding. If she didn't qualify for special ed, they would have held her back. But this way, she'll continue. Now she can say, "I'm in fourth grade," and she'll get a lot of intervention. They're going to get her a tablet to use for writing, and her reading is also finally starting to take off.

Libby had a very difficult teacher in the public school system, so we left and enrolled her at a charter school right down the street. I can't praise that teacher enough. Libby went from needing to repeat kindergarten, according to the public school kindergarten teacher, to, by the time she finished first grade, being above grade level. She's going into third grade now. She's been at this school for two years, and she reads at a sixth-grade level.

Her teacher this last year knew that Libby gets sensory overload, so they had a special table for Libby with pillows underneath. She's totally welcome to go under the desk when she needs to. They have the psychiatrist and the occupational therapist for the school district come in and evaluate her. They observed that when she isn't under the chair or under the table, she perches on her chair or perches on the counter. For some reason, she pops up and perches. Her joint laxity is out of this world, crazy. They allow it. They know it's something she has to do.

An aide comes and gets her out of class constantly for a break to run outside so that she isn't in this enclosed space. Her teacher says, "Go noodle." She gives all the kids a break. They also do yoga sometimes in class. It's so awesome, because it's totally what she needs.

Liam had a very hard time starting school. He got suspended in the first week for acting out. They told me to keep him home with independent-study packets. Liam and I spent a lot of one-on-one time together. I was already exhausted trying to figure Libby out. But the one-on-one time and using positives paid off, because he wanted to go back to school. He wanted it so bad because he saw what his sisters were doing and he was missing out. These kids just need a little something extra.

Relationship with Biological Parents

One time, I actually went and picked up the bio mom and I drove her with the kids in the car to a court appearance when she was being tried for burning Layla. She didn't have a way to get to court, and I felt bad for her. I remember really feeling sorry for her. I remember going home and saying to my husband, "I'm so confused, because I want her to have her kids back. I feel bad that she doesn't have her kids." I get to reap the benefits of being a mom, but I know that she's somewhere, aching for her kids. No matter what heinous things she's done, she's made some bad choices. What makes me feel better is my own belief system, knowing that [we have previous lives], and I just say, "Maybe I was good friends with her, and maybe I promised her that I would take care of these babies until she could have them again."

Although my sympathy was real and my actions were heartfelt, unfortunately, the bio mom's actions toward me were hostile at times. At a later court appearance for terminating the bio mom's parental rights, she threatened that if she ever found out where we lived, she would come and steal the children.

We did have a couple strange visits at our house. One time, we had two men come up to our house, looking for a certain street, and they were looking around because I answered the door. Luckily, all the babies were in bed asleep. I didn't really have any kid toys out at the time.

One night, we found a truck on the side of our house, and when I approached them, they got in the truck and sped away. I think she was trying to find me. We asked our attorney about privacy. He was like, "You can find anyone nowadays on the Internet."

We've been really open with the kids. They'll tell everyone they're adopted. We never want to bad-mouth their mom. They all know that their mom couldn't take care of them. They know that she loved them. I know she did. She just didn't know how to keep them safe; that's what I tell them. Libby constantly says, when she tells me goodbye as she gets out of the car at school, "You're the best mom I've ever had." Some people laugh—"Oh, that's so cute"—and they don't even know the story. She doesn't remember her birth mom, of course.

You're required to bring them to have a final, two-hour visit after termination of parental rights. At first, I was a little upset at that—two hours! I knew that it would be very uncomfortable and awkward. I had professional pictures taken of the kids, and we gave them to the bio mom with frames. I wrote her a poem and promised that I would love them like she would, that she wouldn't have to worry. She gave me cards to give to each of them when they turn eighteen. I opened one of them and read it. I just wasn't sure; the children's attorney warned me, "She's dangerous. Don't fall into her trap. Do not let her be a part of these kids' lives." They said we needed to cut the string totally.

This is how bad things were. The judge gave a court order to have their Social Security numbers changed for the two girls. They didn't have a Social Security number for the boy yet when they took him away.

I was adopted, and I met my bio mom when I was thirty years old. My adopted mom was great. I never had a want. I started having my own kids, and then I just wanted to meet her. It provided this emotional completeness for me. I will understand if my kids come to me and want to do the same.

I won't lie—I am very fearful of the bio mom's lifestyle. The doctor and the psychiatrist warned me that if the kids try drugs once, they will be hooked. We are working so hard not to expose them to cigarettes, drugs, alcohol, and it could be turned in an instant. The bio mom feels she was very wronged, and she pulled me in. If she sees these kids and tells them something that will make them think that I stole them or took them away unfairly . . . I don't want them to feel sorry for her and then be upset with me. The bio dads don't have anything to do with the kids. I don't know if that day will come. Maybe it won't. Who knows? I do still have the cards to give them when they turn eighteen, and I will let them decide. I'll support them, but I obviously will be fearful.

Family Outings

I've learned that in order to keep them protected, we have to be real selective with where we go. I try not to take them to the grocery store anymore. If something happens, I don't want the ridicule. It sets them up for failure. Whatever we do, it has to be something that we know is going to work.

We tried to take them camping three years ago. That did not work. We were setting up camp, and one was throwing a fit. I don't blame the people who were not too far from us for yelling, "So much for rest and relaxation!" We ended up pulling up and leaving.

We have a spot on the beach this August. Knocking on wood. I hope it will be better for us. I hope they're ready for it.

We're all excited that in two weeks, we're hiking in Zion, the Narrows. A lot of it goes in water, so I thought it would be kind of cool for the kids.

We just have to be real selective with what we try. They love water. They love to build. They love sand, dirt. They love being outside. When we bike to a park, as a mom, you have to be this therapist twenty-four-seven. I made up an obstacle course. They want me to time them. They were doing it, and their times were getting worse and worse, but I was fibbing, because they just want to keep trying to get a better time and I can see they're just getting worn out. That's the only way we can get them to sleep, and they're better behaved.

Three years ago, we bought into a vacation club. They wanted us to buy so many points, and we were like, "We don't need that many points." We explained, "We started all over. We're not going to be going on very many trips. We have special needs kids. We can't even really take them with us." So the guy gave us, just for signing up, all these extra points. We looked at the resorts that they had, and there was one in Puerto Vallarta that we were able to go stay at for five nights. My oldest two daughters came home to stay with the kids so that Lucas and I could go. We had never been anywhere, and we had been married twenty-five years.

It was so incredible. We zip-lined through the jungle, we rode donkeys, we repelled down waterfalls, snorkeled in the ocean.

The older girls were so excited for us to adopt. But none of us really realized that our life was really going to change. We used to have year passes at Disneyland. We would go two to three times per year, with Livia performing. She won a scholarship, so she and I were in New York one summer. We can't do that stuff anymore.

Even going to see shows, they can't do loud very well. We tried to take Layla to a *Little Mermaid* music circus. At the very beginning, the lights went down and the announcer was making the announcement about no flash photography. She started screaming and crying. Lucas and I were looking at each other and realized, *Oh my gosh, this child can't do this either.* A lot of times, with vacuums and stuff, they'll cover their ears. Anything dark and loud, you just can't do. We learned that you just keep trying and see what works.

Advice

Honestly, my husband and I wouldn't change anything if we had to do it all over again. We will be the first ones to tell you that.

I've had a lot of days where I'm like, *I don't know why I thought I could do this.* We have a lot of disappointing days, and some days just getting through a day without a fit makes you just feel so charmed: *Oh, it's a good day!* Honestly, there have been times when I've just wanted to walk out of the house and just keep walking.

Be prepared to learn. Even though our classes prepared us a lot. We honestly had no idea that we could have newborns all over again for twenty years. We have a license plate holder that reads: Girls 6 Boys 1 Game Over. Little did I know that this game would never be over. We don't know what Libby's future is. We don't know what Layla's future is. We just don't know.

There's also no spontaneity anymore. You have to be flexible, you have to be open, and you will be exhausted emotionally. Just going through the foster system before they became ours was the biggest roller coaster we've ever ridden. You have to be prepared for anything. But the love that you get will teach you the honest definition of unconditional love. It doesn't happen unless you're stretched to this.

CHAPTER 12:

RAISING A CHILD WITH
A HISTORY OF TRAUMA

C hildren enter the foster care system for numerous reasons, often related to parental abuse or neglect. Upon
entering foster care, these children experience the trauma
of being taken away from their birth parents. To eventually have parental rights permanently revoked, the child
may have also experienced numerous sudden removals and
reunifications with birth families; temporary stays with
multiple foster families; physical abuse, sexual abuse, verbal
abuse, or malnutrition; and, very often, a combination of
these stressful incidents.

These traumas affect children in many different ways.
In interviews, several families referenced behaviors reflecting their child's difficulty with attachment, or their quick
default to anger. Others described diagnoses of post-traumatic stress disorder (PTSD) and reactive attachment
disorder (RAD), while others did not mention any behaviors
characteristic of children with histories of trauma. In order

to help children recover from traumatic events, it is important for parents to recognize behaviors that signal previous
mistreatment, know the child's history (if available), and
understand how to find the many resources available to
assist in this process.

Responses to Trauma

When a child suffers from stress after a traumatic event,
the ability to recognize behaviors characteristic to trauma
exposure can be the first step in preventing lasting effects.
The National Child Traumatic Stress Network (NCTSN)
provides a wealth of information for anyone involved in
the lives of children exposed to traumatic events: caregivers, parents, educators, etc. The network provides a list of
signs that children are feeling stress after a traumatic event,
including eating poorly and losing weight (for preschool-age
children), worrying about their own or others' safety (for
elementary school children), and developing eating disorders and self-harming behaviors, such as cutting (for
middle- and high school children). For the full list, please
see the NCTSN website.[1]

While these signs may be more likely to occur in the
chronological ages listed above, parents must also consider
a child's developmental age. The authors of *Adopting Older
Children* explain:

> *Parents and educators must not rely solely on the
> child's chronological age when making decisions about
> behavior, development, and ability. The child may
> have a different "developmental age." For example,
> a five-year-old may act and play more like a toddler.
> A nine-year-old may have the social skills of a four-
> year-old. A child's history of trauma, including abuse
> and neglect, may have frozen her development at a*

specific point in time. Skills acquired at a certain age during the period of a major traumatic event in the life of the child may have to be relearned or the child may need help advancing to the next stage of social or emotional development. When parenting children, take into consideration the developmental and emotional age of the child, rather than targeting chronological age.[2]

Furthermore, some children will not exhibit the effects of trauma. In *Adopting Older Children*, the authors ascribe this trait to the child's resilience:

Young people who have experienced trauma or great stress may become more resilient in the face of other life stressors. The attitude is, "I've survived the worst, so nothing else can defeat me." Resilience in young people . . . is an ability to accept what they cannot change, get the help they need, and be able to move on with their lives with hope.

Young people who have experienced past trauma may find themselves drawn toward service to others, helping other children or teens with their struggles, or toward studying for a career in one of the above-mentioned fields.[3]

Obtaining Information About a Child's History

As soon as possible after a child's placement, whether or not a child exhibits signs of trauma, parents must do their best to determine whether any trauma occurred in the child's past. Author and adoptive parent Deborah Beasley advises parents and caregivers to acquire the following: "A moderate knowledge of your child's history prior to placement [,] awareness of any continued high-stress situations after placement, such as changing schools, ongoing parental visitation or court procedures, and even your parenting style [, and] attention to the wide range of subtle to severe behavioral clues."[4]

It can be very difficult to obtain information about a foster care child's history. Families interviewed for this book describe preplacement disclosure meetings, in which social workers provide families with pertinent information. However, the social worker determines what is pertinent and what isn't, and the information given can therefore vary widely. Furthermore, as the child moves from placement to placement or changes social workers, sometimes the paperwork simply is not maintained and the history isn't available.

However, in many cases, even when the paperwork has not been maintained, social workers can be a wealth of information. Author and adoptive parent William Gregory described his experience: "The social worker has so much knowledge about the child and their experience in the foster care system, the issues around the birth parents, and other factors that go into placement." He strongly advises parents, "Do not be afraid to ask any question of your caseworker—they are there to get the answers for you."[5] Asking these questions is vitally important because the more time passes after placement, the more difficult information will become to track down.

In their book, *Adopting the Hurt Child*, authors Gregory C. Keck and Regina M. Kupecky suggest that, in addition to social workers, parents can ask questions of former foster parents, the child's birth-family relatives, and the child's therapist. Keck and Kupecky include a list of possible questions, such as, "When did initial removal occur and how old was the child? How many reunification attempts have there been and why did they fail? How many placements has the child been through and why did they end? Does the child have any diagnosed conditions—such as dyslexia, Attention Deficit Disorder, or Reactive Attachment Disorder? Is there reason to believe that any such conditions exist that have not been diagnosed?"[6]

Acquiring as much knowledge as possible about a child's life prior to placement will aid parents in understanding a child's behavior, and will also guide them toward finding the assistance they need to help their children recover from past trauma.

Diagnoses

Children exhibit a spectrum of responses to trauma, from none at all to a general challenge with attachment to one or more of the behaviors listed above to conduct that may suggest a diagnosis of RAD or PTSD. Although other disorders may also afflict foster care children, in addition to mentioning challenges with attachment, one or more families interviewed cited RAD, PTSD, and ADHD, described as follows:

ATTACHMENT

A common challenge for children with a history of trauma is forming attachments to caregivers. In her book *Attaching in Adoption*, Deborah Gray describes attachment as "enduring relationships that are formed over time and experience, almost always by members of a family."[7] Secure attachments form when a parent repeatedly meets the needs of a child. For example, parents respond consistently and appropriately to hunger, they change diapers when needed, and they provide comfort when the child cries. Gray continues her explanation of attachment by listing potential interruptions to the attachment process as:

1. Separation from parents through foster care moves
2. Adoption after attachment to another parent figure has occurred

3. Prenatal exposure to drugs and alcohol
4. Traumas like sexual abuse, physical abuse, and domestic violence
5. Major depression, schizophrenia, or manic-depressive illness in the parent figure
6. Drug or alcohol addiction in the parent figure
7. Orphanage care
8. Hospitalization of parent or child, during which children lose access to their parents
9. Neglect[8]

Should one or more interruptions occur during a child's attachment process, children may form an insecure attachment in which they "cannot count on their parents as constant, safe bases of nurture and caregiving."[9] The resulting distrust in parents leads these children to have difficulty attaching to adoptive parents and to display behaviors characteristic of insecure attachment, such as lying, hoarding food, and trying to control parents.[10]

REACTIVE ATTACHMENT DISORDER (RAD)

Professionals use the *Diagnostic and Statistical Manual of Mental Disorders* (*DSM-5*), published by the American Psychological Association, to diagnose mental disorders. The 2013 version divides RAD into two types: inhibited and disinhibited, also known as disinhibited social engagement disorder (DSED).

Both disorders are caused in part by inadequate caregiving during childhood. For this diagnosis, an attachment-related trauma must have occurred before age five, and the child will have had multiple caregivers, potentially in an institutional setting that prevented attachment formation. RAD children limit their emotional responsiveness, whereas DSED children attempt to form attachments with unfamiliar people.[11]

Keck and Kupecky provide explanations of common behaviors of children with RAD. They include superficially engaging and "charming" behavior; indiscriminate affection toward strangers and lack of affection with parents on their terms; little eye contact on parental terms; persistent nonsense questions and incessant chatter; inappropriate, demanding, and clingy behavior; lying about the obvious; stealing; destructive behaviors to self, to others, and to material things; abnormal eating patterns; no impulse control; lags in learning; abnormal speech patterns; poor peer relationships; lack of cause-and-effect thinking; lack of conscience; cruelty to animals; and preoccupation with fire.[12]

POST-TRAUMATIC STRESS DISORDER (PTSD)

In their paper "Mental Health Issues in Foster Care," Drs. David Lohr and Faye Jones give brief explanations of RAD, PTSD, and ADHD. They say, "PTSD is diagnosed when someone has been exposed to severe trauma and has problems with intrusive symptoms associated with traumatic events such as memories, dreams, or dissociative reactions. . . . Youth with PTSD may have trouble with irritable and explosive behavior consistent with over arousal. . . . Recovery may be adversely affected by continued compounded stress."[13]

Risk factors include the severity of the trauma, the parents' reaction to the trauma, and the proximity of the child to the trauma.[14] Signs that a young child is experiencing PTSD include a fear of strangers, sleeping problems and nightmares, and repetition of the trauma in their play.[15] Children age five to twelve may also think that they can see signs of trauma and avoid future traumas if they pay attention. Teens may act impulsively and aggressively.[16]

The criteria for diagnosis of PTSD and RAD/DSED overlap closely and are thus sometimes difficult for professionals to distinguish. In her paper "PTSD from Childhood Trauma as a Precursor to Attachment Issues," Christy Owen writes that a RAD child's behaviors, violence, destruction of property, and so on result from PTSD from early childhood trauma—specifically, "the interpersonal betrayal of the child by his or her caregivers (who were supposed to protect him or her from harm) and the fact that, by definition, the caregivers failed to provide the child with the most basic needs (food, shelter, comfort, and safety)."[17]

ATTENTION DEFICIT HYPERACTIVITY DISORDER (ADHD)

ADHD is included here because of the potential relationship between trauma, attachment, and ADHD. The National Institute of Mental Health (NIMH) describes ADHD as a disorder that "makes it difficult for a person to pay attention and control impulsive behaviors. He or she may also be restless and almost constantly active."[18]

Lohr and Jones state that ADHD is "the most common mental health diagnosis for children in foster care."[19] The NIMH does not include trauma in the possible list of causes for ADHD. However, in a literature review examining twenty-nine studies, researchers found that "parental attachment problems and environmental mediating factors were significantly associated with childhood ADHD."[20]

In an article titled "How Childhood Trauma Could Be Mistaken for ADHD," author Rebecca Ruiz interviews Caelan Kuban, a psychologist and director of the Michigan-based National Institute for Trauma and Loss in Children, who "describes how traumatized children often find it difficult to control their behavior and rapidly shift from one mood to the next. They might drift into a dissociative state while reliving a horrifying memory or lose focus while anticipating the next violation of their safety.

To a well-meaning teacher or clinician, this distracted and sometimes disruptive behavior can look a lot like ADHD."

One danger of a misdiagnosis is inappropriate treatment. Ruiz writes, "Though stimulant medications help ADHD patients by increasing levels of neurotransmitters in the brain associated with pleasure, movement, and attention, some clinicians worry about how they affect a child with PTSD, or a similar anxiety disorder, who already feels hyper-vigilant or agitated. The available behavioral therapies for ADHD focus on time management and organizational skills, and aren't designed to treat emotional and psychological turmoil."[21]

In summary, though research does not exist to prove a direct link between trauma and ADHD, the similar behaviors marking the two disorders can potentially result in misdiagnoses and unhelpful, even harmful treatments.

Beasley reminds parents that behaviors will not be severe for all foster care children. She says:

> *Prospective foster and adoptive parents do not have to worry that these more severe behavioral patterns will become evident in every child from foster care. Parents and caregivers benefit from the [ability] to recognize that some children will be more dramatically affected by early traumatic life experiences and they may need additional emotional and psychological support. As parents, you will become vigilant to these patterns and will eventually be able to determine what they mean and, with training, how you can help.*[22]

Finally, in *Instant Mom*, Nia Vardalos lightly reminds readers that all of us may at times exhibit symptoms similar to those described above. She says, "In truth, I'm telling you all these stories to dispel the myth that adopted kids are damaged. . . . Someone once asked me if I think adopted children have abandonment issues. My answer is yes. We all do. That's why so many love songs are written and we play Adele's CDs over and over and wail to our cats about the one who left us."[23]

Parenting and Treatment Resources

No matter where a child falls on the spectrum of any disorder, numerous parenting styles and treatments exist. As the authors of *Adopting the Hurt Child* stress to readers, "*Something can be done. . . .* With patience and understanding, parents can help their child form the bond of love needed to heal."[24] Of course, treatments vary based on diagnosis. For example, Keck and Kupecky provide a long, detailed list of potential treatments for the hurt child. They vary from the more complex, requiring professional assistance (eye movement desensitization and reprocessing, sensory integration dysfunction treatment, and neurofeedback), to those that parents may be able to implement after direction from a therapist (activities involving movement, use of music, and animal-assisted therapy).[25] These treatments are different from those the NIMH recommends, which include medication, education and training, and therapy.[26]

Finding the correct therapist can be challenging, as many therapists do not have knowledge of adoption-related issues or, worse, may immediately place blame on parents whose confidence is already at an all-time low.[27] In 2012, the Child Welfare Information Gateway published a fact sheet on working with a therapist skilled in adoption issues. It recognizes that "professionals skilled in adoption issues often can prevent concerns from becoming more serious problems. An appropriate therapist will understand that although the adoptive family is often not the source of the child's problems, it is within the context of the family relationships that the child will begin to heal."[28]

In addition to treatments listed above and help from therapists, parents can learn to be aware of potential challenges for their children, such as specific triggers, holidays, and transitions. In *Wounded Children, Healing Homes*, Grace Harris tells a story of learning her adopted sons' triggers:

> *One of the most visibly shocking results of the boys' trauma surfaced whenever we moved suddenly, particularly in the perceived direction of either son. They recoiled, cried out, covered their heads with their hands, and cowered. The first time this happened, John was taking off his belt of his pants, after being dressed up for work. As he sort of whipped the belt out of the loopholes, Josh dove across the floor, yelping, whimpering, and crying. He huddled in the corner, as if he were protecting himself from harm. Oh, how our hearts broke. We were stunned and mortified that a sudden movement, especially of our arms, would alert him to danger and violence.*[29]

According to authors Betsy Keefer and Jayne E. Schooler, parents can be alert for "predictable times . . . when adoption issues can become more difficult for children," potentially triggering "emotional pain, grief, divided loyalties, or anxiety." In their book, *Telling the Truth to Your Adopted or Foster Child*, these authors provide detailed descriptions of potential triggers, such as the child's birthday, Mother's Day, placement or separation anniversaries, holidays, any experience of loss (school transitions, loss of a pet, grandparent, or best friend), perceived loss of the adoptive parents through illness, death, divorce, moving, problematic or insensitive school assignments, films or television programs that depict adoption insensitively, and emancipation from the adoptive family.[30]

Indeed, several families interviewed raised instances of concern for their children during these times and their navigation through these situations. When Liam Butler (chapter 11) started kindergarten, his mom followed several recommendations offered by the authors of *Adopting Older Children*: "When starting your child at a new school, take steps to prepare him mentally by making early introductions with teachers and staff. Find out about orientation programs if there is an opportunity to gradually introduce your child to the school. When that is not possible, for instance, when school is already in session, talk with school personnel, including specialists, and discuss your plans, goals, and any concerns you or your child might have and seek other opportunities to lessen the stress and increase chances for success."[31]

Adoption experts, families interviewed, and therapists also have a wealth of tips regarding effective parenting styles. There may be trial and error, and one method or tool may work for a period of time and need to be replaced by another. It may also take time for the parents to grasp and for the child to respond to new parenting styles. Trisha (chapter 4) describes her family's efforts to encourage positive attachment in her daughter, Celeste, using a "love and logic" approach:

> *We disrupt that cycle of reactive attachment and heal it through more appropriate attachment, which includes loving communication. There have been lots of times when we've disrupted the reactivity process. For example, during the morning routine, she used to refuse to get ready. She'd curl up in bed, scream, and kick if we got near her—tantrumming, tantrumming, tantrumming for months.*
>
> *Then we got coached by our social worker to do this love-and-logic approach, to say, "Oh, sweetheart,*

I'm sorry that you're having such a hard time getting dressed today. I really see how hard this is for you. At the same time, going to school is not a choice. We will leave at eight fifteen, just like always, and if you're dressed and walk out nicely, that is one choice, but if you're still in your pajamas, I will pack up all of your clothes and bring you to school." We've done that twice.

Then it's a reset behavior: "All of this tantrumming is not going to work, and I'm not going to fight with you during it. I'm going to stay calm and enjoy my coffee and do my thing"—which is really hard to do, by the way.

"You can do whatever you need to, but I'm going to put you in the car and sit with you and hold your seat belt on and drive you to school and give you a hug and leave you on the front lawn and drive away while you go in. If, on the way, you're calm and respectful and say, 'Mommy, can you pull over the car? I'd like to get dressed,' of course I will."

She kicked and screamed the whole way. In the weeks following, she said, "Mommy, I'm having a hard time getting dressed. Can you pick out my clothes?"

"Of course. I'm so glad you asked."

We don't have to say, "I'm never going to help you get dressed again." We can say, "If you're kicking and screaming, I won't engage with you. I love you, and if you're calm, I can't wait to give you a hug. But I'm not going to fight with you in that way. I don't fight. When you're being calm and respectful, I'll be so happy to help you get dressed and with your morning routine."

It's reprogramming. That's positive attachment: responding to how we are being treated, reinforcing positive attachment, and disengaging from reactivity.

One important element in this story is Trisha's ability to remain calm despite her daughter's stressful behavior. Adoption experts agree, "The key is for parents to resist allowing the child to activate them. . . . When parents do not emotionally overreact, the child is assured that they will be able to handle anything and keep him safe."[32]

Sherrie Eldridge adds, "When surging emotions and startling statements are hurled, try to keep your cool. This will communicate unspoken strength to your child and will help him gravitate toward wholeness instead of rage. If he can draw you into the cyclone of emotions, the chaos has won."[33]

The authors of *Adopting Older Children* recommend several parenting methods, including Authoritative Parenting, developed by Diana Baumrind; Emotion Coaching, developed by John Gottman and Joan DeClaire; and the Kazdin Method, developed by Alan Kazdin. They say, "Parenting styles that focus on strengths and positive behaviors are more likely to set up children for success. Effective 'positive parenting' styles promote a healthy, secure attachment between child and parent, have a high rate of success, and reduce parenting stress. The opposite is true of punitive methods which increase aggression, have a high failure rate, increase parental stress, and deteriorate the parent-child bond."[34]

Lori Butler (chapter 11) describes parenting methods she uses with her children:

> *We've done parent-child interaction therapy (PCIT) with these little guys, I've done everything, gone to classes. We used the same philosophy as we did with Libby and Layla, trying not to say, "Don't do that" and use positive words. We don't say, "What would you like to do?" We ask them, "Do you want this or that?" Instead of saying, "Will you do this?" we say, "Libby, please pick that up." You don't give them the option. If you say, "Will you?" it lets them say yes or no.*

Clearly, there is a range of responses a child might have to move past trauma, and parents can take advantage of resources offered by their schools (several families mentioned Individualized Education Programs [IEPs]),[35] or by their county or fost-adopt agency, and suggested by other parents, therapists, and adoption experts. *Successful Foster Care Adoption* author Deborah A. Beasley advises the following for parents:

Seek classes and workshops offered in your area on topics like:

- Understanding childhood trauma
- Facilitating healthy attachment and bonding
- How traumatic events shape a child's life, relationships, and abilities
- Helping children to develop stress coping strategies
- Stress management for special needs caregivers
- Cultural competency in transracial adoptions

Parenting our children is one of the most demanding and critically important responsibilities we share as adults. Yet it is the one for which we are least likely to seek sound advice, help, or education.[36]

The sound advice, help, or education that Beasley mentions above can help tremendously as parents develop strategies to assist their children's healing from past traumas. Many families interviewed for *All the Sweeter* do not mention a history of trauma or lingering effects of trauma on their children. Other families describe difficult, often repeated situations that have challenged them in unexpected ways. In the latter case, Keck and Kupecky have found that "parents who adopt a hurt child who is eventually able to attach and become part of the family seldom regret the experience. They often learn more about themselves than they bargained for and may work harder than they wished, but they invariably share a deep pride and profound joy at playing such an important role in a child's life."[37] Indeed, as many of the families in *All the Sweeter* exemplify, parents are able to strengthen their family when they seek assistance to learn and apply new parenting skills that can help their children overcome past trauma.

CHAPTER 13:

UNEXPECTED BLESSING:

THE WALTERS FAMILY

A nna Walters fostered her son, Colby, from the age of five months to his adoption at age three. Their story is unique in that Colby's first foster parents became his god-parents and a second family for Anna. In addition, as part of the parental rights termination agreement, Anna takes Colby for visits to his biological family three times per year. Anna tells her family's story.

Adoption Story

I always felt a calling to adopt. The concept of physically having a child was not something that I cared about. I have loved kids since I was a kid. I always loved the concept of being a mom. I was a teacher and a coach, and I loved all of my students and athletes so much that I knew they didn't have to be my own physically for me to love them as much as if they were. I got serious about adoption in my early thirties, but there was a lot of hesitation on my family's part.

People in the Walters Family's Story

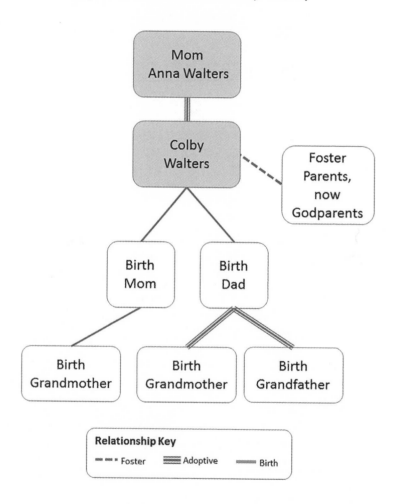

They felt it's very hard to be a single mom and didn't want me to get in over my head.

I held off partly because I was a teacher and the cost of an adoption, the cost of raising a child, is a lot. Then I found out that the foster care system gives you a subsidy. I know a lot of people misuse it, but for me it was the avenue that allowed me to be able to do this. I signed up for a twelve-week training at the CPS offices.

I hadn't really thought of fostering. I knew that adopting through the system meant that there was a chance that the child would not stay with me. However, usually they place children who are less likely to return home to their biological families in preadoptive homes, the goal being to start bonding as quickly as possible. I knew there would still be some risk, but it was less than if I automatically went in as a foster.

They knew very clearly what I wanted. At my last class, they came up to me and said, "We really want you to consider fostering, because for the children out there who have potential to be preadopted, we have hundreds of families waiting."

My state has a computer system that matches a child with five families. Those five families get sent to the child's social worker, who narrows it down to two families. An entire group, including physicians and nurses and psychologists, then picks the family. Because I was a single mom, the computer would not pick me [as a candidate to adopt]. They didn't put it that way, but they said they have other single women who are phenomenal and would be incredible moms but have been on the list for two years. These moms were not willing to take the risk to foster.

My thought was, *Maybe this is God telling me just to foster, because I may be getting in over my head. Maybe I'll do this and say, "You know what? Maybe I really couldn't handle this by myself."*

I agreed to foster. They clearly knew what my goals and intentions were, so I think they were looking for a child who was not necessarily denoted as preadoptive but who they had some reasons to believe likely wouldn't go back home.

I finished my course in January, and it was sometime in April when they called and said all of the paperwork had gone through. I was a big thorn in their sides, because as soon as they finished the last home visit, I was like, "All right, let's go!" I was calling at least once a week: "What's the holdup?"

It was everything from fingerprinting not going through to my paperwork being sent to the wrong office—ten million bureaucratic issues. [The paperwork finally] made it to the office that I would be working through, and they told me, probably two days later, that they had a child in mind for me. I got to meet him at the CPS office first, then went to his first foster home to meet him there. I talked to the foster mom about his situation: when was he happy, did he like baths—all of the things that a lot of people don't get to find out with foster kids.

They made it fairly clear that I would likely get an emergency phone call sometime between 4:00 and 10:00 p.m., saying, "Can we bring you a child in an hour?" Usually, they'd have been removed from the home, so the parents would be upset and unlikely to share any information, like what kind of formula they used or what their favorite toys were. I had gone into this expecting that situation and had the absolute opposite of everything they told me.

I met Colby in advance. He happens to be a white child (it didn't matter to me). He is healthy; he was born addicted to crack but has, thank God, had absolutely no repercussions from that.

Colby's biological mother has schizophrenia. She and his biological father are, to this day, still together. At the time of Colby's birth, they both had violent tendencies. There had been a fight that broke out, where she was beaten. When he was born, his father was in prison and his mother was living in a homeless shelter. Her attorney claimed that she didn't take her antipsychotic medication while she was pregnant because she thought it would hurt the child. Of course, it's difficult to believe that, given that she used crack while pregnant. This delayed the process of terminating parental rights.

Colby went from the hospital to his first foster family. Absolutely amazing people, they have five children of their own and are Colby's godparents. His middle name is their last name. They wanted to be emergency foster care for infants who were born addicted, because Marion, his god-mother, had learned how important it was for those kids to be held all the time.

"I can strap this kid to me and do everything I've always done." That's really what she did. I give them an immense amount of credit for Colby's success. He lived with them for five months.

The really frustrating part was that during those five months, his biological parents were at their most extreme of behaviors and the social worker who had his case at the time kept no records. The day that Colby came to me, he was given a new social worker, who stayed with us until he was adopted. When she went to get his records, there were none. I know that the first social worker got fired. But it meant that Colby's adoption, which likely should have happened before he was a year old, was delayed until he was three and a half.

He came to me at five months and was with me from that point on. About a year after he came to me, his god-father was appointed to a high-level government position in another state. He began commuting between states and finally said, "This job is too hard. I really need my family with me, and I can't keep commuting."

They said, "We feel like you are family, and if you would ever consider coming, we would love for you to come."

My parents had retired and moved out of state, and Colby's godparents truly were my support system. If Colby was sick and I needed to be at work, his godmother was at my house at six thirty in the morning. He sees his godfather every week. We go to church together on Sundays; then they go and spend what we call "guy time" together on Sunday afternoons. They do everything from wash the car to mow the lawn. His godmother picks him up from school a couple times a week so that he doesn't have to be there the whole day. She really is like a coparent for me.

We did have to wait until he was adopted to move, and I had to make sure that I got a job. When we initially said yes, we want to do it, we still weren't sure that the adoption would go through.

Relationship with Biological Parents

The first year and a half that Colby was with me, his birth parents were still pretty involved. They mandated that he still have visits with them twice per week,[1] and because I worked, CPS would pick him up from day care and take him to the visits. They were supervised visits, but there was no question that he left the visits traumatized. It was truly a heartbreaking, devastating thing to see him go through that. The time that really drove home for me how hard it was, he was probably thirteen months old. I had to go to the CPS office, and the minute he saw the building—he was still so little; he was only four pounds when he was born, five weeks early, and even at a year old, he was still only about nine pounds—his face just went totally blank. He had been smiling and laughing with me in the car, and his little fist just grabbed my shirt as tight as he could, like, *Don't let me go, don't let me go.*

He was a cute kid, and all the social workers wanted to hold him and play with him, but his parents wouldn't allow it. When we walked in, they were like, "His parents aren't here. Now we can actually hold him."

I would pack bags for his visit, and they would go through an entire tube of Desitin, diaper cream, in an hour and a half. They would literally change Colby's diaper six times in an hour and a half because they just didn't know what to do with him.

It was obviously very hard for him. Sometime around his second birthday, they stopped showing up to the visits, and we did not see them until after the adoption.

The parents are very devoted to each other. They had an expectation that if one couldn't go to the visit, nobody went. If one was doing drugs and not able to go, neither of them went. I am very lucky that his biological grandparents on his father's side are wonderful people. I've actually gotten very close with his biological grandmother. She and Colby's grandfather adopted his father from an Eastern European country during the Cold War. He was in one of those orphanages where they just lined up the cribs and never held the kid. His parents adopted him when he was four months old. At four months, he weighed less than he did when he was born. He truly had been neglected.

He struggles with drug addiction and reactive attachment disorder. They believe he has bipolar disorder. The hardest thing is that he functions like a child, and there's just no way to know if it is nature or nurture, because nobody knows his biological parents.

After about three years, the parents had stopped showing up. We knew that it was essentially coming to an end, but the parents were unwilling to sign the termination agreement unless it was an open adoption. At that point, I really didn't want to delay things any further. It is written into the adoption agreement that they have the right to see Colby under my supervision as often as three times per year. It is fully my choice if I think that it is not in Colby's best interest, but I have so far upheld that. I never want him to get to adulthood and say to me, "You kept me from knowing them."

At this point, I am leaving it to him. If he feels uncomfortable, we certainly will stop. At the visits, I have to be present, and I have it written into the adoption agreement that his grandmother must be present at every visit—really so that I have some backup.

It's very hard to be around them, because they have so many challenges of their own. When you put Colby into the mix of it, it's even more challenging, because you want to protect him, but you don't want to be disrespectful to them. But they truly don't have any parenting skills. They do things like grab his sleeve and say, "Hey, let's go do this." He'll be busy doing something else, and so then they just grab his arm, but they grab it very hard and forcefully. It's not with malintent. They're not trying to hurt him; it's just not a natural thing for them.

They're supposed to give me paperwork before the visit that tells me that they have been drug tested, are clean, and are both psychologically capable of being with a four-year-old. One of their psychiatrists has to deem them in a good position to be around Colby.

They are drug tested consistently as part of their programs—psychological programs and support-type programs—so getting a drug test is not hard. Our last visit, I asked for the drug test. I really made a huge error in that we had two good visits before we moved, and both parents were sober and doing about as well as anyone had seen them do. It's never going to be easy, but it was much easier than I had anticipated. When we went back at Christmas, I did not ask for the drug tests because I had had these two other visits and they went really well. I thought, *Oh, Colby's grandmother would tell me.*

I am now fairly certain that his mother was using at that point. I think the grandmother didn't know. I don't think she was trying to hide it from me; I think she figured it out a few weeks later. The mother tends to fall off the wagon, more often than the father, and she typically hides it from him until he starts to say, "Okay, we need money from your welfare check for rent" and she doesn't have it. That's usually his cue that she's using. In this situation, I don't think that he knew either, but I could tell that something was just different.

I required it the next time, and I know they were not really happy that I was requiring it. They said, "We can't really get it to you." They don't have a lot of access, they don't drive, things are hard. They eventually said that it is really difficult for them to get me the letter before the visit.

I said, "I will trust you to tell me before the visit if you have the letters, and, if so, we'll plan the visit and you can give me the letters at the visit." The first time that we did that, it worked well.

We then planned to see them a few months later, and the father told me, "Yes, we have them." But during a conversation with the grandmother, she said to me, "I don't think that the mother actually has it."

I said, "Please let him know that it really will backfire on him, because I won't be able to trust him. Then they'll have to figure out how to get me the letters in advance, mail them to me, etc."

Colby's grandmother spoke to them, and the mother did not come to the visit. It was definitely hard to hold that line. The father was confrontational. I was lucky that both of Colby's grandparents were there when we all went out for breakfast.

He said, "You guys won't come to our house just because she doesn't have the letter? You know that she would never actually smoke crack in front of Colby."

I said, "I'm glad to hear that, and I'm sure that she wouldn't, but it's really that it affects your behavior for an extended period; it's not just while you do it."

Then it kind of clicked and he was like, "Oh. Okay."

It's that type of disconnect for them. They truly believe, *If I'm not smoking it in front of you, then there's nothing wrong with it.*

Colby's grandparents are very aware of their son's limitations and have said that they anticipate that the time will come when Colby does not want to see them. The mother does not have quite the developmental delays that the father does, but there is not a lot of affect. She just kind of watches.

Colby has not really voiced an opinion about the visits. He's still so young. He'll be five in a month. The best way to describe it is, he can't voice how he's feeling. Whenever I think maybe he's not comfortable, I'll say, "How was that? What did you think? Did you like having the visits?"

"Yeah."

"Do you want to see them again?"

"Yeah."

There's not a committed yes, like, "Yes! That was awesome!" But so far, there hasn't been a no either.

Our second-to-last visit, the father's siblings were there, as well as the grandparents and a social worker. They were all downstairs, and I went upstairs to go to the restroom. I knew that I was not leaving Colby alone. As I came back down the stairs, I heard the father saying, "Well, Colby, why can't I say that? Why can't I say, 'I love you'?"

Colby said, "Stop talking."

Typically, Colby is not at a loss for words. He went into speech therapy for about four months when he was two. Since then, he has not stopped talking. Anytime someone tells Colby they love him, he responds, "I love you." Truly. It can be his friends in his class, it can be his teacher, it can be our neighbor—we have lots of people we love. So to have his father say that and for Colby's response to be "Stop talking" told me that there is something there.

From the very beginning, I have tried to talk about

adoption. When we had the adoption, we celebrated it. We talked about it for months and had a big party. It got to a point where he thought we should just adopt everybody. But whenever I try to ask if he really understands—"Do you know that you came from Gwyneth's belly?"—it's the only time he'll look at me and say, "Stop talking."

It may be too confusing for him to know how to explain himself—to be able to say something like, "I'm uncomfortable with what's happening, and I don't get it, so we're just not going to talk about it." He may just not have the words to explain it.

On Being a Single Mom

My parents were concerned about me being a single mom, but I really never have been, because I do have, as a single parent, the support of this other amazing family. I am very close to my parents, so I tried to respect them, and there was still the financial piece that hadn't been resolved at that point, but I'm very glad now about the way it has all turned out. I feel like I have been blessed with the right child for me, and just an incredible situation.

The initial first few months for any parent, regardless of whether the child is adopted or whether or not you are doing it by yourself, are utterly exhausting, beyond anything I had thought they would be. I've talked to other moms, who have said they had multiple days where they broke down. I had one day when I truly was just so beyond exhausted, when I really would have loved to have somebody else who could step in. In general, probably the hardest part is the times when Colby wants to know where his dad is or why he doesn't have one.

From a selfish standpoint, one of the benefits is that I am really able to raise him in the way that I think is the best. In that way, I don't have to compromise, although

I do very much take his godmother's point of view into consideration almost all the time—she has five incredible kids. Even when there are times when I'm thinking, *Oh, jeez, I don't know about that,* I'll stop and think, *That actually probably is a good idea.*

Advice

Adopting through the foster care system is an amazing and wonderful way to adopt, and because of the financial support, it opened up a lot of doors for me. It needs to be a path that you are really ready to take, because there are lots and lots of ups and downs, as there are for any adoption situation.

When you do it this way, there are a lot of people who are very heavily involved who you don't normally think of when you think of parenting. We had his social worker, who came to visit once a month to the home. They also gave the family a social worker, so I had my own, and she came to the home almost once a month. A lot of times, the adoptive parents don't necessarily understand all the rules and how CPS works, so the social workers are there to really help guide them through that.

You have this constant threat and concern that at any time, something can happen: a biological family member can be found, or the court decides that they want the child to go home, to see how the child will do with the family. There are a lot of concerns that you wouldn't normally think about. In no way is it meant to deter anyone from doing it; I certainly am in the best position that I could have ever wanted to be. But there were a lot of times where I just thought, *Okay, I'm ready to know that he's mine and know that nobody is taking him from me and not have anybody show up to my house, evaluating everything that's going on.*

I had a situation where I knew that the birth parents were going into court [to determine their ability to parent] and had literally been told that if the court decided that he needed to go back to his parents, they would pick him up from day care and take him and that I would not have the opportunity to say goodbye.

As you can imagine, I spent the entire day crying at work. There are those ups and downs, but it has truly all been worth it. I have huge faith in God, and, as hard and painful as a lot of that stuff is, it was also possible for me to say, "I see God in all of this." And if, God forbid, it had been decided that he wouldn't stay with me, it would have been unbelievably painful, but in time I would have been able to accept God's hand in it.

What I didn't do very well was have a real conversation with my family, my parents, my brother and sister-in-law, my niece and nephew, about what they really thought about my doing this and what role they thought they could play. I helped raise my niece and nephew, and then when Colby came along, my brother and his family were fairly distant. I think a lot of it was the fear of falling in love with him and then losing him; it was just something that they couldn't handle. I can understand it. At the same time, I was looking for that support and I was expecting a very different reaction.

My parents were awesome and love him immensely, but it had already been in the works before he came that they would be retiring across the country. Four months after he came, they moved. They, too, had essentially raised my niece and nephew while my brother and sister-in-law worked. I had seen my brother and sister-in-law and how my niece and nephew were raised and how much support they had gotten. I just didn't communicate. My own fault. They knew what my plans were, but I never really had the conversation "How much a part of this do you want to be?"

In my mind, I expected that they would be this huge part of it. In reality, that was not the case. That became something that was really hard.

Had I not had his godparents, it would have been incredibly difficult. Even CPS kept saying, "Oh my gosh, we've never seen anything like this." We spend Christmas and Thanksgiving together. We really have become a family. It's a very neat and special thing for me.

CHAPTER 14:

SUPPOSED TO BE:

THE OLSON FAMILY

....

Brooke, Shelby, and Dakota live in a densely populated neighborhood of a large city. Brooke isn't married but knew she wanted children. After exploring several other options, she decided to adopt two sibling daughters from foster care.

Shelby graduated from fifth grade in 2018 and Dakota will start fifth grade in 2019. All three have birthdays the same month, and the girls are one week short of one year apart in age.

Each summer, they travel as a family to a horse-back-riding camp where the girls spend a week playing Ping-Pong and volleyball, barbecuing, making friends, and riding horses twice a day. Brooke says, "My youngest daughter writes me poems and love notes. Often! She is an amazing artist and draws photos of our family, including pets. My older daughter is an old soul, wise beyond her years, very empathetic and nurturing to all. She is sensitive and is always looking to see what she can do to help others.

People in the Olson Family's Story

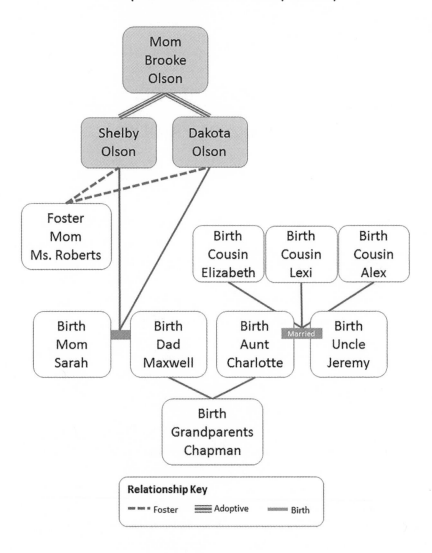

I'm touched by how important it is to both of my girls to help others. They warm my heart beyond measure."

Brooke, Shelby, and Dakota shared their story together.

Adoption Story

DAKOTA: Shelby was born; then I was born. Shelby and I were born in a hospital in the Northeast, and our first mommy was named Sarah.

Our birth father's name was Maxwell. Once I was born, Sarah gave Shelby to Maxwell's mom, our grandma, to take care of her, which is why we have so many pictures of Shelby and not so many of me.

BROOKE: Maxwell's sister, Auntie Charlotte, just sent us a few pictures. We are still in touch with her.

DAKOTA: We still call her Auntie Charlotte. She couldn't take care of us. They were thinking about adopting us, but they just couldn't because they already had three kids. When Sarah passed away—she was asleep, I think, and she never woke up—we were in the room, and the door was just closed, and then they came in to check and she was not alive anymore. So we went to Maxwell's.

BROOKE: No. Maxwell was in the Northeast, in jail. Sarah brought both girls out to the West Coast. She was struggling. It was her choice to go to the transitional house for mothers and children, but if she wanted to leave, she couldn't take her kids at that point. The kids were under CPS. So it was drugs and mental health, all of that stuff. She was being cared for well, and she was doing her best. I'm not exactly clear when they came out here, but they were very young. When Sarah passed away, Dakota was one year and eight months, and Shelby was two years and eight months, so they were little.

SHELBY: Show her the book that we got when we went to meet Auntie Charlotte and our grandparents.

DAKOTA [flipping through pages of a picture book]: This is Sarah. This is Maxwell. This is the house we lived in when Sarah died. This is Ms. Roberts's house. She was our foster mom for six months. She was very strict.

SHELBY: You loved the dad.

DAKOTA: I had a bond with the dad, and Shelby had a bond with the daughter. Then my mom saw a picture of us and said that she wanted to meet us. Mom, can you talk about that? I forgot.

BROOKE: When I was very seriously thinking about adoption, I'd gone to an attorney in the city and talked about private adoption. She thought that I seemed open enough and suggested I try fost-adopt. She didn't know exactly how it worked but offered to support me pro bono if I needed her. She was the one who basically introduced me to it.

At the time, I worked with my friend Joseph. He married Derek, and the next thing I knew, they were adopting three kids. I went over to their house and met the boys. The youngest introduced himself and told me he was a chick magnet, which I will never forget.

They provided me with so much information, including the best advice. They told me, "Be really clear on what you can and can't do, and don't judge yourself for that. It's not fair for you or a child to do what you can't do. Be open to everything else." That's how I ended up with two toddler girls, when I was looking for an infant boy. And I don't get to talk that much, do I? I just listen.

When I went to the fost-adopt agency, I had this mentality that I was just going to go full steam ahead. If something told me to stop, I'd know I'd given it my best shot. Nothing ever told me to stop, so I kept plugging along.

The path didn't scare me, because I really felt like if it is supposed to be, it will be what it is supposed to be. This is absolutely what it was supposed to be. There is no doubt in my mind.

When I was certified as a foster parent, the social worker I was working with literally had a book of kids. This was crazy to me—it really was just a binder of kids. I was looking through it, and near the end I saw a picture of these two little girls and thought, *What are they doing in here?* It just was very—

DAKOTA: And immediately, she wanted to know our story!

BROOKE: The social worker told me she needed to find out about their status. I was like, *Oh my God, what am I doing?* I went back to work and—Shelby likes this part—I caught myself brushing my teeth in the coffee bar, out in the open. We did have bathrooms. I went back to my desk, then got on the wrong bus to come home.

When the social worker called me a couple days later, she said the girls had an aunt and uncle in the Northeast who had been trying to adopt them, but the situation wasn't perfect because they had three kids from a blended marriage already. The county felt very strongly that these girls would do better in a home without other kids, so that they could get all the attention, because they needed all the attention. I think it was a little bit of a positive that I was single, because they'd had some very rough experiences.

DAKOTA: Sarah had a boyfriend, 'cause she wanted to be loved—that's all she wanted. His name was Jeff, and he was not very nice to Sarah or to Shelby. He did some nasty things—like, he burned Shelby with a cigarette, and he pulled her ear.

SHELBY: I remember that very strongly.

BROOKE: They were very popular in the shelter. As you can see, they are very social. Everybody was really concerned about them. In fact, one of the women who worked there was a student, and she wanted to try to adopt them. A social worker at the transition home asked my social worker, "What about this woman makes her think she can do this? These girls have been through a lot. What does she have in her background?"

I said, "Hey, I don't want to be placed with kids that I can't [support]. If they need something that I can't give them, that's fine. I'm happy to talk to her." I did, and she loved me.

She called their auntie Charlotte and said, "We think we've found somebody." Auntie Charlotte was pretty happy and just wanted to know if I would allow her to be in touch with the girls. I said, "Of course." I moved forward. It happened very, very fast. There wasn't a risk of Auntie Charlotte's family or anyone else trying to adopt.

The social worker set up a visit with the foster parents, and I went to Ms. Roberts's house. Five weeks later, they moved in.

DAKOTA: During those five weeks, we visited Mommy on the weekends.

Shelby pulls out a book that Sarah compiled after Shelby's birth. It includes information about the family, pictures of Sarah's ultrasound of Shelby, and information about the hospital where Sarah gave birth.

SHELBY: Sarah smoked, so that's why this smells.

BROOKE: I picked the girls up from Ms. Roberts's house. Everything they had was in huge trash bags. There are non-profits that talk about foster kids with big black trash bags to carry their stuff. It makes me want to cry, because it is absolutely true.

I started going through the girls' bags and found this book from Auntie Charlotte. She would send them gifts. In the back of one of the books, Auntie Charlotte drew the whole family tree, like a map, so that the girls would know how to find her if she completely lost touch with them.

Auntie Charlotte had also bought gifts for them, which she'd kept if she didn't know where to send them. After they moved in, I got all the things that she had bought, including ornaments every year for Christmas, so now we have them all on our tree. She loves them very much.

The second year that they were with me, we went back to visit Auntie Charlotte. My mother, their grandmother, came with us. It was very emotional but very, very special for everybody. Auntie Charlotte's husband is in the military and he was away, but we met all three kids and the grandparents.

Shelby reads from the book:

The special things that Sarah wants to remember are that:

1) Through the good times and bad times, we care. Always there for each other, always.
2) We so wanted you. We all love you very much.
3) We will always be there for you. Everybody is really close in our family. Anytime you need one of us, we will be there in a heartbeat.
4) We all love you very much. We are so very lucky to have you.

BROOKE: The state of California locked our file, which isn't common anymore. The state doesn't want Sarah's parents to ever look for us.

DAKOTA: Why?

BROOKE: There was a lot of abuse and a lot of drugs—really, Sarah's whole life. When Sarah passed away, she had been trying to correspond with her family and they weren't responding. After she passed away, they called and asked her social worker to send them her belongings. The social worker told me, "They wouldn't support her, and now they think there might be something in there. The belongings are yours." I went through all of Sarah's stuff and pulled out a few items for the girls. [Shelby tries on Sarah's sunglasses, and Dakota puts on a scarf.]

The other side is completely wide open. Maxwell has had his struggles, but he has definitely loved them.

SHELBY: Is he out [of prison]?

BROOKE: I think so.

DAKOTA: Mom said she might let us meet him when we're very old.

BROOKE: It will be your choice when you're older.

The first time I visited them at Ms. Roberts's house, it was just a crazy feeling, in a crazy-good way. Here were these little girls, and they were a little bit shy initially. I got down on the ground with Dakota and played with her. That was a Wednesday. I went back on the following Saturday, and then I was by myself and the caseworker left me. The family who lived there let me be by myself with the girls, and I brought them little things—sunglasses and clips. They had just turned two and three. Right after that, I think I only had two visits at Ms. Roberts's house, and then it was my house. My house was ready, though the room wasn't done. My parents basically did their entire room. It's bubble-gum pink. I had the crib from Joseph and Derek and a hide-a-bed that Shelby slept in.

Their first visit to my house was the night before Easter. I had planned to have a bunch of people over—this all happened pretty darn fast. I asked their social worker if I should cancel. She said, "With any other kids, I would say yes, too many people is not a good thing. But these girls are so social and they were in the shelter for so long that they'll probably love it."

So we did it. That Saturday, I picked the girls up and brought them home. We went to the playground with our upstairs neighbors, who had two kids. The kids were all around the same age, and we went to the playground right down the street, and we were playing and playing. Afterward, I put together the dinner while they were napping, and I thought, *This isn't that hard. They're sleeping, I'm making an Easter roast.*

That night, I put the girls to bed and then the work really started.

DAKOTA: I slept and Shelby cried.

BROOKE: Dakota slept all night, and Shelby cried all night. My neighbor came down the next morning with a few Easter things and asked if I'd gotten any sleep. Not much! Then the Easter bunny came. They had no idea what Easter was. They had had no holidays in their foster home—they were Jehovah's Witnesses—so they really had no holidays. Pretty exciting for us.

DAKOTA: The next night, I couldn't sleep and Shelby slept. So I went into my mom's room and I slept on her belly, and whenever I fell off, I'd start crying, so my mom had to put me back on.

BROOKE: The third visit weekend, we went to Grandma and Grandpa's house, and they slept all night and so did I.

The fourth weekend, I didn't have them, and then the fifth week, they moved in. We had a move-in calendar set up with the caseworker. Every weekend we would bond more and more, and Dakota started calling me Mommy by the third weekend.

DAKOTA: First we both called her Brooke. Then I started calling her Brookemommy. Then Shelby started calling her Brookemommy. Then I started calling her Mommy, and then Shelby kept calling her Brookemommy, and theeeeeen she started calling her Mommy.

BROOKE: The things about bonding and stuff were super happy and by the book. They didn't take long [to get attached to me]. Every time I took them back to the foster family, it was torture. Shelby was quiet and kind of stoic about it, and Dakota would bawl.

They were very ready. Ms. Roberts got them on a routine—they were safe, they were clean—but I don't know that she nurtured them.

We finalized the adoption about a year and a half after they moved in. It took time only because the courts are slow. At one point while they were living with me, Sarah's boyfriend tried to say that he was the dad and wanted custody of them. He never showed up at court, and the judge threw it out. He has a very big drug problem.

The day we finalized, all of the social workers came and my family came, and a couple of really, really good friends came.

The judge was awesome. She was one of the strictest judges in the city. The judge who does adoptions was out on vacation or something, so she was doing adoptions that day, and, oh my gosh, she was awesome. She said it was the best day of her life, doing stuff like that, because she's usually with the really bad guys.

Current Challenges

BROOKE: They had been in a university hospital program. Shelby was in it with Sarah because Sarah had a hard time bonding and nurturing. She tried very, very, very hard, but she was never set up for success. Then Shelby and Dakota had counselors there as well, and they were in a big research study on the effect of childhood trauma on children's brains. We continued there for a while with a really great woman who works with a lot of foster kids, and then didn't really need to do it anymore. Shelby sees a social worker and has since third grade. She does a lot of somatics work, and Shelby loves her very much. They have a good relationship.

SHELBY: Sometimes we see her Monday and Wednesday, and sometimes we see her just Monday. Dakota doesn't go.

BROOKE: Shelby did a course. Shelby has some challenges. Right?

SHELBY: Yes.

BROOKE: Okay, I'm just checkin'. [Shelby laughs.] Shelby wasn't nurtured and didn't have a great opportunity to learn how to work through things when those habits usually develop, ages two or three, when your brain learns how to regulate itself. She has a hard time. She definitely has triggers, and kids know that, so they go at her. It's the freeze, fright, flight. She can go there really fast. [Turns to Shelby.] I'm speaking like you're not next to me, but you *are* next to me, and I know that. You can speak up whenever you want to.

She's worked very, very hard to have lots of different things that she can do to calm herself. For the most part, the school has been very supportive.

SHELBY: I have a 504 now.

BROOKE: I am only now learning what that is. It's a plan that will go with her to middle school, where, by law, they have to provide her with the services that she needs. And what that means for her primarily is, if she needs to walk out of a classroom to cool down for two minutes, they have to let her.

SHELBY: I would only stay out there for three minutes.

BROOKE: Sometimes all she needs to do is get out. With a 504, she can do whatever she needs to do, then go back in. You can imagine if a teacher has thirty kids and all thirty kids decide they want to go out for two minutes, it's a problem. The kids know Shelby and have known her for a long time and know that she can get very upset easily. That's another reason why she wants to go to another school. She's been asking for it: "I want a fresh start. I want a fresh start." She deserves and needs a fresh start, and I imagine that many of these kids will be friends of hers at some point in time, but right now it's time to switch it all up.

Shelby's social worker has been awesome. Though Shelby usually sees her alone, for the next several appointments, we're going to do it together. We'll do work focused on what she should have learned when she was two and three. The good breathing is the best. I forget about it; then sometimes I remember for Shelby, and then I think, *Remember for yourself!* Shelby is better now, but all of her friends, all of her classmates, know her trigger points. They know what to do and say to get her upset. They probably think it's funny. I don't think it's funny, and Shelby doesn't think it's funny.

The social worker has been great for us. I found her through my fost-adopt agency.

Logistics and Support

BROOKE: A little more room would be good. We live in a two-bedroom, and one-and-a-half-bath. The girls share their room. I have a nanny in the morning; she just left for vacation, and I sent her a note today and said, "I miss you already." [Laughs.] She comes every morning at seven, and she gets the girls to school by eight thirty. They just walk, and she feeds them breakfast and makes them lunch, which is a godsend. When they were at day care and preschool, which was all close by, I put them in the stroller and walked them down and took a bus to work.

After school, they participate in the YMCA elite program and they do STEM and LEAP (Learning Enrichment After-School Program). They do field trips every couple of months.

SHELBY: We did a partnership with a neighborhood senior services center and took eight bags of food with protein on the bus and delivered them to the elderly. Some of the people were super sweet and would give you candy. Some of them were Russian, so they would give you Russian candies like the ones we ate at our Russian preschool. They were good.

BROOKE: I also have really good neighbors who are like family. I have family that's not very far away, and my work has been flexible. In fact, my work didn't offer any adoption benefits. I put in a proposal for it, and we got it, and I was the first recipient. It was for a lifetime maximum of two kids, and it paid for me to be out for six weeks. Prior to that program, there was no real leave, except for family leave, which doesn't really pay you anything. Having the girls gets me out of my job on time or early. I get online at night if I need to.

When I was doing all of the classes with my fost-adopt agency, I was the only single woman, and I was the only straight woman. I thought, *Wow, I'm the minority.* It's a good experience to feel that way.

Have you ever heard of Single Mothers by Choice? It's an organization that was started in New York maybe twenty years ago. There are women who tried to get pregnant on their own; there are women who are thinking about adoption. I met a friend on the website who has a daughter one week younger than Dakota.

Of course, there are things that can be scary, but you're responsible for what you go for, what you decide to take on. And there is support. It would be very hard without my support system—not impossible, but it would be way different. Now that the girls are a little bit older, it's easier in some ways, I'm sure harder in others, but it keeps changing.

The Fun Stuff

BROOKE: Our fost-adopt agency has a holiday gathering and a summer picnic every year. We try to go to every one of them. They get more and more fun every year, I guess because we're really comfortable and we meet new people. Everybody has something in common.

We went to Italy. Our neighbor had a sabbatical two summers ago, and she rented a five-hundred-year-old farmhouse in Tuscany. We flew into Florence, stayed with them for a week in Tuscany, went back to Florence for three nights, then took the train to Positano, on the Amalfi coast. We stayed in a resort there for seven nights and met really nice people from Ireland. We went to Capri and Rome and ran into friends of Dakota in Pompeii.

One summer we went to London, and another to Paris. We went to France for two and a half weeks, and my parents organized all of the logistics. We took my nephew and rented a flat.

SHELBY: In Paris, we were going to leave, and the flight attendant gave up our seats, but we were actually really early.

BROOKE: We were there first, and they did that to four families. It was terrible. I did end up getting half of my airfare back, though I was so furious. They oversold the flight, and there were four families that were all standing there, and I had the girls and my nephew, who was twelve. They said, "We will give you a hotel room, but there cannot be more than two children in any room."

SHELBY: *Bonjour. Parlez-vous français?*

BROOKE [laughing]: It's often a comedy show around here, though sometimes it's funnier than others.

Advice

SHELBY: I'd say keep a journal of your children's quotes, because later in their life, they will want to know what they said. My momma keeps quotes on me, and it is really cute to listen to all of the funny things I said, and it's fun to laugh with her about what we said.

DAKOTA: We were sitting in front of a barbecue, and I asked my mom, "Mom, how do you spell *in*?"
    She said, "*I-n.*" I asked, "Mom, how do you spell *sex*?" And then she said, "*What*?" And I said, "Mommy, I'm trying to spell *insects*."

BROOKE: She was four. We were sitting there with a bunch of friends, and I was like, "*What*?"
    I would always pass on Joseph and Derek's advice: keep as open as you can, know what you can't do, and don't feel

guilty about it. It's really easy to feel like you should do something that you can't.

I am forever thankful for our family. Our story feels fated to me—the stars totally aligned—and I still pinch myself that it happened. I always wanted children and honestly feel like the luckiest mom alive.

CHAPTER 15:

RELATIONSHIPS BETWEEN
ADOPTIVE AND BIRTH FAMILIES

....

These twelve family stories highlight many different types of relationships with birth parents. There can be no current relationship with the birth family but a possibility of one in the future; there can be family visits contingent upon the child's interest and the parents' health; sometimes there is contact with cousins after the birth mom passes away; sometimes contact is a professionally mediated work in progress; and sometimes there are relationships to maintain with birth siblings adopted by another family.

The literature on relationships between adoptive families and birth families recognizes the variety of situations that the families in this book describe. Experts in the field generally agree that positive relationships between birth and adoptive families ultimately benefit all members of the adoption triad: birth parents, adoptive parents, and adoptee. However, they also agree that when children adopted from foster care have a history of trauma with their birth parents, interaction has potentially negative repercussions for the child.

Overcoming Fear

Adoptive parents can have a laundry list of fears related to biological family members, such as fear that the child will love a birth parent more than an adoptive parent, fear that biological parents will want to be more involved in the life of the child than the adoptive parents want them to be, and, in the case of children adopted from foster care, fear that a harmful part of the parents' world will reenter the child's life.

Some of the fears surrounding adoptive-family relationships with birth families can be traced back to the early and mid-1900s. Some adoptive parents, feeling inadequate about their inability to bear children, may not have told adopted children of their adoption.[1] Post–World War II, as the public stigma around adoption dissipated, the system that orchestrated adoptions maintained a high level of secrecy and usually prevented birth parents from meeting adoptive parents.

Prior to legal abortions and birth control pills, parents sent pregnant teens to deliver babies at homes for unwed mothers, surrounded by clouds of shame, with little to no choice regarding the child's placement for adoption. This secrecy led to a paralysis around discussions surrounding adoption, adoptees' fears that their birth parents did not want them and therefore would not want to meet them, and birth parents' fears that an outreach to their birth children would be an invasion of their adoptive family's privacy. Because of fear, families had, and may still have, an inability to even broach the subject of adoptees meeting birth parents.

Knowing the benefits of relationships between birth and adoptive families may help all members of the adoption triad overcome their fears. As the authors of *Adopting Older Children* wrote, "At one time, closed adoption was the only choice biological parents and adoptive parents had, but more recently adoption experts have realized that openness in adoption is healthier for the child, the biological parents, and the adoptive parents. Openness can help adoptees learn about inherited medical conditions, strengthen their sense of identity, and alleviate feelings of abandonment."[2]

In addition, many adoptees refer to "filling a void," when describing the need to meet their birth families. In an interview with Jill Krementz, adoptee "Sue" (age thirteen) said:

> *I have a friend who lives next door, and when I showed him the pictures of my birth mother, he asked me, "Are you going to move back down to Florida now?" And I laughed really hard and said, "That just goes to show that some people don't understand—when you're adopted by people, these people are your real parents. Finding your birth mother is just filling up a gap that makes you feel you belong. . . . Everyone goes through an identity crisis at one time or another and everyone needs to know where he or she came from. As soon as I searched and found the information that I was looking for, I felt more worthwhile in the world—as though I belonged better. Beforehand, a part of me had always been missing.[3]*

In addition to this feeling of filling the void that so many adopted people reference when considering contact with birth parents, interaction with birth parents dispels a child's tendency to fill the void with fantasies. According to David Brodzinsky, "As children mature, they quickly realize that they may have birth parents, birth siblings, and other birth relatives. Moreover, it is extremely common for adopted children to fantasize about meeting these individuals."[4]

Author and adoptive parent Adam Pertman relates adoptee Gail's story:

She sometimes thought about what adoption meant and used to daydream about her birth mother. Sometimes she appeared as an ogre who was mean to her daughter and didn't deserve to keep her; that made Gail glad to have been adopted, but afraid she might grow up to be like her birth mom. Occasionally, the faceless woman seemed to be afraid, as though her little girl had done something terrible to her; then Gail thought she must have deserved to be given away. Most often, she was a kind, enchanting princess who gave her child toys and understanding; this is the mother who materialized when Gail was angry or upset or felt her [adoptive] parents weren't giving her enough attention.[5]

Pertman goes on to say that these fantasies "underscore the importance of providing accurate information [about birth parents] in a positive manner, so the children don't think they did something wrong. . . . Adoptive parents have a choice: to acquire information and possibly establish relationships that give their kids a true picture of the people who created them, and deal with the consequences; or to allow unpredictable, uncontrollable phantasms to become their partners in child rearing."[6]

Author and adoptee Sherrie Eldridge described the implications of her own fantasies: "I also fantasized about my birth father. I imagined him as a knight in shining armor. This transferred to the significant males in my life. When I met my husband, I idealized him by believing he could do no wrong and that he would provide for my every need. Needless to say, [this fantasy] interfered greatly with my emotional and relational health."[7]

In addition to benefiting the child, interaction between birth parents and their children can benefit the birth parent. In her book, *Come Rain or Come Shine*, Rachel Garlinghouse shares a birth mother's perspective:

I once spoke with a birth mother who shared that she often feels as devastated as a mother whose child goes missing; the mother knows the child is "out there," but the loss remains unresolved, causing heartache, distress, and confusion throughout the mother's life.

The fact is that adoptive parents must recognize that their gain (a child) only comes from the birth parent's loss.[8]

While the benefits of relationships between adoptive and birth families are easy to understand, in the case of children adopted from foster care, it can be difficult for adoptive parents to consider the birth parents' perspective. Adoptive parents may hear only of the events leading up to their child's placement in foster care, and without empathy, they may not understand how birth parents could permit and even enact the cruelty that led to their child's removal. It's rare to have the opportunity to hear and understand a birth family's story from the perspective of a birth parent.

Ruth, a birth mother whose loss of parental rights to her four children was the price of her addiction before she achieved sobriety, offers her story to potential foster parents in preservice licensing classes, to foster children, and to birth parents struggling to parent their children. She offers this advice to adoptive parents wanting to instill positive feelings in their children about the children's birth parents:

- Always explain what's going on with age/development-appropriate language.
- If [the child is in foster care and not yet adopted and] a parental visit is scheduled, tell the child, "We have a chance to see your mom/dad tomorrow, and hopefully she/he will be feeling well enough to make it. In case he/she can't come,

ALL THE SWEETER

let's make a special drawing/art project so we can
leave it with the social worker and let your mom/
dad know we hope they feel better."

- Use a calendar for elementary school–age kids.
  Make an X on the days leading up to a visit and
  a heart shape on the day of the scheduled visit.
  Continue to remind the child that there may be a
  reason if Mom/Dad doesn't show up.
- Get involved with Al-Anon or Narconon, and
  work the entire twelve-step process, because you
  will have a better understanding of what type of
  recovery the parents are required to do and you
  will inadvertently do some healing and have an
  outlet amongst like-minded people.
- Do not voice frustration or judgment [about the
  birth parents]. You may think the child cannot
  hear you, but they can, and they also pick up on
  your vibe/nonverbals.
- Say a prayer, light a candle, and say positive
  wishes/desires for the birth parent. Basically, have
  a positive routine so the child knows it's okay to
  talk about the parent and you have kind feelings
  toward the parent.

Unhealthy Birth Parents

When a child's past is filled with significant trauma and/or
if a birth parent is not sober or suffers from an uncontrolled
mental illness, adoptive parents must be extremely careful
with their child's relationship with their birth family. The
authors of *Adopting Older Children* advise, "Adoptive parents should be cognizant of their child's emotions regarding
contact and look for cues that the relationship is helpful or
harmful. . . . In the case of a child who was abused, contact may lead to worsening of trauma symptoms or mental

health conditions such as anxiety or depression and should be carefully considered."[9]

In her book *Raising Abel*, Carolyn Nash provides an example of this recommendation, based on her own experience raising her adopted son, Abel:

> *The closer the time of the visit [with his birth parents] drew, the more agitated Abel became. One night he was wound up, almost unable to sit still. He had knocked his dinner plate on the floor and left the toilet full of feces and great wads of toilet paper. Just as I stacked the last dish in the dish drainer, there was a crash in the living room and the sound of breaking glass. Abel knocked over a favorite vase.*[10]

In addition, on many occasions, interactions with birth parents may not be possible. Laura Bolton (chapter 17) describes her hope for a future relationship with Hannah's birth parents:

> *Right now, there isn't contact with the birth parents because they aren't in any sort of recovery. My dream is that someday they're healthy and we can be in touch. I really hope that.*
>
> *I check up on them on Facebook and google their names to make sure that they're still alive. I hadn't seen Dad for three and a half years and just saw a mug shot on the Internet. At least he's alive. It breaks my heart to know that someday Hannah will see that.*

Ruth mentioned that in cases like this, where parents are not yet sober, children may still have a desire to know their birth parents:

If the child wants to meet their birth parent and you know for a fact that birth parent is not a healthy person, then, when the child is the appropriate age, offer to accompany them. If you wait until they are eighteen, they will do it on their own as an adult, behind your back, and either they'll get sucked into the world that their birth parent is in or something bad will happen and [the adoptive parent] will not be available to help ease that fall or prevent it. [When the child is] fifteen/sixteen, start having that conversation and do what is comfortable for the family.

Even in these situations, there exists potential for interaction that can benefit the adopted child. Lois Ruskai Melina and Sharon Kaplan Roszia, authors of *The Open Adoption Experience*, suggest adoptive parents "keep in mind that *painful* is not the same as *harmful*. They may want to protect their child from a difficult truth about the birth parents, but it may be important for the child to know that fact so she can understand why it was necessary for her to be placed for adoption."[11]

They list several other benefits of an adoptee's interaction with unhealthy birth parents:

- They can also see that the problem that led to their placement was their birth parents' and not theirs. This frees them to believe they deserve better treatment than they received from their birth parents and allows them to accept it from the adoptive parents, which is an important step in attachment.
- For some children, having contact with their birth parents forces them to confront extremely painful events they experienced at their birth family's hands. However, by facing the issues, they can grieve for them and eventually move on.

- Once they are removed from a dangerous situation and begin to heal from the trauma they suffered, children can also forgive their birth parents and see that they also have good qualities. They learn they can love them without approving of their actions.[12]

Roszia and Melina remind their readers, "Adoptive parents also benefit from open adoptions because their children benefit—when their children can face the reality of their past, grieve for it, and move beyond it to accept a new future, parenting is more fulfilling."[13]

Adoptee Feelings

Adoptive children can have very different feelings about their birth parents, feelings that may be unique to their age, to the situation in which they left their birth family, and to their general view of being adopted. Laura Bolton relayed this story about her four-year-old:

> I worry about parents who don't talk to their kids about their biological parents. Hannah is four years old now and asks me about them all the time.
> At three, she'd ask, "Did they not love me?"
> I would say, "They loved you" and explain to her what happened.
> The other day, I said to Hannah, "I have a surprise for you. Guess who's in the other room?" It was a puppet toy.
> She said, "Mommy Holly?" Her birth mom is part of her.

David Brodzinsky wrote, "Adolescents are highly variable in the extent to which they are interested in their adoptions. Some show intense curiosity in their origins and are helped by contact with birth family members; others exhibit little interest in adoption or their birth heritage."[14]

Jaiya John, who reunited with his birth mother in his twenties and with his father later, described his relationship with both of his families after his reunification with his birth family:

> *Wounds were closing and my spirit was rearing up rapidly—fueled by knowing my biological family. I had filled in trenches and canyons in my being as I opened myself to my root. This was new earth within me. I could stand on it and use it as a foundation for improving my relationship with my adoptive family. As with Mary, Allan, and Arnold, knowing the Jenkins[es] allowed me to strengthen my attachment to Mom and Dad, and my adoptive siblings, even Greg. My adoptive family seemed to notice from afar that my reunion with my biological family was a good thing. They could tell that it was not driving me further from them, but was instead allowing me to heal and develop in a way that caused me to drift toward them.*[15]

While adoptees will have different feelings about interaction with their birth parents as children, Beth Hall and Gail Steinberg write that adoptees of closed adoptions, like Jaiya John, who do not have any knowledge as children of their birth parents, "grow up feeling confused about where they came from, as if they didn't fit, that something was missing, and that it would be a betrayal of their adoptive parents and family, *whom they love*, to ask questions or seek information about their birth family." Adoptees who have interaction with birth parents are able to acknowledge and accept that "each adopted person has two families, and that each family is critical and central to who they are."[16]

Degrees of Interaction

The first hurdle in a potential relationship between adoptive and birth families may be an adoptive family's discussion regarding the birth family. As outlined in chapter 3, the content of the discussion will depend on the age of the child. Experts advise that no matter what the child's age, adoptive parents must refrain from making negative comments about the child's birth family. Brodzinsky says, "To feel worthy as human beings, children need to believe they came from worthwhile beginnings." He continues to say that if parents provide children with derogatory descriptions of their pasts, "there is a risk of undermining the children's self-esteem and identity. Such comments can also undermine any contact the adoptive family may have with birth relatives, which in turn can further compromise the children's psychological adjustment. In short, adoptive parents must find ways of discussing their children's histories so as to be supportive of connections with their origins."[17]

Sherrie Eldridge advises adoptive parents to continually support their children in talking about their birth families. She explains, "There is a mixture of feelings about the birth mother in your adoptee's heart. Fantasy. Anger. Victimization. Love. You can be a powerful resource in helping him identify and process these conflicting feelings—or you can be a major obstacle. What determines your role as a facilitator or a hurdle is your willingness and skill in drawing your child into productive conversation about her birth family and her complex feelings about them."[18]

Trisha and her wife, Susanna (chapter 4), embrace the idea that if parents can love multiple children, children can love multiple parents. Trisha describes how she and Susanna try to speak with their daughter, Celeste, about Celeste's birth family. "In her current stage of development, she struggles with the idea of two families. Some of the language that we've been offered is, 'All of these families belong to you. We all belong to you. Your heart is big enough to hold all of us.' We have extended family in other states; she has her birth family. We talk about how she has invisible strings from her heart to all these places."

Laura Bolton (chapter 17) describes how she helped Hannah understand her relationship to her biological sister, whom another family adopted:

> *Hannah sees her biological sister a couple times a month. At first, I referred to her by her name, Jaden. Then I realized everything about Hannah's adoption should be part of her consciousness. Because Hannah's story includes Jaden, I can't randomly tell Hannah, "You know your friend Jaden? She's actually your sister," so I now refer to Jaden as "your sister, Jaden."*
>
> *At about three years old, she asked, "My sister?" I explained it to her. Now that we've told the story enough times, she knows both of them grew in Mommy Holly's tummy. They have different adoptive moms. They'll eventually go to school together and have a relationship.*

The degree of interaction will be different for every family. Experts and those with experience offer suggestions for several situations. The authors of *Telling the Truth to Your Adopted or Foster Child* relate the story of a nine-year-old who was adopted when she was three:

> *Mindy was adopted due to neglect resulting from her birth mother's chronic depression. Mother's Day used to be a troubling day for Mindy as she struggled to honor her adoptive mother without being disloyal to her birth mother. Mindy's adoptive mother recognized her daughter's dilemma and suggested that Mindy*

write her birth mother a card on every Mother's Day telling her about her accomplishments and feelings, and including drawings and collages about her life. Mindy works very hard on the letters she makes for her birth mother every year, and they are kept in a special album for Mindy to review when she wants to feel close to her birth mother or proud of herself. The understanding and acceptance of the adoptive mother has given Mindy "permission" to love both mothers. Mindy no longer holds herself behind a wall of fear in her relationship with her adoptive mother—she is now free to love her because she understands that to do so, she does not have to stop loving her birth mother.[19]

While Mindy's letters don't appear to have been sent to her birth mom, adoptive mother and author Rachel Garlinghouse describes a friend and adoptive mother who "buys two of the same ornament each Christmas. She sends one to her daughter's birth mother and she hangs the other on their own family's Christmas tree. She chooses an ornament that reflects something significant in the child's life over the course of that year."[20]

While these suggestions do not all require in-person interaction with the birth families, Don Romesburg and his family think it important to foster relationships this way. He says:

We are headed to Sacramento to visit our daughter's birth family following our finalized adoption over a year before. Social workers and mandated visitations have stopped, leaving us to manage the relationship. The common foster-adoptive approach of just sending pictures and letters didn't feel right for us. So we kept up visits, at roller rinks and playgrounds, in our town and theirs. Each time was exhausting for all, but our daughter left feeling so much love. With every visit she became more casual and upbeat about the experience.[21]

Adoptive families can work with birth families to set interactive boundaries that are in the best interests of the child. These boundaries may limit interaction to letters; they may include visits with an intermediary; there may be a contract that describes how often contact will take place.[22] However, in the case of Don Romesburg's family, in-person visits, though sometimes uncomfortable, felt right for all.

Summary

This chapter scratched the surface of many topics related to relationships between adoptive and birth families: overcoming fears, filling emotional voids, dispelling birth-family fantasies, a birth parent's advice after finding sobriety too late to maintain custody but in time to build relationships with her children, potential relationship benefits even with unhealthy birth parents, different levels of adoptee interest in knowing birth parents, and options for interactions between adopted and birth families.

Though adoption triad relationships can be complicated, the authors of *Adopting Older Children* provide a simple summary: "Contact with biological parents can be healing or harmful depending on each child's unique situation."[23]

Author and adoptive father Adam Pertman adds, "The glorious, reassuring realization that eventually dawns on most adoptive parents is that our children love us deeply, even if they care deeply about other people as well. But the hard accompanying truth is also that the best adoptions—or any other relationships for that matter—entail accepting and dealing with their complexities."[24]

While it is much easier said than done, when parents overcome their fears, they can work toward the best-case scenario of creating an extended family that includes both birth and adoptive families to provide their child with support and love. Our best hope for children adopted from foster care is that they have positive relationships with each of their family members so that they are able to relay feelings such as Emma did to her adoptive mother, Debbie (Trevino family, chapter 2): "I am lucky because I have three moms—my birth mother, my foster mother, and you."

CHAPTER 16:

OUT OF THE ORDINARY:
THE McPHERSON FAMILY

Leah and Gavin McPherson always knew they wanted to adopt. After they had one biological child, they could not have a second. They chose to skip fertility treatments and signed up to fost-adopt. Although they chose an agency that came highly recommended, they had a difficult experience. Throughout the process, they felt as if the agency did not prioritize their son's best interest and that it was highly disorganized. Further, they believed that CPS neglected to adequately follow their son's case.

Leah tells her family's story.

Adoption Story

We took the foster care route because we wanted to go for kids that not everyone fought for. We began the process when our daughter Amelia started kindergarten. We finished our ten-week course and moved on to our home

People in the McPherson Family's Story

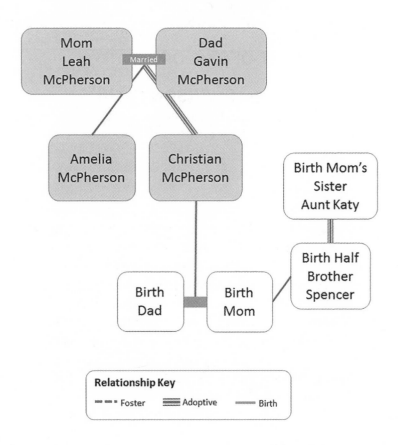

study, but the social worker didn't really know us. During the home study when asked, "What kinds of children are you comfortable with? What age ranges and what behaviors and what nationalities?" I felt like I was picking a child from a catalog.

The classes include scary descriptions: "This little boy had these issues, and he pulled a knife on his adoptive sister at four years old." So I only cared that the child had no major violent history. I had to look out for my biological daughter.

We told our agency we wanted a child under three years old, because after three, the time frame that birth families have to prove themselves stretches out. Our agency told us birth parents of children under three have six months for their reunification services and over three have anywhere from one and a half to three years. I felt we put ourselves at less risk with the younger age group, and we expected to be placed with a three-year-old because it's harder to place older kids than a baby.

While eating pizza one Friday night, our social worker called. "There is a little boy in the hospital who was just born. Birth parents will be out of the picture because he was born positive for methamphetamines."

The birth parents had had multiple children in foster care and were still doing drugs, so the court would likely terminate rights.

I said, "Yes, absolutely," though my husband had expressed apprehension about a newborn exposed to drugs. We didn't know how we could physically change our lifestyle to take care of a child with special needs.

Calls about kids contain a few bullet points: "Little boy, born early, positive for methamphetamines, seems to be eating well." Then I received a call from the NICU's social services. She told me a bit more—he was doing great, born seven weeks early, breathing on his own, no respiratory problems, eating well. She kept saying, "He's been such a good baby, we all just love him." She told me his labs, which made me feel so much more comfortable. Just five sentences more of information was huge.

They told us, "You can come at any time, but if you want to speak to the doctor, you need to be here by twelve thirty." It was ten o'clock. I didn't have a car seat. We had been thinking we would bring home a three-year-old, so we hadn't set up a crib. We had nothing.

My husband picked me up, and we went to Walmart. We were both walking through Walmart, and I looked over at him pushing the shopping cart, and thought, *What are we doing? We're going to go pick up a baby who we didn't even know was there yesterday? Really?*

In the waiting room, our social worker said, "Okay, I have some paperwork for you to sign before we can go up to the NICU."

I couldn't even stop trembling. How would I sign my name to these official documents, which, really, were very unofficial-looking? It was a piece of paper, a folded copy, not even a straight copy, of a letter from the county saying we could take the child home.

I will never forget walking into the NICU and seeing these babies with their feeding tubes and their breathing machines. I thought, *What are we getting into?*

Our social worker was sick and couldn't come in with us. How did they know I was the right person?

The nurse pointed to Christian. I looked on the wall and saw a wooden lion with his name written on it. I looked in his bassinet; he looked like a fake, porcelain baby. He was so beautiful, and he looked so perfect. He didn't have any tubes; he had nothing. It was too good to be true.

I didn't have time to mentally prepare to go pick up this baby. With my daughter, I had time. I knew she was coming. I was pregnant.

The nurse started rambling about how often I'd be

feeding him, and his diapers, and "This is the last time he had this or that."

The nurse side of me wanted to soak it in and have every detail, yet I just wanted to hold him. But I didn't know how to hold him and take him in, because this wasn't my child and I was going to take him home just like I gave birth to him. I thought it would be harder to care for somebody else's child, treat him like my own. But my thoughts quickly turned to action: change his diaper, feed him.

He had to pass the NICU's car seat challenge—sitting in the car seat for two hours—before he could go home. As we sat staring at him, the doctor told us he was very anemic, his hemoglobin was low, they were giving him iron, and the birth mom is a cystic fibrosis carrier. I tried to soak it all in.

I didn't tell my daughter where we were going and arranged for a friend to pick her up at school.

We had told her, "There are many kids who need good homes. Sometimes they need them for their whole life, and sometimes they just need them for a couple of weeks or a couple of months, until their families can get into a good place where they can take care of them again."

I tried to prep her, because you don't know what is going to happen. We put our whole family at an emotional risk. My daughter was six. She'd been asking me for a baby brother since she was two. She was three years old and sat on Santa's lap and told him she wanted a baby brother for Christmas.

At the hospital, the nurse told us the birth parents were really nice, young, had had a rough life, but were good people. "You need to be prepared he might go back to them," she said. We'd told our agency we did not want to just foster. I didn't want to put my daughter through that.

I struggled with how to prepare her that he might leave. "You are going to call this person your brother, which he will be regardless of whether he stays or not."

My friend texted me and said, "I slipped." She had told her boys, and they didn't know that we hadn't told Amelia. So they told Amelia, "Your mom and dad are picking up your baby brother at the hospital right now." She'd been waiting a year and a half for her baby brother. It was like prepping her for a baby that I would be giving birth to—I just didn't know when it would happen.

My daughter doesn't usually show emotion, even when she's happy. But when we pulled up, she came running out, tears in her eyes, jumping in the air, yelling, "My baby brother's here! My baby brother's here!"

I wondered, *What did I just do to her? If this little boy leaves in three months, did I just totally crush her?* My friend had told me, "Leah, you are teaching her to love no matter what happens. You can never go wrong."

Once we brought him home, the birth family's story began to emerge. Birth mom, age twenty-six, had other children. The first lived with its birth father. She chose not to visit. She had had custody of the second one, named Spencer, off and on, until her aunt Katy adopted him. Then she got pregnant with Christian. Our social workers told us when we were bringing Christian home that parental rights would automatically terminate because of repeat history. Normally, if a parent's rights are terminated and he or she is in the same lifestyle when the next child is born, rights are automatically terminated.

We brought Christian home on Monday, December 16. We didn't hear from CPS or our agency, but we knew we needed to start birth-family visits, so we contacted the manager at our agency, who set one up for the next Friday. She said, "When you meet the birth parents, tell them how Christian has been doing and what's been going on."

The birth parents came together. It was much harder than I thought it would be to give him to somebody for an hour that I didn't know—someone who, in my opinion, had harmed him. I showed them how to change his diaper and feed him. I trusted that the manager would sit there and watch them. She did.

We didn't have a schedule set up, but I knew that they had three one-hour court-ordered visits per week. From my perspective, that was so much. I would try to see the other side and think, *Gosh, they only get three hours.* At the same time, did they deserve any of him?

Our social worker struggled to find visit times that worked for everybody. We soon found out the pecking order for scheduling visits. The birth mother falls first, despite not having a job. Other agencies pick up the child and take the child to the visits. We had no say when those visits happened, so we had to adjust our family's schedule.

At one point, our agency social worker said to us, "You are not his parents. The county looks at you as long-term babysitters." She also didn't want us at the hearings. She told us, "Those hearings have nothing to do with you. They are regarding the birth family, and you are not his birth family." Then, on another occasion, she said, "You guys are acting like you're going down the street and you're buying the house out from your neighbor, when the house isn't even for sale."

When we finally met the county social worker, we had a really good rapport with her. She was furious at those kinds of comments. That is exactly what they are pushing for foster families *not* to feel like.

She told us to be involved, have a say, and come to all of the hearings because we were with him 100 percent of the time. I am not opposed to the birth family having social-worker support. However, it felt like we received more support from Christian's CPS social worker than our agency social worker, who seemed strictly there for the birth family.

As we tried to understand the process, we were told that birth parents of a child under three years old have six months [to prove their fitness as parents], and that in Christian's case, they definitely were not going to offer the birth mom any services but weren't sure about the birth dad.

The birth mom wouldn't show up to visits, or she would show up thirty minutes late, or she'd call and say, "I had a flat tire," and they would give her another hour for that week.

The birth dad started skipping visits in February, two months after Christian's placement with us. Sometimes the birth mom would show up, sometimes she wouldn't, and we learned that they had separated. The visits also separated, and they attempted to coordinate them so that they were back-to-back, first with Mom, then with Dad, or vice versa.

Then they got back together and wanted to do joint visits. CPS said, "No, we aren't doing this back-and-forth. Your visits are separate."

I would take Christian to his visit. Let's say she showed up, never on time, and got her visit. The birth father would sit in the car in the parking lot, and then it would be his visit. He would choose not to go in.

Other times, I would take Christian in, holding him as I walked into the room. The birth father would walk right past me to go get a drink of water, and the social worker would say, "Would you like to see your son?"

"No, I'm good," he'd say, and then he'd just walk out.

The social worker made requests about the visits: "Please make sure that you don't feed him before the visit, so that the birth family can feed him" or "Don't give him a bottle. Bring a bottle to the visit."

Over the next two months, there were visits when I would interrupt Christian's nap and the birth family wouldn't show up. One visit, I interrupted Christian's nap, the birth parents weren't there, and our social worker had me sit there without feeding him for forty-five minutes.

We pushed back, letting our social worker know, "He's hungry. We're trying to keep him on a schedule." Kids need to be on a schedule; they have to have a routine. I didn't understand. I signed up to take care of this child like he was my own, to put him on a routine to do what is right for him, so I questioned our agency, "Now you're asking me not to do that?" That was the hardest part for me—trying to do what I know I needed to do for him as his parent, yet letting them tell me to do what was best for the birth family.

Throughout this ordeal, during every conversation, our agency told me I needed to have more empathy for the birth parents: "Can you even try to understand what it's like to give birth to this child and then not get to take him home? You don't get to care for him? You get to see him three times per week?"

I have empathy for his birth mother. But I can have empathy for her and still put Christian first. I want to encourage and support the birth family but not enable them.

The birth mom's reunification services were terminated, but after months of not showing up for visits, the birth father was trying to get the birth mom back. His only way of getting her back was to get Christian back. So he decided to go to court, and they said, "Birth father will be given reunification services. We will meet with him and set up a plan. He will get so many visits per week, and we'll go from there."

We prepared for reunification with the birth father, and then he didn't show up for the meeting that was set up with CPS to lay out his six-month plan. We were still going three times per week. Finally, after a couple of months, the social workers agreed not to schedule visits until he called them back.

Somewhere in there, the birth mom tested positive for drugs again, and she agreed to go to rehab. I worried that they'd change the plan again and offer her services. Now I have to drive Christian over an hour for visits— this child who hates the car, screams bloody murder, and hyperventilates all the way there. He's there for an hour or two hours, depending on if we're making up a visit or not. Then I drive him an hour home while he screams.

If I didn't do all this, they would take Christian away because I'm "interfering" with the plan, even though the plan was not to reunify her. When we questioned it, we were told, "This is a little abnormal [compared with] what usually happens."

We had a hearing scheduled in November to terminate the birth father's services. He still wasn't showing up. He was incarcerated by then. They had to bring him from the jail for the hearing, but the lawyer failed to notify him, so they had to reschedule it. I can't tell you how many hearings we went to that were canceled because somebody didn't fill out the proper paperwork.

At the hearing, they terminated services for the birth father but didn't reduce mom's visits. Our new agency social worker was outraged. She said, "I have no idea what's going on. She should not be getting these visits."

Our agency and CPS still weren't speaking very often. The CPS social worker wasn't crazy about working with the agency and never returned their phone calls; instead, he would call us. Our agency social worker didn't like that and told us, "You should not be talking to him. You need to have him call me, and then I will talk to you." When we finally talked to him, he said he forgot to reduce the mom's visits.

My husband, Gavin, was so frustrated. He'd missed countless days of work. I'd missed work so that I could go to hearings and take care of Christian and go to visits. It put a huge strain on our family.

Still, they were treating us like we didn't matter, like nothing we said mattered, yet we were the ones who were with Christian 100 percent of the time. At this point, Christian was eleven months old. He was my child. I'd been through surgery with him to put tubes in his ears for chronic ear infections. When Christian was six months old, he started having bad asthma; we were taking him to the doctor twice a week sometimes. We were the only family he knew. He recognized us, he knew us, and he was starting to get stranger anxiety (he was on target with his development of stages).

While we felt Christian to be part of our family, Gavin also started to have empathy for the birth mom. He had had some conversations with her while waiting for the visits. He liked her. He felt like she just wasn't a good mom, but she wasn't a bad person.

They had always encouraged us to maintain a relationship with the birth family for Christian's sake, and so my husband went and talked to the birth mom at her rehab. They hadn't told us that we couldn't talk to her. He said, "It's no secret that we want to adopt Christian. You know that; everybody knows that. I just want you to know that we have never intended on cutting you out of his life." We really wanted her to know that, as it looked like her rights would terminate soon.

Then Gavin told our agency social worker, "I talked with her, and this is what I said." He had also called the CPS social worker, who had said, "Okay, that sounds fine."

Our agency went to the birth mom and told her, "We think it is very inappropriate that this foster parent came and talked to you, and we want to know what he said."

She saw an opportunity to get her son back and reported that Gavin threatened her, that he told her she would "never see [her] son again and should give up."

We had another meeting with the manager at our agency, and she presented it like, "You totally failed at foster parenting, and you might not be able to do this anymore."

That was on a Friday. Tuesday, November 25, seven o'clock at night, I was making dinner, my husband was at the gym, I had half a glass of wine on the table, Christian was playing in the drawer behind me, my daughter was sitting on the couch. I remember the garage door opening. Gavin came home, and I heard him sobbing.

I'd never seen my husband cry. I'll never forget it. He couldn't even talk. He pointed outside, and I looked through my garage door.

We're good people, right? I work at the hospital. I'm a good person, I'm doing the right thing, I have a good family, we're good people in the community, and I saw two policemen standing on my sidewalk. Then I saw the CPS social worker. He said, "You need to put Christian in the car."

Dumbfounded, I couldn't respond.

"You need to get Christian's things, and you need to put him in the car right now." Then our agency social worker got out of the car.

Gavin asked, "Can you come in? Can we talk about this?"

Our agency social worker said, "We are not getting into this right now. You need to get him and put him in the car."

I was shaking. *This is my child, and you want me to put him in your car? Where are you going? What are you going to do with him? What do you mean?*

Gavin came out of the house, holding Christian, and he was sobbing. He said to the CPS social worker, "Just please explain this to us. Let us work this out. I don't know what's going on. Can you please explain to me why you're taking him?"

I tried to put pieces together quickly in my mind. I couldn't understand why our agency social worker, our representation, was standing there, not talking to us. When she jumped in front of the CPS social worker and said, "We're not doing this right now," I realized, *She's not on our side.*

I said, "I don't know what I'm supposed to do."

Our social worker said, "Go inside. Get a bag. Get his things, get his sheet from his bed, get his bottles, get his formula, get some clothes, and get a blanket."

I stuttered, "I-I-I don't even know how to do that right now. I don't know." I physically could not do it.

I went inside, shaking, and I went into Christian's room, thinking, *Does he need one pair of clothes? Does he need two pairs? How many days is he going to be gone? I'm not going to pack all of his clothes, because he's coming back.*

I pleaded with our social worker, "Please come inside and help me. I don't know how to do this. Please come in and help me."

And she said, "We are not going in your house right now. You need to get his stuff and bring him out here right now."

I walked in, and I saw Amelia sitting on the couch, and I thought, *What do I say to her?*

I grabbed his medicines and tried to explain, "He's had a long medical history. He has to sleep with a humidifier; he has to have his nebulizer." I remember trying to take the nebulizer out of the bag to show them, and they said, "Put it in the car." They wouldn't even look in the bag. Nothing.

He was sick at the time, he was wheezy, and I was doing nebulizer treatments.

They just threw it in the trunk of the car.

I put him in the car, and I buckled him up. He was screaming.

As I put him in, Gavin said, "When can we see him? Tomorrow can we come by the office and talk about this?"

The CPS social worker said, "No, we're closed tomorrow. We're closed for Thanksgiving. Call the supervisor next week and maybe set up a meeting."

They're taking him away. This is going to be his last memory of me? Pinning him down in this car seat, trying to strap his seat belt on?

I remember the car. I remember the color. I watched them drive away.

One police officer said, "I don't know what's going on here, but something doesn't feel right. I think you guys need to get an attorney."

Gavin called an attorney the next morning. The attorney immediately filed a request to get us in the court to talk to the judge. We met with another attorney, who had specifically dealt with foster care cases. He said, "I've done this kind of work for a really long time. I have never seen something like this."

Another lawyer said, "Why did you let them take him?"

"What do you mean?"

"Did they have a court order?"

I said, "I don't know."

She said, "I guarantee they didn't have a court order, or they would have shown it to you."

Had I known, I would have said, "Call me with a court order" and shut the door.

We researched all of the reasons why they could take a child out of a foster family home. Nothing fit. He was not in harm's way. The night they took him, even the CPS social worker said, "Gavin, I have no doubt in my mind you guys have been taking excellent care of him. Nobody questions that at all."

We learned a child can't be removed from a home if the home has a valid license. After they removed Christian, we received a letter from our agency saying, "Your foster care license through us has been revoked. If you'd like to contest it, call this number."

As soon as we could get ahold of somebody at CPS, they transferred us to the CPS program manager, now three days after Christian's removal.

Gavin introduced himself as Christian's foster parent and said he wanted to know what happened. She responded rudely, "Christian is no longer your foster child, so none of this concerns you."

"I don't understand," Gavin said.

"Did you or did you not threaten his birth mother?"

"What are you talking about? No."

She asked, "Sir, did you go and speak with her?"

"Yes, I did. I went and spoke with her because I wanted her to know that we intend for her to know Christian and to be a part of his life."

She cut him off. "This is the deal. Christian has been removed from your home. He is not your foster child. You will never see him again. He is never coming back to your home, so please don't call me again." She said, "Are you recording me, sir?"

"No. You're on speakerphone."

"You know this is a violation if you're recording me!"

The attorney couldn't get us in Thanksgiving week; the judge was out of town. We finally got into court two weeks later. Over the next few days, I had letters to the judge dropped off at my door, speaking to our character, our relationship with Christian, and our intentions. Letters came from friends, family, colleagues, and leaders in the community. Within five days, we had over 120 letters.

Christian's eight-year-old half brother, Spencer, was in and out of foster care his whole life, until the birth mom's Aunt Katy adopted him. We developed an excellent relationship with Aunt Katy. We called her when they removed Christian. She didn't know his location. She said, "I don't know what my niece is thinking." We learned that two days after Christian was removed, the birth mom got kicked out of her rehab for using.

Aunt Katy continued, "She is such a liar. She ruins people's lives. This is what she does. She's done it to me."

Aunt Katy called our agency and CPS. She wrote us an amazing letter speaking to our character and how much she enjoyed getting to know us and how she prayed every day that Christian would stay with us his whole life.

We decided to stay with the attorney in our county because he knew the county system well. He knew the other attorneys involved in the case; he knew the judges. We gave him all of the letters. I don't know how many thousands of dollars we spent on attorney fees, but he didn't even charge us a tenth of what he normally would have.

At the first hearing that we had, about two weeks in, we found out that Christian's attorney was beyond angry with his client, CPS, because he wasn't notified that they removed Christian from our home with a court order.

The CPS attorney requested a continuance because he had received a stack of paperwork and hadn't had time to review it. That was all of our letters. Our attorney had made copies of every single one of them, given copies to all of the parties involved.

The judge said, "I have never seen something like this" and granted the continuance.

Three weeks in, our attorney arranged for us to meet with Christian's attorney. We told the attorney the whole story from our point of view. He asked us a few questions that he knew the significance of but I didn't understand. "Has your agency reached out to you? Have you talked to them since?"

"No." The week after Thanksgiving, five days after Christian was removed, I tried calling because he needed this other medication. They didn't call me back. I tried contacting the CPS social worker, but he would never call me back. Finally, our agency social worker called me back and said, "What do you think he needs? You can just drop it off at the office next week." That was it.

The final hearing was scheduled on a Friday at one o'clock. We arrived an hour early, just in case. Our attorney said, "They delayed the case until about five o'clock because the director of CPS wants to be there. I don't understand why."

We waited. People went in and out of the courthouse. I saw a man walk in that I'd never seen before. He gave us a nod and kept walking. Nobody from CPS had looked our way in those four weeks—people we'd known for an entire year dealing with Christian. People who *knew* us, had been in our home, had interviewed my daughter. No "hi." Nothing.

But this man looked and nodded at me. What did that mean? I kept praying, using a prayer card. The one for that day said something about completely submitting, it's out of my hands, let it all go. *Whatever happens, it's for Christian's best. I can't do anything about it.*

As five o'clock approached, the CPS attorney walked out of the courthouse and asked to speak with us. We went into a room, and he got tears in his eyes and said, "I want you to know that in my entire career of being a CPS attorney, I have never seen something like this happen. I don't understand it fully, but I want you to know that I can't put it into words." He said to us, "We want Christian returned to you. We think you are his family and he belongs to you."

We went into the courtroom for the hearing. In the courtroom, the judge asked the purpose of this hearing and what was happening with Christian. The CPS attorney began by saying, "After thorough review, my client feels it is in the best interest of this child to be placed back into his original foster home. It seems as though there have been many miscommunications between agencies, and we would request the court to return Christian to the home of the McPhersons. This is the only family he has known, and they have proven to care for all of his needs." Then Christian's attorney chimed in and agreed, as did ours.

The judge said, "Well, good, glad we all agree, because that's what I was going to order anyway."

My mind started spinning in disbelief, like I was in a foggy dream, as I had lain in my bed countless hours, having this dream. It took me a bit to realize this was reality. I remember stuttering something about "When? What happens next?" I was shaking. The judge told us they would like to approve us for a non-related extended family member placement. He said they wanted to send someone to assess our home (at this point, it was around six thirty at night). I was shocked that they would send someone that night, on a Friday night, to assess the home and sign off.

As I walked outside the courthouse, a man standing outside in the rain with a hat on caught my attention. "Leah?"

"Yes."

He stuck out his hand and introduced himself as the director of CPS. "You don't know me. I feel like I know you because I've read a lot about you and your family."

I was putting it together: *This is the director who needed to attend the hearing, why it got delayed. He was the one who nodded to me as he walked into the courthouse.*

He said, "You're Christian's family. The right thing is for him to be in your home. I'm going to make sure that happens."

We learned that CPS had requested a meeting with our agency after Gavin had sat with the birth mom. Our agency said we lacked empathy toward Christian's birth mom. They reported that they had revoked our foster care license, though they hadn't at the time of the meeting. CPS had to remove Christian immediately from the home because they believed that we had no foster license. The director did not attend that meeting. The program manager, the woman from the brusque phone conversation we had after Christian's removal, represented CPS at the meeting. I later found out CPS fired the program manager.

CPS came to our house at eight o'clock that night and made sure it passed all of the CPS requirements.

I didn't know if Christian was coming home that day, in two weeks, or the next day. The weekend went by, and no call. Monday morning, they called and said, "Your home checked out. You need to go down to get fingerprinted. We also need to come to your house."

The CPS supervisor and adoption social worker met with us on Monday, wanting to write down the story from our point of view.

We told them everything—about the bottles, the pacifier, everything—and a few times they said, "Did your agency ever tell you [such-and-such]?"

When we answered, "No," they would give each other eyes and then write something down.

CPS took full responsibility and apologized profusely, but they still wouldn't tell us exactly what happened.

As they packed up their books, I asked, "What happens next?"

"Pending your fingerprint approval, Christian will come home to you today."

I cried.

They called later that day. "Something is wrong with your fingerprints."

The company we used put down the wrong account number or something silly. They corrected it.

We waited.

I didn't want to tell Amelia anything about the court hearing or anything she didn't need to know.

We went to get our nails painted.

Gavin called me partway through with news from CPS. I told Amelia, "We're going to go pick up Christian and bring him home."

We arrived early, in time to see our agency social worker pull up with Christian in the backseat.

My heart melted. He looked like he had just woken up from a nap, different. We all got out of our car and walked toward her. She took off and walked toward the building.

We let her walk in. She sat in the waiting room, and we sat across from her, about three feet away. I whispered, "Hi, Christian."

She was holding him away from us, kissing his head, saying to him, "Oh, baby," pretending she didn't see us.

The CPS social worker came out. The agency social worker tried to give Christian to him. He said, "You can give him to Gavin."

She handed him to Gavin and said, "He's been doing really great, you know."

Gavin put him in the car, and I was going to get in and sit next to him, and he freaked out crying. It broke my heart. Then Gavin banged his elbow on the car and Christian started laughing. So Gavin sat by him and I drove home, Christian laughing at Gavin and Amelia making funny faces at him.

When we took him out of the car, he looked at me, a little more assured, and smiled. *He's been with me his entire life. He knows me.* I have a picture of him giving me the biggest hug, just snuggling—that kind of deep, *I know you* snuggle.

He laughed when he saw our dog. He crawled over and lay on top of him and closed his eyes. He was looking at his toys, and he would crawl over and grab one and look at it for a while; then he would crawl over and grab another one. We took him in his room and put him in his crib, and he started jumping and laughing and jumping and pointing at things. *He knows it—he's home.*

The first couple of nights, he screamed to the point where he was hyperventilating and we had to turn on all the lights. We would walk him up and down and show him the pictures on the walls.

He came home December 23. Our families came over for Christmas. He had just woken up from a nap. I instructed, "Don't grab him. Don't get in his face. Let him warm back up to you."

We brought him out to the living room and put him on the floor. He looked at everybody, but then he would just look down. He fixed his eyes on my dad. He crawled into my dad's lap and buried his face and stayed on his shoulder for at least twenty-five minutes. He didn't move, just looked around a little. My dad said Christian had the tightest grip on him ever.

We got no report about what had happened to Christian over the last four weeks. Did he have new foods? Did he go to the doctor? Did he get his immunizations? His booster flu shot? He's at high risk—he has asthma. It was a bad flu season; he needed his flu shot if he hadn't gotten it.

His CPS social worker kept saying, "We'll have to look into it."

It bothered me that there was no documentation, no handoff, no report. I told the director, "I'm a nurse. When I go to work, I take care of very sick adult ICU patients. I get thirty minutes' worth of report. I get to know the last time they washed their hands, brushed their teeth, the medicines they got, the last time they used the bathroom, their whole life history." Here I had a one-year-old child who had been gone from my care for four weeks, and I got nothing.

The two things the agency social worker said were, "The family that he was with discovered that he had acid reflux, and he is now being appropriately treated, and they also discovered that he is allergic to milk, so he is drinking almond milk."

We had already determined that several months ago. I didn't say anything, but it was in his medical records, it was in their files, had they looked. Had the agency appropriately reported to this family, this family wouldn't have struggled.

How much trauma did that put him through unnecessarily?

He's only one child, but this happens all the time.

After a year and a half, they stopped visits and the birth mom's rights were terminated. His birth mom requested another hearing contesting his return to us. We went to court. I had to testify. It felt good to be able to truthfully, openly, and honestly, knowing that he is safe at my house, say how I felt and say what happened.

It is important for us to know the birth mom's whereabouts and know somebody who knows her. I still believe it is in Christian's best interest to know where she is if he wants to meet her. Gavin and I both agreed that will never change for us. It's about him. Her rights were terminated. After the birth mom's rights were terminated, she had sixty days to file an appeal. She filed it on day fifty-nine. She didn't have an attorney. She was using again and eventually missed a deadline, and they dropped her appeal.

We continued visits with his brother and his aunt. Spencer is such a good kid. We have his pictures up in Christian's room. Aunt Katy is older and asked us to take Spencer if anything happens to her.

Our county doesn't file their own adoptions. So we found another fost-adopt agency. We had a new home study, another interview. They were easy to work with.

We finalized Christian's adoption on November 16.

Our county does adoptions one day a month. We could have chosen to go elsewhere, but we wanted to have closure in our county. This was a huge day for us. We'd been through so much.

So many people were there for us. I hate for that four weeks to be the defining moment in our first two years with him, but I go back and forth. It really showed me how many people there are in our lives and what a strong support system we have. The judge emphasized this: "What is amazing to me is that Christian doesn't just have an amazing foster family, he has an entire community supporting him, and that is what this is all about."

I would do it again in a heartbeat. Christian has, from day one, molded into our lives as if that was the plan all along. It's never felt awkward, or like we're a family of three with a fourth wheel. Not once. We have so many family memories that I could never imagine without him here. We have taught him and treated him exactly as we did Amelia. We love to go camping, boating, snow skiing, play baseball, go on bike rides. We have wanted both of our kids to have as many experiences in life as possible, expose them to anything, so that they have the knowledge to choose what is important to them. My dream for my kids is for them to have open hearts and minds. For them to always keep in mind that we don't know people's stories and we don't judge or criticize. It's so very important to me that they believe in themselves and truly believe they are capable of anything. Life is hard. Things don't always make sense. I wish for them to understand how special and unique each individual person is. We should support and respect every individual for the qualities they bring to this world.

I hope for Amelia that she stands up for Christian, understanding that he may have emotional challenges in his future when it comes to the word *family*. I hope that she never lets him forget what we taught her about that word.

My hope for Christian is that he always feels safe and comfortable to express himself and any questions he may have about his families. I hope he never questions our love or intentions when we first brought him home. I hope he never resents the actions of adults who made the decision that he should not live with the family which gave birth to him. I hope he never resents his birth family yet can look for the good. I hope he can use his past experiences as a positive in this confusing world. I hope he never, ever questions his place in this family of his. I am so in awe of him already. His heart, his mind. Each day, I think I couldn't possibly love him any more.

Advice

My advice to families considering foster adoption? *Do it!* Do it wholeheartedly, and don't look back. Do it with the intention of doing what is best for the child(ren) involved, even if it means putting yourself last and risking your heart being hurt. If you have kids you're worried about, you can never go wrong teaching your kids to love. You can never go wrong loving/caring for a child when they need it the most. Even if they leave and your heart hurts, you will have given that child your best when they needed it the most—and quite possibly have helped them live the best life they can. Do it.

CHAPTER 17:

ALL THE SWEETER:

THE BOLTON FAMILY

....

Laura and Philip live in a medium-size college town on the West Coast with their six daughters. They had four biological daughters when they adopted their youngest, Hannah. Over the years, they've fostered numerous children and have thereby developed an identity as a foster family. Laura says that she feels the most love for Hannah "right before she falls asleep. I like to hold her, rock her, rub her back, and tell her how much I love her, that she's my 'angel baby,' and that I am the luckiest mommy in the world because I got to adopt her. . . . This bedtime routine is good for both of us. It brings us back together at the end of the day, reminding us that no matter what the day held, we are still a forever family and we will always love each other."

Laura shared Hannah's adoption story.

Adoption Story

We started fostering when our biological daughters were five, seven, nine, and eleven. We always knew that we

People in the Bolton Family's Story

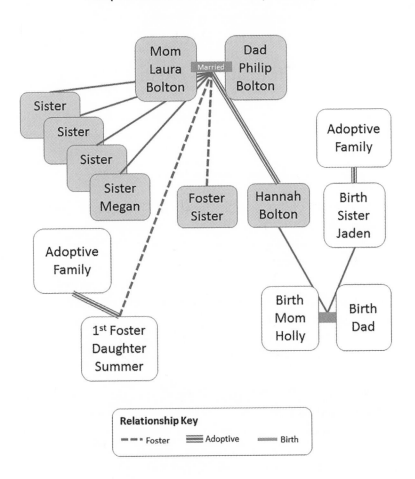

wanted to adopt. We also felt lucky that we could have biological children. So we did those first. It sounds awful. I'm so thankful. I get pregnant really easily. We also have good insurance, so, ten bucks for a copay, and I could be pregnant in two weeks.

We started to look into adoption stuff, and it looked overwhelming. On the last kid, we felt, *It's easier; let's just get pregnant.* After I had her, I decided no more pregnancies, but I knew I wanted more children. My husband had moments of uncertainty but then would say, "I trust you."

We were waiting for the right time. Our youngest was going off to kindergarten, and I'm a stay-at-home mom who didn't want to retire. We got licensed to be foster parents. After fostering one girl, we thought maybe we should just be foster parents. We were really good at fostering and maybe not so good at the adoption part. Then Hannah came and we just fell so in love. She needed to be adopted by us, no-brainer.

We were ready to take a placement but didn't specify what age or sex; we were just going to take the next child who was younger than four—though we weren't planning on a newborn.

I was at the school, running a party, and didn't have my phone on me. When you're ready to take a placement, you always have your phone with you. When you receive a placement phone call, you need to call back immediately. Philip called me on the school phone. I worried, *What happened? Why is he calling me on the school phone?* Despite being adamant about never taking a newborn, he asked, "Did you just get the call? It's a newborn. You gotta call in!"

The social worker told me they had a newborn little girl with very young parents. She said, "The judge will give them many chances. She may be in foster care with you for a year to eighteen months and still go home. She will likely have a lot of visits. Are you okay with all that?"

I didn't think about it too much and just said, "Yeah, I'm okay with that."

Usually with newborns you have a little bit of time between notification and pickup. We had twenty-four hours. We didn't have any baby things. We never thought we would take a newborn. I sent an email out to everyone I knew with two-year-olds: "We're getting a baby tomorrow. Does anyone have anything?"

Within twenty-four hours, the baby's room was full to bursting. My daughter and I bought a stroller.

Hannah's birth parents were very upset and sad and angry that their baby was being taken from them. Her dad was especially volatile. The hospital staff didn't want the parents to see us. Of course, they didn't tell us that—they just kept demanding, "Come now."

Then backpedaling: "No, don't come now."

Reconsidering: "Come three hours from now."

Finally: "Come at six a.m."

We met the social worker outside and signed the county paperwork. Inside, a nurse whisked us out of the hallway, into a room. A scrawny security guard, swimming in his adult uniform, stood outside.

Part of my brain thought I might be meeting my daughter. The other part reminded me, *Her mother is in this building. Her mother and her father. I'm not her mother, Philip's not her father. We can't let ourselves think,* This is our baby! *It's not our baby. This is their baby that we are going to be watching until she can go home.*

I wish I'd taken a picture of that meeting. I didn't. Me, Philip, the nurse, the assistant, the security guard—we all seemed jittery in that small room. We didn't get a picture. My previous experiences with birth parents had been so positive, it was hard for me to understand.

Happy and excited, we met our daughter for the first time that day. The nurses treated us like baby-nappers. A nurse told me she connected with the birth mom while supporting her though labor and delivery. Feeling sympathy for Mom, the nurse had a hard time understanding the foster-parent perspective.

I knew the hospital, knew the hallways, knew the delivery rooms—I'd delivered four babies at that hospital—and I still shook through the whole experience. Imagine if that was your first baby—being ushered in and told to leave with a child two seconds later!

We took the baby, and we left.

First thing the next day, we received a call from the manager in the hospital, asking us to come back to sign papers.

They were so nervous and so tense the day before, they just handed us the baby and we left. We signed paperwork with the social worker outside. But the hospital didn't take our IDs or ask us to sign discharge papers. From the hospital's perspective, they had lost the baby. They didn't even know our names. When the nurse cut Hannah's ID bracelet, she said, "Usually I check this against Mom's bracelet, but oh well." She cut it off and said, "Here you go. Bye."

For the most part, they were super nice to us that next day. They kept giving us gift cards to Safeway and thanking us. Though, while I waited for a photocopy, a nurse asked if we would adopt Hannah.

I said, "I don't know. We will be her family for as long as she needs one."

She said, "Well, don't get attached to her."

I said, "Well, I will. That's the whole point of this."

She said, "Well, don't let your kids get attached to her."

I said, "They'll get attached to her, too. That's why we do this, so that kids have attachment."

I was so angry! Why *wouldn't* we get attached to her? The thing that makes me the angriest as a foster parent is when people say, "I would do that, but I would grow attached."

I always think, *Do you think* we *don't get attached to these kids? Do you think we are that hard-hearted that we could have a newborn live with us for a year and not get attached?*

Since then, I've learned a lot about prenatal attachment. Hannah was born drug-free, full term, nine pounds. Perfect. Healthy. But when we got home, I had her an hour, and knew this was very different than my birth kids. She didn't relax against me. She was totally tense, tight tight tight, like a little peanut. Clearly, I was not Hannah's mom. She didn't know me. She didn't know us. We were strangers.

Hannah had a visit with her parents right away. I told the social worker that whenever the birth parents were ready, I would like to meet them. They were understandably still angry, upset, and not interested. I can't imagine having your baby taken from you, then two days later having to meet foster parents and say thank you.

When the social worker brought Hannah back after the visit, I didn't recognize her face. It was so totally relaxed. When she was with me, she always had a furrow between her eyes, a worried look.

Two days later, we had another visit and the social worker said, "Mom and Dad are ready to meet you now." I walked in, and Hannah was lying on her mom's belly, spread-eagle, arms out, legs out, totally relaxed, melted into her mom, sound asleep. Dad was cuddled in with them and had his arm around both of them. What a wake-up call. *I am not her mom. She knows that's her mother. She's trying to nurse on her mother; she's never tried to nurse on me.* Hannah knew this woman, and she didn't know me.

We learned over the next few years that Hannah had a strong attachment to her mom even at birth. Being separated from her mother traumatized her. She never relaxed against me; she was always pushing me away. She never pushed her mom away.

Perhaps because of her mental illness, Hannah's mom created a relationship with Hannah while she was still in her belly, as if Hannah had been born. "Oh, Hannah likes it when you sing to her. I sing to her all the time," Mom would tell me. "We love to take baths. We love to sing in the bathtub together. We like to play with the cats together. The cat will jump on my belly, and then Hannah will hit the cat's paw, and then the cat will hit my belly. These are some of her favorite songs."

At first, I thought, *She is so crazy.* Then, *No, something in this really worked. This baby is so bonded to her.*

The first three months Hannah was with us, she had visits three times a week. We thought she would go home. Her birth parents made it easy to be really supportive, though there were times when I wasn't. I remember thinking, *I'm finally going to get her sleeping through the night, and then she's going to go home.* Then I would think, *Her parents probably couldn't handle being up with her in the night. Maybe my purpose is to foster this family, do the night feedings until she is old enough to sleep through the night, and then she'll go home.*

We knew Hannah would go home. Her parents presented well to the judge when they came to court. We hoped I'd built a strong enough relationship with her parents that I would be able to see her regularly. Philip and I would always keep a bed open at our house for Hannah if she needed to come back.

I worried about her. I saw her parents at unsupervised visits. We'd meet at the library, and they'd take her for three to four hours; then we'd meet back at the library. I knew they weren't caring for her the way I would, but they're her parents and I had to accept that. You can't keep a child based on what you think is going to happen.

As we approached month four, I said to them, "Next time we have a visit, I'm going to start bringing her things so that you can start getting her room ready at home."

About that time, Mom found out she was pregnant. Something happened. They knew they couldn't take care of Hannah. They had a huge fight, broke up, everything fell apart. Without Dad, Mom couldn't hold it together with visits. The county asked if we could keep Hannah for another six months.

I allowed myself to start thinking, *Maybe she'll stay.* My heart opened up. I remember thinking, *Oh, crap, I'm in trouble.* I cry thinking about how vulnerable I felt. I already loved her so much, and to think they could take her away anytime. My heart felt like a tetherball on the end of a string, suspended in air for anyone to whack. Visits stopped, and I didn't have a reminder that Hannah had this mom. *I* started becoming her mom.

I'm big on trying to spin it: *If Summer, our first foster daughter, had stayed, we would never have had Hannah. If Hannah is meant to go, someone else is meant to come.* We had to hold on to that.

As more and more time went by, we had a plan that if Hannah left, we would drop everything and go to Hawaii.

We didn't hold back.

I fell in love with Hannah and got really scared because Philip wasn't in love with her. He cared about her, but he would come in the front door and say hi to the other kids and say, "How's the baby?" With our biological kids, he'd come in the front door, and the first thing he would say was, "Where's the baby?"

I kept wondering, *What if I fall in love with this kid and Philip doesn't?* But then, right around six months, he started coming in the front door and asking, "Where's Hannah? Where's Hannah?"

I got to watch the two of them. They'd just stare at each other. He couldn't get enough of her, and she would watch for him.

She loved music, and this was when she and Philip really bonded. He would play music, and she would just look at him, and if he was on the floor, she would roll over and put her hand on the guitar.

We were all in love. Despite the potential heartbreak, Philip and I just kept saying, "It's worth it." *I'm not going to hold back. If I hold back and we don't adopt her until she's three years old, then I've missed out. She deserves all of my love, and if she goes home, then she deserves to know that feeling of complete attachment, that she is completely loved.*

Then—I didn't expect it—I grew to care about the parents, too. Hannah had visits with her biological grandmother once a month. Once a month, I would hear how her parents were doing. I would finish the visit and call Philip.

"How's it going?"

"Great, they're doing terrible," I responded, bursting into tears. To adopt through foster care means for you to get the baby, someone else loses it, not necessarily by their choice. For us to get what we wanted, their lives had to tank. It wasn't congruent with how I try to live my life—I wasn't hoping for their failure, their homelessness, their return to drugs. On the other hand, if her parents were doing well, I'd get worried she might go home.

Hannah's usually homeless mom told me during a visit, "Oh, we're doing so great. We have a home. We live with six other people and eight pit bulls."

I just imagined Hannah in this house with all of these strangers and pit bulls everywhere and drugs. I had to have faith in the system, trust the social worker, and know that if Hannah was taken from us, it would open our lives to another child.

The court date was the next week. The longer we went without seeing Hannah's parents, the more my mind wandered to images of adopting her. I ran into her parents at the grocery store. Hannah wasn't with me. They asked, "Do you want to adopt her?"

I waffled. "Of course. Well, we'll take care of her as long as she needs a home. You're her parents. It's up to you." I encouraged them to speak with the social worker, and just before saying goodbye, I offered, "See you at court next week."

"It's next week?"

After making sure they had their lawyer's number, I kicked myself. If they didn't show, it would reflect poorly on them. I debated whether or not I should have sabotaged them, told them nothing.

They both arrived at the courthouse dry and clean, despite the pouring rain and their homelessness. The three of us sat in the hallway of the old courthouse, and they told me they wanted me to adopt her. They'd lived their own lives bouncing in and out of foster care homes. "We don't want her to have the life that we've had, to see the things that we've seen. We want her out of the system. We want to stop fighting."

That day, they would have lost her anyway. For them to feel that it was their choice . . . I just never imagined being the recipient of someone saying that they wanted me to have their child. It was one of the greatest gifts of my life. They went into court and told the judge. The judge told them to be proud of themselves.

I watched the two of them hold hands—they're children, teenagers, sitting there holding hands, crying because they'd just lost their child.

I stepped into the pouring rain and phoned Philip. "Oh my God. She's ours. We get to adopt her."

The actual adoption process took forever, eighteen months. A comedy of errors. We'd get one adoption worker, and then they would quit and we'd sit on someone else's desk. Eventually, we got an adoption worker and she went on a medical leave for four months and they reassigned all her cases but ours.

They decided that we could wait on desks for months and months and months.

The state contracts with a private agency for the home

studies. The agency was great. A representative came to our house three times to interview us. Separately and together, they interviewed the kids.

The home-study interview included questions about Philip's childhood. I had stuff, and I wrote how I dealt with it—I went to counseling, I talked to my husband, I have support systems, and then it was a nonissue. However, the interview was appropriately invasive. It should be—you're taking someone's child.

I hated our state adoption worker. She held her power over us. She could take our child, and she made sure that we knew that. She was so disrespectful to Hannah; she made rude and disrespectful comments about Hannah's birth parents in front of Hannah. I couldn't complain or report her, because she had this power.

Then you get the court date to finalize adoption, and this is so much fun. Our court date fell on St. Patrick's Day. We invited our parents, the little girl we fostered first, and my best friend.

We're very lucky with Hannah. Her mom is mentally ill, so we will have to watch for mental health issues. Before we adopted Hannah, someone warned me, "She has addiction and mental health issues in her genes."

I responded, "My birth children have more!"

Luckily, Hannah was not exposed to drugs prenatally. Mom's not an addict. Yes, she takes drugs and alcohol, but what she really needs are mental health services. And she keeps having babies.

People have said, "Just sterilize her." But that's not the answer. Are you going to sterilize all mentally ill people in this country? The answer is, eight to ten years ago, why wasn't anyone taking care of this child? You can't blame the twenty-year-old who no one took care of when she was two.

Once we knew we were on the road to adoption, my goal was to give Hannah five years before fostering other kids.

Hannah has a biological sibling who we declined to foster for this reason. Many foster parents will keep taking kids.

It's hard when you keep receiving call after call to take baby after baby. It's really common to have a baby and a one-year-old and a two-year-old and a four-year-old. I kept saying no because I wanted to have some quality of life. I have other kids. I didn't want six babies all at once, and I really wanted to focus on Hannah.

In our four and a half years together, we've made a lot of progress. Hannah's come a long way, and she's going to be fine in life.

Overcoming Challenges

Her parents exposed her to trauma in the womb: domestic violence, homelessness, huge amounts of stress hormones. At birth, separating from her birth mom added even more stress, flooding her brain with cortisol. She would go from normal crying to hysterical at the flip of a switch, and it would take a very long time to calm her down. If I tried baby massage, it was torture—she would scream and kick.

At the baby store, the woman said, "Get an Ergo; every baby loves the Ergo." I thought I would wear her. She haaaaated it. She never wanted to be held. She never wanted to be fed. As soon as she could feed herself her bottle, she didn't want me to feed it to her. The first time she ate food, even then, she grabbed the spoon from me and fed herself.

That was Hannah. She walked early. She crawled early. She advanced much faster than any of my other kids. It seemed her brain was wired [to say,] *I better get self-sufficient, fast.* I've gone to enough classes on brain development to know very early on, her brain received the message *The world is scary, the world is bad, the world is stressful, and I gotta take care of myself.*

She would not rest her head on me, not even in her sleep. She'd arch away. She was a prickly kid. She was very advanced in some areas. And yet the two milestones she didn't hit were smiling and laughing.

We had to teach her how to laugh by tickling her. She made this choking, painful sound, and the doctor was like, "I don't . . . um . . . hmm." Hannah couldn't laugh! She was just a prickly personality, not a people pleaser.

She talked very early, very clearly. People would say, "Hi, little girl."

She'd respond, "Get away" or, "Mommy, I don't like her." Perfectly clear. We couldn't hide anything she said. You either loved Hannah or hated her. It was about even. Some found it endearing. My friend Wendy loves Hannah so much, "because she is real."

If you said, "Give me a hug" when she was little, she'd say no. Now, she'll say, "No, thank you." If you got a hug from Hannah, it was real. She wasn't going to smile because you told her to smile or be cute because she was trying to please you. She does her own thing. So we surround her with people who like her. At the gym, I knew what time the day care lady liked her, and I would always go at that time. I wanted her surrounded by people who cared about her because there were just as many people who would think, *What an obnoxious baby.*

Hannah's biological sister had the same biological parents and prenatal experience as Hannah. Hannah's mom was still homeless and getting beaten up while pregnant. That baby came out relaxed, giggly, happy, and smiley. Someone in our town adopted her, and I was holding this baby at a picnic while talking to her adopted mom.

Hannah walked by, and the mom said, "Hi, Hannah." Hannah scrunched her face, sneered, "Ugh!" and kept walking. I looked down at her sister in my arms, batting her eyes and smiling, and I was like, "What the heck?"

Luckily, Hannah's personality fits our family.

Many people wanting to adopt through foster care miss that yes, she had a lot of issues, she didn't want to be held, she didn't want to be touched, she pushed me away, all that stuff. Then, one year old exactly, she hugged me for the first time. I don't remember the first time my [biological] kids hugged me. For them, it's a nonevent. With Hannah, I yelled to Philip, "Get the camera!" She rested her cheek on my shoulder and lay there. I remember the first time that she laughed when we didn't tickle her.

With Hannah, there have been issues, but that just makes it all the sweeter.

I always tell Philip it's not that I love her more than my other kids, but I had to work so hard for that love that I don't take anything she does for granted.

Many people think of adoption as the ending point, that all of the problems go away once the child is yours. I'd gone to many classes and knew that wasn't the case. I could either choose to ignore the issues or address them head-on.

We consciously made an effort by going to water classes to work on physical contact and trust. She loves water. It was a lot of skin-on-skin, eye contact, and trust stuff—she would sit on the wall, and I'd have to say, "Waaaait. Okay!" I'd make eye contact, she'd get into my arms, and I'd say, "Okay, I've got you." Hannah learned to trust me.

At about two years old, she had finally accepted us, but we had to redo all of those things we missed. When kids are in foster care, you don't sleep with them—they aren't your kids. So she never learned how to snuggle. She never learned you can crawl into bed with Mom and Dad in the middle of the night and snuggle with them. It took months for her to learn how to relax lying next to us.

It's been a long time coming, but five or six months ago, she surrendered. She says, "I love you, I love you" all the time. Her temperament will always be fiery, but the attachment stuff we've overcome.

We were somewhere, and I think this person meant it as an insult, but it was a total compliment to me. They asked, "Does she always do that? Run off and play for a second, then run back and check with you, run off and play, and come back and check on you?"

"Yes, she does!" She didn't use to. Now she checks back with me, and when I leave her somewhere, she cries.

Adopted Family Relationships

My biological daughters think Hannah is the best kid in the world. My biggest fear for Hannah is that she will have a God complex, thinking the world revolves around her. She can't do anything wrong in our eyes. I have six girls now. They're all independent and powerful. Hannah fits right in.

Our older girls were totally on board with adoption. We were very honest with them about what was going on with Hannah's parents. Until Hannah's parents told me they wanted us to adopt her, we always said, "She might go home."

I made sure they met Hannah's parents and grandparents. Kids understand fostering if you explain it to them. They understand there's another family when they meet the birth parents.

When they met Hannah's birth grandmother, they were all polite and shook her hand and told her it was nice to meet her. She started crying and said, "No one's ever treated me with respect like that." She had a rough life. It's all generational, a cycle that repeats itself.

When we started fostering, that really united us; it gave our family an identity. My kids take pride in being foster sisters. As a fourth grader, Megan came home from school one day and told me, "We were supposed to give an oral report on how we help our community. I gave a speech about being a foster sister."

Afterward, kids came up to her, patted her on her back, and said, "You made me cry."

This nine-year-old knows that she helps the community by being a foster sister–well enough to be able to articulate it to her class.

Biological Family Relationships

Just because you're in foster care doesn't mean you don't know your parents. Hannah's birth father was in foster care, living with his grandmother, who I think was also an addict. This family had babies fifteen years apart. I was really nervous about meeting Hannah's grandma, the birth father's mom. In my mind, she would be this sweet granny, like my grandma, who would take Hannah and fall instantly in love with her.

I walked up to a woman exactly my age, tattoos and piercings all over. Her husband, who looked younger than me, stood next to her. I said, "Nice to meet you. What would you like Hannah to call you?"

"Uh, Grandpa?"

"Okay, Grandpa!" He was thirty-three years old! "Hey, Grandpa!"

Hannah saw her birth mom when she was three months old and not again until she was a year old, at our last visit after the court date. The social worker told the parents, "Hannah is not going to know you. Don't expect her to run in. Don't scare her. Come in quietly and sit down, and Laura and Hannah will be playing. You can start to play with her."

Hannah looked up when they came in, and kept playing. She got up and stood next to me and looked at them. Then she walked over, sat in her birth mom's lap, and leaned into her. At the time, she wouldn't sit on my lap like that.

I told her mom, "She knows you. She does not sit on anyone's lap, and she definitely does not lean back into their chest." Even after eight months of her not seeing her mom, there was still a connection there.

That last visit, the parents told me to stay. Dad said, "We like it when you're here."

I took pictures and videos. They played with Hannah for a bit. Thirty minutes in, Mom lost interest and started talking to the social worker and me. Forty-five minutes in, Dad lost interest. Then the hour was over. People fear biological parents stealing kids back; our situation did not support this myth. That visit meant more to me than to them.

I've run into her mom a few times and excitedly whipped out my phone. "Let me show you pictures!" She reluctantly obliges.

At court, the parents clearly felt heavy and sad. Three days later, we had this visit. It was like they'd lost one hundred pounds. They seemed at peace. They didn't have a place to live and were fighting such odds. To accept they were done fighting for their child must have been a huge relief.

Hannah sees her biological sister a couple times a month. At first I referred to her by her name, Jaden. Then I realized everything about Hannah's adoption should be part of her consciousness. I started talking to Hannah about her story when she was very young. It's awkward, so I practiced before she could understand it.

Hannah's story includes Jaden. I can't randomly tell Hannah, "You know your friend Jaden? She's actually your sister." I now refer to Jaden as "your sister Jaden."

At about three years old, she asked, "My sister?" I explained it to her. Now that we've told the story enough times, she knows both of them grew in Mommy Holly's tummy. They have different adoptive moms. They'll go to school together and have a relationship.

Even in the short time I had with the birth parents, I made a relationship with them and their people. We come from such different paths, and I feel lucky that I get to know them. They bounce around and are likely living on the streets. Mom is really beautiful, and I think she's sex-trafficked. It's pretty easy for her to find a man who will take her in and feed her. Her life is horrific. She was eighteen when she gave up Hannah, but developmentally, she was probably six. She's lived in the streets since she was about twelve. The only way that we could help her was by changing the cycle—Hannah is not going to live the same life that she lived. Hannah's children will not be in foster care.

I care about the biological family. I grew very attached. Hannah's mom will always be part of our family. I think about her almost every day. She and the biological dad are a mess, but they gave us our daughter. I will always be indebted to them. I will always know that they had to give up so much for us.

Favorite Memory

Hannah was about ten months old. I loved her and thought, *All the other foster moms are so jealous of me because I got the best baby.* I honestly felt guilty going to the Baby Signs classes with other moms.

My inner dialogue told me, *I don't know if I should go, because I have this baby who is so good and I don't want to rub it in the other moms' faces. She's the best baby in the world, and they have to look at her and realize they didn't get the best baby.*

One night, I said to the leader out loud, "Is everyone jealous of me?"

"Of what?" she replied.

"Because I have the best baby?"

She looked up at Hannah, running around the room, screaming, and at all the other babies, sitting on their moms' laps, and said, "*Nobody* thinks that you have the best baby."

"What?" I scanned the room and knew I'd better adopt her.

Philip and I had reached the point where we thought our kid was so much better than every other kid.

Logistics

When we bought our house, it had three bedrooms and a garage and we had four kids. When we decided to foster, we expanded our living room for more living space. We made half of the garage into a laundry room and a bedroom. Since then, we've changed the other half into two bedrooms. We have another area, where we added a wall for another bedroom.

Everyone has their own space. The only thing that's hard right now is, the girls all share a bathroom. That's a lot of hair.

I take care of them as far as getting them to and from school until fourth grade. In fourth grade, they switch to a school that's right near our house. So, from fourth grade on, they get themselves to and from school, they make their own lunches. Right now, I only have one kid I really need to take care of. Because we have a big family, my kids didn't do after-school activities unless they could get themselves to them. One of my daughters does swimming, but it's because she can ride her bike to the swimming pool.

I'm probably one of the slower-paced people I know. I don't run around, taking them to activities and playdates. They do it on their own.

We don't have to drive much. We walk downtown all the time in twenty minutes. Now, I'm totally spoiled because I have all these babysitters at home.

Support

Regardless of the fact that I didn't give birth to Hannah and regardless of the fact that we didn't know how long she'd stay with us, we had a baby. Some people didn't acknowledge her at all. They may not understand; they don't know whether or not the baby is staying. It's not biological. I don't know, but their answer was to not say anything. It hurt.

After we brought our biological kids home from the hospital, people brought us dinners. There were no dinners with Hannah. Even if Hannah didn't stay, I was still up all night.

I don't mean "acknowledgment" like they didn't have a present. I mean it was like the baby was invisible. One person brought us a baby gift—the only gift we received. It was a baby bathtub filled with baby stuff, none of it used. It brings tears to Philip's eyes. She wasn't even a close friend, more of an acquaintance.

It reminds me of when you fall in love with someone. You bring him for the first time to meet your parents, and your parents ignore him. I was so in love with this kid. I wanted my friends and family to meet her, and no one wanted to meet her. This cranky kid with a prickly personality and bad eczema always looked like an uncomfortable mess. I loved her so much, and it made me really sad that others only saw the uncomfortable mess.

Philip's parents held back a little bit. They didn't acknowledge Hannah until she was adopted. They needed to know she would stay. They'd say, "Look, we have a new granddaughter!"

"You had one before. You just didn't talk to her."

My parents really surprised me. They came down to meet her right away and always referred to her as their granddaughter.

Before we started fostering, we sent out a letter to our friends and family letting them know if they saw us with a new child, it was likely a foster child and I was just going to introduce the child as part of our family.

If I did it again, I would be more proactive in asking for support: diaper donations, meals, etc.

Our county is perfect for fostering, big enough that we receive funding, small enough that everyone knows everyone. We have a network of foster-parent support on Facebook. I am a hub leader, and I have ten families under me. Someone in my hub can text me, "I got a newborn yesterday." I get on Facebook and write, "Sandra just got a newborn. Here's what she needs." Within ten minutes, I have ten responses. People will request support: "We are heading out of town, and we need respite for the week." If the kid is in foster care, you may not be able to take them with you. Also, foster parents need to connect with other foster parents, someone who gets it and isn't going to tell you there is something wrong with your kid.

In many places, you get twelve hours of classes, you're handed a kid, and you're on your own. Our county offers tons of classes, and they're always free. They helped me know what to expect and how to help Hannah. Every kid in foster care wouldn't be there unless something happened to them.

We've had some pretty difficult kids come through our house, and yet there is nothing that the child has done or said that I was shocked at, because it is all something I learned about in class. I could say, "I know where this behavior comes from."

Benefits of Adopting from Foster Care

As far as starting a family goes, I don't think people realize foster-to-adopt is free. You are reimbursed while you are fostering and even after you adopt. Hannah gets a stipend every month until she turns eighteen. She receives Medi-Cal until she is eighteen. If she needs any services, she gets services—therapy, physical therapy, any kind of therapy. Financially, it's a great deal.

You also get to know the child to find out if it's a good fit. You can love any child, but it's not always that crazy, motherly, love-them-so-much love, and I've learned over the years that it's about temperament. Does the child's temperament fit with your family? Do their rhythms match your family's rhythms?

Hannah was not the first kid we fostered who needed to be adopted. We fostered a little girl named Summer for ten months. We didn't adopt Summer, but I see her almost every day. She lives just three blocks from us. The day care provider we hired to provide care for her adopted her.

We were all morning people, and Summer hated the morning. Our rhythms were off. All of my [biological] kids are screaming, yelling, temper-tantrum kids. Summer cried silently. It threw me. I didn't know what was wrong with her. I kept asking myself, *Why isn't she screaming?* I didn't know what to do with silent tears; they would send me over the edge.

Everything was just a little off.

Summer landed in just the right family. It's a perfect fit. They're crazy about her, and I get to be her auntie. Then Hannah came along, and we knew, *Now,* this *is the perfect fit.* She screams and yells, and I can handle that. [Laughs.]

We have lots of social gatherings with foster and adoptive parents. We can't tell which kids are adopted, which kids are foster kids, which kids are birth—they're all the same. They're all beautiful kids.

The news reports are terrible, and people miss all of the good stuff. There are a million stories about perfectly normal, beautiful families. I love that about fostering and adoption. It is only in this world where families can change so much in one year. One year, the family is two people thinking, *We may want to have a family.* The next year, they have four kids.

I love meeting different foster parents and birth parents and thinking, *I would never have met these people had we not fostered.*

Advice

It's totally worth it. Even when I was at my most vulnerable. I wouldn't trade a minute. If Hannah had left, I wouldn't have given away the year I had with her. She deserved all of my love, and I deserved to have that relationship. It's a beautiful relationship.

We don't want to admit this, but we don't know how long anyone is in our life. Our biological children could die tomorrow. Enjoy it while you have it.

It's not easy to not be in control and not know what's going to happen, but I think it's been such a good lesson in life. You just live each day. Many families say, "God is in charge." Look, we're not religious, so for us, no one is in control. We just feel like whatever is meant to be will be—we're just along for the ride. You can love someone so much, but you don't have a guarantee that they're going to be there.

It wasn't that I was afraid of my heart breaking. I knew that might happen, but I knew I would survive. Foster parents will do it again and again. We have faith that we're strong enough to handle a broken heart.

People worry, *I couldn't do that, I would get too attached, and it would be too hard*. Yeah, it's hard, but you are stronger than you think, and you can handle it. It's worth it. When she belly-laughs, I cry. Every morning, she opens her eyes and says, "I love you."

When Hannah did stay, it was totally worth it. Had she left, it would have still been worth it. And we would have done it again.

CONCLUSION

....

I began *All the Sweeter* with the intention of creating a resource for parents who wanted to learn more about the true lives of families who adopt children from the US foster care system. My appreciation for the importance of this project in my own life continued to grow as I interviewed and became acquainted with families, spoke about the project with friends and family, and dove into the literature. I've taken note of themes that I thought were relevant to me, and I've summarized them below as my concluding thoughts. These are the first points that my family will refer to as we begin foster care training and, I hope, eventually adopt children through foster care. Please feel free to add to them as you begin your own foster-to-adopt journey.

1. SET BOUNDARIES, BUT BREAK THEM IF IT FEELS RIGHT.

It's okay to say no. The most pronounced example of this occurs when families, during the matching process, feel discomfort about a certain child or general characteristics of potential children.

Daniel Fletcher described telling his family's social workers they would prefer a toddler (as opposed to an infant), and that they didn't feel comfortable caring for a child with certain characteristics, such as fetal alcohol syndrome. They also preferred to foster children whose biological parents' reunification rights were already terminated. The Trevinos limited the number of children to two. In addition, they told the story of having to decline fostering a little girl with a troubled background and a potential syndrome that they weren't sure they could care for. Jason Trevino provided this advice to potential parents as they consider their boundaries: "You have to be honest with yourself. You have to really do some serious soul searching in terms of *What is my capacity?*"

Hugh Booker set boundaries when he and his husband started the foster-to-adopt process. After meeting, fostering, and adopting his boys, he has this advice: "Leave the options open. Know what you want, and start there, but when you are presented with something that may not fit your parameters, really consider it."

In other words, potential foster parents may need to set a number of boundaries to maintain their own health and happiness throughout the process of fostering and adopting. However, should an opportunity outside those boundaries present itself, give it some careful thought and remember, it's okay to say no.

2. ADOPTED OR NOT, IT HAPPENS.

Jason Trevino referenced his initial tendency to attribute his children's misbehaviors or negative characteristics to being adopted and advised other parents against this. As referenced in chapter 3, Keefer and Schooler named this thought process "insistence upon difference."[1] It's easy to want to place blame for difficult situations elsewhere—in this case, on adoption. In reality, whether or not children are adopted, parents and children have challenges; any parent won't have to think beyond the last thirty minutes to find an example. Recognizing and correcting a tendency to insist upon difference will decrease shame around adoption and will even allow children and families to take pride in being a part of a family that includes adopted children.

3. LEARN AND USE TOOLS TO AVOID ANGER.

Children, adopted or not, can test a parent's patience beyond what they previously thought possible. Traumatized children may push adopted parents to repeat a previously learned cycle of anger and abuse. Experts advise parents to learn and use tools to avoid being drawn into a child's cyclone of emotions. The Allen Pierce family references the "love and logic approach" (chapter 4). The authors of *Adopting Older Children* recommend the authoritative parenting style. In the book, *Telling the Truth to Your Adopted or Foster Child*, the authors remind parents to learn their children's triggers. Above all, rather than get angry, recognize that the child, like all children, may be progressing through a difficult phase. I think back to the example in chapter 3 of a donor-conceived son who, in a moment of anger, yells, "You're not even my father!" The father understands that his son's accusation is a symptom of puberty, and that that will pass. Instead of taking it personally and blaming the behavior on the child's being adopted, parents can avoid anger by using available tools and seeking therapeutic help whenever they need it.

4. WORK THROUGH PERSONAL ISSUES FIRST, BEFORE THEY ARISE WITH KIDS.

This theme came up in several contexts. Working through one's own issues prior to adopting will minimize the effect those issues have on children. Laura Bolton and Trisha

Pierce both referenced previous traumas they needed to work through. Several books made reference to families turning to foster care after having trouble conceiving and recommended working through the feelings of loss. The issues themselves will, of course, be different for each parent: anger, alcoholism, difficulty raising challenging topics, sexual abuse, etc. What is important is our willingness to recognize them, work through them, and be aware of the effect they can have on adopted children.

5. SOLIDIFY A SUPPORT SYSTEM.

Support systems can come in many forms. Nearly every family mentioned some type of support in their life. Daniel Fletcher described a Friday-night program sponsored by his county that his daughter can enjoy while he and his wife have a date night. The Allen Pierce family's daughter, Celeste, participates in an after-school program that helps her with homework. They also have a network of friends who spend time with Celeste when Susanna and Trisha need a respite. Aaron Keller talked about overnight care that he hires when he needs to be out of town on business trips. Hugh Booker is thankful for their family's "angel," who shares his sons' cultural heritage and includes his sons in her family's outings and celebrations. Anna Walters found an unexpected relationship and a second family in her son's first foster family. At several points during our interview, Brooke Olson mentioned her gratitude for the tremendous role her extended family plays in the lives of her daughters, Shelby and Dakota. The Watts and Schneider parents mentioned family and friends who are the same race as their children, and how that gives their kids opportunities to learn about and participate in their birth culture. Laura Bolton mentioned other parents whom she can text when she wants to express frustration. All of the families interviewed emphasized the importance of therapists, friends, school and county programs, and community and family members who provide essential support.

6. RAISE ISSUES FOR CONVERSATION.

It can be scary to talk about adoption, race, trauma, gender, birth parents, and many other topics that surround foster care and adoption. Experts agree that even if children aren't raising these topics, they're thinking about them. Having conversations about these issues reminds children that these topics are safe to discuss with parents. By listening, parents can understand their child's thoughts on a subject and provide guidance and a sense of normalcy regarding any important issues in their family's life.

7. POSTADOPTION ASSISTANCE IS A MAJOR NEED.

Many, though not all, of the families interviewed mentioned a need for postadoption assistance. Some parents did not express frustration with finding assistance that met their needs. Brooke Olson, for example, worked with her daughter's school to set up an IEP. Others, such as the Allen Pierce family, had trouble keeping the attention of the social workers responsible for facilitating the relationship between them and their daughter's birth family. The Butlers have been on their own in finding assistance for autism-related symptoms and have been frustrated by trying to locate services.

Author and adoptive parent Adam Pertman wrote:

> *The research on adoptees shows they generally grow up to be pretty much like everybody else. However, there is no question whatsoever that boys and girls who have been abused and neglected (which is why they were placed in foster care) or who have spent considerable time in*

orphanages or other institutions will invariably have problems that must be addressed—often in a long-term and sustained manner—and that their parents will require assistance to help their families succeed. This is why, as the percentage of children adopted from foster care and from other countries has risen, post-adoption services have undeniably become the biggest need in the field.[2]

Any parent moving through foster care training will want to pay attention to how to access these services and organize them in advance of fostering a child. As Daniel Fletcher pointed out, it's easy to disregard aspects of foster-parent training that don't seem immediately relevant. His advice is to keep that resource information handy, even if parents don't think they will use it.

8. PARENTS NEED TO BE "GOOD ENOUGH," NOT PERFECT.

There are many times when parents, whether or not their children are adopted from foster care, become frustrated and question their ability to parent. Lori Butler told me a story about crying in her car after one of her children acted out at the grocery store and a fellow customer questioned her parenting skills. Carolyn Nash, who wrote *Raising Abel*, describes a conversation she had with her therapist after many disheartening moments with her son. Her therapist starts the conversation:

> *"There's one thing to keep in mind: the only kind of parent you need to be is good enough. That's all anyone can hope for. You are going to make mistakes. Try to learn from them and move on. Don't spend time punishing yourself. Key words?"*
> *"Good enough," I said.[3]*

When questioning your own ability to parent, remember that no one has to be perfect, only good enough. This premise allows parents to refrain from being unnecessarily hard on themselves.

9. SUCCESS COMES IN MANY FORMS.

When I began talking about writing this book, I mentioned the idea to an acquaintance at a retreat. I told her my motivation: One day, I would like to adopt from the foster care system. I would like to enter the process as prepared as possible and be able to share what I learn with others.

She thought for a second and asked, "Have you thought about how you will feel when you speak to other parents and you aren't able to boast about your child?"

It was an innocent question but also a marker of assumptions easily made about kids from the foster care system: first, that it would be impossible for a foster care child to have accomplishments similar to any other child's; second, that my genes would combine with someone else's genes to become a child to boast about; third, that accomplishments of a child who got off to a rough start would be less valuable than those of a biological child, and that I therefore would not be able to boast about them. This third and last point warrants additional discussion. It's not about a kid's first-place finish in a spelling bee or admission to a top college, although those accomplishments would be wonderful and are entirely possible. While I was writing this book, what struck me was the value of raising a child who did not have a good start in life, and how one finds value not only in the joy that child will bring to any family, but also the difference a family can make in that child's life. It may be a challenge for parents who adopt children from foster care to maintain a conscious awareness of the many opportunities to boast about their children. Boast worthy accomplishments may be SAT scores, soccer championships, and acceptances to Ivy League schools, but also may be less traditional.

For the Bolton family, the story of the hug that Hannah finally gave to Laura brought tears to my eyes. The Butler family's perseverance on behalf of Libby to ensure she had correct medications was awe-inspiring. An entire community sending letters on behalf of the McPherson family to facilitate Christian's safe return was unheard of. The fact that the Walters family created a relationship so strong with Colby's first foster parents that they became his godparents and often coparents with his adoptive mother, Anna, filled me with hope about potential support systems for anyone adopting from foster care.

Families who adopt children from foster care have plenty of options for boasting, should they choose to. Like the families themselves, the topics for the kind of pride that results in boasting just may not be thought of as traditional.

10. LIFE WITH A CHILD ADOPTED FROM FOSTER CARE WILL BE ALL THE SWEETER.

Before I left for Peace Corps Malawi, a returned Peace Corps volunteer who had served in Malawi many years before told me that when she encountered situations that she was unsure she could handle, she repeated to herself, "People adapt." When I faced similar situations in my own Peace Corps service, that mantra helped, and I still use it today. As I consider embarking on the journey through foster care and adoption, situations that I have not encountered before will no doubt arise. However, unlike those Peace Corps experiences that required me to adapt to things that would not change during my time of service (living without running water and electricity, for example), experiences of the fost-adopt journey can be addressed, worked through, and improved upon, and those involved can ultimately benefit from having worked through the challenge.

I will be forever grateful to the many families who provided an intimate view into the situations they've encountered and conquered. They have allowed me and other potential parents to better prepare for fostering, adopting, and raising children. Their stories exemplify how the joy of parenthood is that much greater because of their challenges, rather than in spite of them. As with my Peace Corps mantra, "People adapt," remembering that life will be all the sweeter on the other side of difficulties makes tough situations seem less daunting and more surmountable. It might even become an aspect of parenting to eagerly, albeit cautiously, anticipate.

Finally, the families in these stories clearly emit super-hero-like qualities, although not a single one would identify himself or herself as a superhero. The families of *All the Sweeter* are just like you and me; in fact, we may have stood behind them the last time we were in line at the grocery store. As Jeffrey Schneider said, "If you have the heart, if you have the desire, you will overcome any sort of issues or any sort of problems. If you are really thinking about taking the step to expand your family, and that's what you feel in your heart that you want to do, do it." When it comes to those involved in the lives of children adopted from foster care, everyone can be a superhero.

FOSTER-ADOPTION STEPS

....

1. Initiate contact with an agency specializing in foster care and adoption, or work directly with your county's office responsible for foster care. To find an agency, speak to others who have adopted through foster care for their recommendations. An Internet search will also likely turn up several agencies available in your county and state of residence.

2. Attend agency orientations. Agencies hold orientations on a regular basis to introduce potential parents to the process and allow parents a chance to meet the staff. Attend several to get an idea of how each agency works and which might be a good fit for your family. Consider the resources they do and do not provide.

3. Complete foster care training and a home study. The requirements may vary from state to state and even agency to agency. Generally, foster-parent training consists of eight to twelve two- to three-hour classes, but it can also comprise several all-day classes.

A home study is a written report completed by a caseworker that includes information about your family and home (relationships, financials, health status, background checks, etc.) and serves as a foster-parent application to your state's licensing agency. The home-study process takes three to six months, depending on how quickly your family can complete the requirements.

4. Match with a child or children. Once the state has licensed your family for foster care, your home will be available for a foster child. The time from approval to placement varies dramatically, based on a family's openness to children. Generally, the fewer restrictions a family requires for its potential child's characteristics (number of siblings, ethnicity, religion, health status, age, etc.), the shorter the time to match will be. The way the match occurs will vary by agency and by a family's participation in opportunities to meet children.

5. Foster-parent. After a child's or children's placement in your home, there is a statutory waiting period before adoption finalization; this varies case by case and state by state. During this time, if the child's parents have not yet had their rights terminated, the child may have visits with one or more biological family members in an effort to reunify them. If reunification is successful, the child returns to his or her biological family. Once a parent's rights are terminated, which may occur before the child enters your home, the child becomes legally free for adoption.

6. Finalize the adoption. Once the child is legally cleared to move forward with finalization, you will likely receive case files on your child and need to fill out additional forms. Eventually, you will work with your state and agency to set a date for finalization. Again, this varies by case and state, from the simple issuing of a legal decree to a celebration in a courtroom.

7. Forever-family bonding and growth. Postadoption, each parent and child will intentionally attach and bond. Some require more focus than others. As desired and needed, families can access postadoption services through their agency, governments, or community resources. Parents can create life books with their children to tell their story preadoption and track their lives as they create family memories together.

ENDNOTES

....

INTRODUCTION

1. Nia Vardalos, *Instant Mom* (New York: HarperOne, 2013), 52.

2. Children's Bureau, AFCARS Reports #10–#25, US Department of Health & Human Services, https://www.acf.hhs.gov/cb/research-data-technology/statistics-research/afcars.

3. Ibid.

4. Ibid.

5. Joyce A. Martin et al., "Births: Final Data for 2015," *National Vital Statistics Reports* 66, no. 1 (January 2017): 4, http://www.cdc.gov/nchs/data/nvsr/nvsr66/nvsr66_01.pdf.

6. UCSF Center for Reproductive Health, "Risk Factors for Men and Women," http://coe.ucsf.edu/ivf/risk.html.

7. A. R. Appel, "Legal Issues in Lesbian and Gay Adoption," in *Adoption by Lesbians and Gay Men: A New Dimension in*

Family Diversity, eds. David Brodzinsky and Adam Pertman (New York: Oxford University Press, 2011), 36–51.

8. J. Jones, "Who Adopts? Characteristics of Women and Men Who Have Adopted Children," NCHS Data Brief 12 (January 2009): 1–8.

9. US Department of State—Bureau of Consular Affairs, "Statistics," 2015, http://travel.state.gov/content/adoptions-abroad/en/about-us/statistics.html.

10. Ibid.

11. S. Vandivere, K. Malm, and L. Radel, *Adoption USA: A Chartbook Based on the 2007 National Survey of Adoptive Parents* (Washington, DC: US Department of Health and Human Services, Office of the Assistant Secretary for Planning and Evaluation, 2009), 4; US Department of State—Bureau of Consular Affairs, http://travel.state.gov/content/adoptionsa-broad/en/country-information/learn-about-a-country/china.html; Adam Pertman, *Adoption Nation: How the Adoption Revolution Is Transforming Our Families—and America* (Boston: The Harvard Common Press, 2011), 30, 72, 75.

12. Child Welfare Information Gateway, "Planning for Adoption: Knowing the Costs and Resources," Factsheet for Families, US Department of Health & Human Services, November 2016, https://www.childwelfare.gov/pubPDFs/s_costs.pdf#page=2&view=Adoption-specific%20expenses.

CHAPTER 3: HELPING YOUR CHILDREN UNDERSTAND FOSTER CARE AND ADOPTION

1. Joshua Gamson, *Modern Families* (New York: New York University Press, 2015), 204.

2. Stephanie Bosco-Ruggiero, Gloria Russo Wassell, and Victor Groza, *Adopting Older Children* (Far Hills, NJ: New Horizon Press, 2014), 99–101.

3. Betsy Keefer and Jayne E. Schooler, *Telling the Truth to Your Adopted or Foster Child: Making Sense of the Past* (Westport, CT: Bergin and Garvey, 2000), 17.

4. Jill Krementz, *How It Feels to Be Adopted* (New York: Alfred A. Knopf, 2006), 16.

5. Friends in Adoption, "Adoption Terminology," http://www.friendsinadoption.org/adoption-resources/for-potential-adoptive-parents/resources-for-adoptive-families/adoption-terms/.

6. Rachel Garlinghouse, *Come Rain or Come Shine* (North Charleston, SC: CreateSpace, 2012), 164.

7. David Brodzinsky, "Children's Understanding of Adoption: Developmental and Clinical Implications," *Professional Psychology: Research and Practice* 42, no. 2 (April 2011): 200–207.

8. Betsy Keefer and Jayne E. Schooler, *Telling the Truth to Your Adopted or Foster Child: Making Sense of the Past* (Westport, CT: Bergin and Garvey, 2000).

9. Vardalos, *Instant Mom*, 182.

10. Brodzinsky, "Children's Understanding of Adoption," 201–202.

11. Ibid., 203.

12. Sherrie Eldridge, *Twenty Things Adopted Kids Wish Their Adoptive Parents Knew* (New York: Dell Publishing, 1999), 5.

13. Keefer and Schooler, *Telling the Truth*, 59.

14. Eldridge, *Twenty Things*, 10.

15. Keefer and Schooler, *Telling the Truth*, 87.

16. Brodzinsky, "Children's Understanding of Adoption," 202.

17. Keefer and Schooler, *Telling the Truth*, 61.

18. Veerle Provoost, "Do Kids Think of Sperm Donors as Families?" TEDxGhent, filmed June 2016, http://www.ted.com/talks/veerle_provoost_do_kids_think_of_sperm_donors_as_family#t-474440.

19. Keefer and Schooler, *Telling the Truth*, 78.

20. Ibid., 63.

21. Betsy Keefer and Jayne E. Schooler, *Telling the Truth to Your Adopted or Foster Child: Making Sense of the Past* (Westport, CT: Bergin and Garvey, 2000).

22. Deborah A. Beasley, *Successful Foster Care Adoption: A Guide to State Adoption and Parenting Adopted Children* (Deadwood, OR: Together at Last Family Press, of Wyatt-MacKenzie, 2012), 37.

23. Pertman, *Adoption Nation*, 228.

24. Guest Contributor, "Favorite Adoption Themed Children's Books," Children's Home Society of Minnesota/

Lutheran Social Service of Minnesota, accessed February 2017, https://chlss.org/blog/favorite-adoption-themed-books/.

25. Creating a Family, "Books to Help Prepare Kids for the Adoption of a Sibling," accessed February 2017, https://creatingafamily.org/adoption/adoptionsuggestedbooks/books-help-prepare-children-adoption-sibling/.

26. Bosco-Ruggiero, Wassell, and Groza, *Adopting Older Children*, 83.

27. Ibid., 87

28. Garlinghouse, *Come Rain or Come Shine*, 116.

29. Keefer and Schooler, *Telling the Truth*, 5.

CHAPTER 4: AN INSPIRING TOOLBOX, RITUALS INCLUDED: THE ALLEN PIERCE FAMILY

1. Adoption & Disclosure, Alaska Center for Resource Families, http://www.acrf.org/assets/Files/Adoption%20Disclosure%20Guide%20Final%2010_2015(1).pdf: "Disclosure is the sharing of information about a child who is in the child welfare system and is moving from foster care into a more permanent placement such as adoption, foster care or relative placement. Information often cannot be shared during foster care placement because of confidentiality restrictions, but as children move toward adoption, potential adoptive parents need and have the right to more complete information."

CHAPTER 5: UNINTENTIONAL FOST-ADOPT: THE KELLER FAMILY

1. "A Foster Care to Adoption Guide," Together We Rise, https://www.togetherwerise.org/foster-to-adopt.pdf: Between the time when a child comes to live with a family and the adoption finalization, a family's adoption agency will "monitor the placement for a period of time that averages around six months, but can also range from a few weeks to a year." During this time, the court may allow birth parents to call and or visit with the child.

CHAPTER 6: DIVERSE FAMILIES REFORM THE NORM

1. Sandra Coontz, *The Way We Never Were* (New York: Basic Books, 2016), 31.

2. Sandra Coontz, *The Way We Really Are* (New York: Basic Books, 1997), 38.

3. Dates and basic plotlines retrieved from Wikipedia entries:

> *Leave It to Beaver*: en.wikipedia.org/wiki/ Leave_It_to_Beaver
>
> *Ozzie and Harriet*: en.wikipedia.org/wiki/ The_Adventures_of_Ozzie_and_Harriet
>
> *The Brady Bunch*: en.wikipedia.org/wiki/ The_Brady_Bunch
>
> *Diff'rent Strokes*: en.wikipedia.org/wiki/ Diff'rent_Strokes
>
> *The Fresh Prince of Bel-Air*: en.wikipedia.org/wiki/ The_Fresh_Prince_of_Bel-Air

Gilmore Girls: en.wikipedia.org/wiki/Gilmore_Girls

Modern Family: en.wikipedia.org/wiki/Modern_Family

"17 TV Shows That Celebrate Nontraditional Families,"CafeMom, thestir.cafemom.com/tv/193443/17_tv_shows_that_celebrate/149413/the_fresh_prince_of_bel/1?stir_start_slideshow_btn=1.

4. "Obergefell et al. v. Hodges, Director, Ohio Department of Health, et. al.," syllabus, Supreme Court of the United States, https://www.supremecourt.gov/opinions/14pdf/14-556_3204.pdf; "Landmark US Supreme Court Ruling Legalizes Gay Marriage Nationwide," Reuters, June 27, 2015, www.reuters.com/article/us-usa-court-gay-marriage-idUSKBN0P61SW20150628; MAP, LGBT foster care laws by state, www.lgbtmap.org/equality-maps/foster_and_adoption_laws; LGBT adoptions laws by state: www.lgbtmap.org/equality-maps/foster_and_adoption_laws.

5. Rosanna Hertz, *Single by Chance, Mothers by Choice* (New York: Oxford University Press, 2006), 13.

6. Child Welfare Information Gateway, "Home Study Requirements for Prospective Foster Parents," US Department of Health & Human Services, 2014, https://www.childwelfare.gov/pubPDFs/homestudyreqs.pdf.

7. Gamson, *Modern Families*, 8.

8. Susan Golombok, *Modern Families: Parents and Children in New Family Forms* (Cambridge, UK: Cambridge University Press, 2015).

9. Gamson, *Modern Families*, 88.

10. "More Support for Gun Rights, Gay Marriage Than in 2008 or 2004," Pew Research Center, April 25, 2012, http://www.people-press.org/files/legacy-pdf/4-25-12%20 Social%20Issues.pdf.

11. Andrew R. Flores, "Examining Variation in Surveying Attitudes on Same-Sex Marriage: A Meta-Analysis," *Public Opinion Quarterly* 79, no. 2 (May 2015): 580–93.

12. Gamson, *Modern Families*, 9.

13. Bosco-Ruggiero, Wassell, and Groza, *Adopting Older Children*, 211.

14. Child Welfare Information Gateway, "Frequently Asked Questions from Lesbian, Gay, Bisexual, Transgender, and Questioning (LGBTQ) Prospective Foster and Adoptive Parents," US Department of Health & Human Services, 2016, https://www.childwelfare.gov/pubPDFs/faq_lgbt.pdf; Pertman, *Adoption Nation*, 208: "Nearly everyone who works in the fields of reproduction, child care, and adoption agrees that the rate of gay and lesbian parenting is climbing exponentially."

15. Don Romesburg, "Where She Comes From: Locating Queer Transracial Adoption," *QED: A Journal in GLBTQ Worldmaking*, Michigan State University Press, fall 2014, 4.

16. Hertz, *Single by Chance*, 18.

17. US Census Bureau, "Families and Living Arrangements, Marital Status, Table MS-2. Estimated Median Age at First Marriage, by Sex: 1890 to the Present," accessed February 2017, http://www.census.gov/hhes/families/data/marital.html.

18. Coontz, *The Way We Really Are*, 79.

19. KIDS COUNT Data Center, "Children in Single-Parent Families," http://datacenter.kidscount.org/data/tables/106-children-in-single-parent-families#detailed/1/any/false/573,133,16,11/any/429,430.

20. Children's Bureau, "AFCARS Report #25," US Department of Health & Human Services, https://www.acf.hhs.gov/sites/default/files/cb/afcarsreport23.pdf.

21. Children's Bureau, "AFCARS Report #12," US Department of Health & Human Services, https://www.acf.hhs.gov/sites/default/files/cb/afcarsreport12.pdf.

22. We Hear the Children, http://www.wehearthechildren.org/We_Hear_The_Children/Welcome.html; Jennifer Luden, "Single Dads by Choice: More Men Going It Alone," NPR, June 19, 2012, http://www.npr.org/2012/06/19/154860588/single-dads-by-choice-more-men-going-it-alone; Elizabeth Kramer, "More Single Men Are Choosing to Become Fathers," KHOU11, June 19, 2016, http://www.khou.com/ext/news/nation-now/more-single-men-are-choosing-to-become-fathers/285/5v6XlwyGLSkeiQmyuKieso; 411 4 Dad, http://www.4114dad.com/4114DAD/411-4-DAD.html.

23. Hertz, *Single by Chance*, 11.

24. Steve Inskeep, "When Grandma's House Is Home: The Rise of Grandfamilies," NPR, December 15, 2014, http://www.npr.org/2014/12/15/369366596/when-grandmas-house-is-home-the-rise-of-grandfamilies.

25. Vandivere, Malm, and Radel, *Adoption USA*.

26. Pertman, *Adoption Nation*, 115.

27. Gretchen Livingston, "Fewer Than Half of US Kids Today Live in a 'Traditional' Family," Pew Research Center, December 22, 2014, http://www.pewresearch.org/fact-tank/2014/12/22/less-than-half-of-u-s-kids-today-live-in-a-traditional-family/.

CHAPTER 9: TRANSRACIAL ADOPTION

1. A survey referenced in *The Family Nobody Wanted* showed that social workers continue to believe that it is valuable to match physical and mental characteristics of adoptive parents and children. The beliefs of these contemporary social workers mirror those of adoption practitioners Carl and Helen Doss encountered in the 1950s. One social worker dismissed the couple's request for a mixed-race child because, she said, "I would rather see a child raised in an orphanage than by parents who look so different."

2. Helen Doss, *The Family Nobody Wanted* (Boston: Northeastern University Press, 2001).

3. "Our History," Holt International, accessed March 2017, http://www.holtinternational.org/about/.

4. Rhonda Roorda, *In Their Voices: Black Americans on Transracial Adoption* (New York: Columbia University Press, 2015), 5.

5. Jacqueline Macaulay and Stewart Macaulay, "Adoption for Black Children: A Case Study of Expert Discretion," *Research in Law and Sociology* 1 (1978): 265–318, http://law.wisc.edu/facstaff/macaulay/papers/adoption_black.pdf.

6. Josie Crolley-Simic and M. Elizabeth Vonk, "White International Transracial Adoptive Mothers' Reflections

on Race," *Child & Family Social Work* 16, no. 2 (September 2010): 169–78.

7. "History," National Association of Black Social Workers, accessed March 2017, http://nabsw.org/?page=History.

8. William Gregory, *Adopting Through Foster Care: Lessons & Reflections from Our Journey Through the Maze* (William Gregory, 2013).

9. Children's Bureau, AFCARS Reports #10–#25, US Department of Health & Human Services, https://www.acf.hhs.gov/cb/research-data-technology/statistics-research/afcars.

10. Elizabeth Vonk, "Cultural Competence for Transracial Adoptive Parents," *Social Work* 46, no. 3 (July 2001): 246–55.

11. Deborah Gray, *Attaching in Adoption: Practical Tools for Today's Parents* (London: Jessica Kingsley Publishers, 2002), 158.

12. Vonk, "Cultural Competence."

13. Jaiya John, *Black Baby White Hands: A View from the Crib* (Silver Spring, MD: Soul Water Rising, 2005), 189.

14. Krementz, *How It Feels*, 16.

15. Garlinghouse, *Come Rain or Come Shine*, 199–207.

16. Roorda, *In Their Voices*, 193.

17. Beth Hall and Gail Steinberg, *Inside Transracial Adoption* (London: Jessica Kingsley Publishers, 2013), 22.

18. Keefer and Schooler, *Telling the Truth*, 140.

19. Hall and Steinberg, *Inside Transracial Adoption*, 42.

20. Roorda, *In Their Voices*, 22.

21. Ibid., 290.

22. Roorda, *In Their Voices*, 217.

23. Garlinghouse, *Come Rain or Come Shine*, 134.

24. John, *Black Baby*, 205.

25. Ibid., 206–207.

26. Keefer and Schooler, *Telling the Truth*, 147.

27. Ibid., 148.

28. Vonk, "Cultural Competence."

29. Garlinghouse, *Come Rain or Come Shine*, 128.

30. Rhonda Roorda, *In Their Voices: Black Americans on Transracial Adoption* (New York: Columbia University Press, 2015), 309-316.

31. Richard R. Massatti, M. Elizabeth Vonk, and Thomas K. Gregoire, "Reliability and Validity of the Transracial Adoption Parenting Scale," *Research on Social Work Practice* 14, no. 1 (January 2004): 43–50.

32. Beasley, *Successful Foster Care Adoption*, 153.

CHAPTER 11: GIRLS: 6, BOYS: 1, GAME OVER: THE BUTLER FAMILY

1. "Older Parent Adoption," Adoption.com, https://adoption.com/older-parent-adoption: "In the past, the upper age limits for adopting parents followed by domestic private agencies was set by a 40-year 'rule of thumb:' adopting parents shouldn't be more than 40 years older than the child they wanted to adopt. Today, that age limit is creeping up as the Baby Boomer generation changes definitions and perceptions about age, health, physical limitations, and life span. More and more agencies are encouraging older persons to consider infant adoption."

CHAPTER 12: RAISING A CHILD WITH A HISTORY OF TRAUMA

1. Resources for Parents and Caregivers: Understanding Trauma, retrieved March 2017, http://www.nctsn.org/resources/audiences/parents-caregivers.

2. Bosco-Ruggiero, Wassell, and Groza, *Adopting Older Children*, 180.

3. Ibid..,123.

4. Beasley, *Successful Foster Care Adoption*, 122.

5. William Gregory, *Adopting Through Foster Care*.

6. Gregory C. Keck and Regina M. Kupecky, *Adopting the Hurt Child: Hope for Families with Special-Needs Kids* (Carol Stream, IL: NavPress, 2009), 94-95.

7. Gray, *Attaching in Adoption*, 17.

8. Ibid., 21.

9. Ibid., 69.

10. Gregory C. Keck and Regina M. Kupecky, *Adopting the Hurt Child: Hope for Families with Special-Needs Kids* (Carol Stream, IL: NavPress, 2009), 70.

11. Jamie Marich, "Post-Traumatic Stress Disorder: Reactive Attachment Disorder & Disinhibited Social Engagement Disorder Criteria," retrieved March 2017, http://www.gulfbend.org/poc/view_doc.php?type=doc&id=55745&cn=109.

12. Keck and Kupecky, *Adopting the Hurt Child*, 34–49.

13. W. David Lohr and Faye Jones, "Mental Health Issues in Foster Care," *Pediatric Annals* 45, no. 10 (October 2016): 342–48.

14. US Department of Veterans Affairs, "PTSD in Children and Teens," http://www.ptsd.va.gov/public/family/ptsd-children-adolescents.asp.

15. US Department of Veterans Affairs, "Very Young Trauma Survivors: The Role of Attachment," (PTSD: National Center for PTSD), retrieved March 2017, http://www.ptsd.va.gov/public/family/very_young_trauma_survivors.asp.

16. US Department of Veterans Affairs, "PTSD in Children and Teens," (PTSD: National Center for PTSD), retrieved March 2017, http://www.ptsd.va.gov/public/family/ptsd-children-adolescents.asp.

17. Christy Owen, "PTSD from Childhood Trauma as a Precursor to Attachment Issues," *Fidei et Veritatis: e Liberty University Journal of Graduate Research 1, no. 2* (2015), accessed

March 2017, http://digitalcommons.liberty.edu/cgi/view-content.cgi?article=1036&context=fidei_et_veritatis.

18. "Attention-Deficit/Hyperactivity Disorder (ADHD): The Basics," National Institute of Mental Health, accessed March 2017, https://www.nimh.nih.gov/health/publications/attention-deficit-hyperactivity-disorder-adhd-the-basics/qf-16-3572_153275.pdf.

19. Lohr and Jones, "Mental Health Issues."

20. Ole Jakob Storebø, Pernille Darling Rasmussen, and Erik Simonsen, "Association Between Insecure Attachment and ADHD: Environmental Mediating Factors," *Journal of Attention Disorders* 20, no. 2 (2016), accessed March 2017, http://journals.sagepub.com/doi/pdf/10.1177/1087054713501079.

21. Rebecca Ruiz, "How Childhood Trauma Could Be Mistaken for ADHD," *Atlantic*, accessed March 2017, https://www.theatlantic.com/health/archive/2014/07/how-childhood-trauma-could-be-mistaken-for-adhd/373328/.

22. Beasley, *Successful Foster Care Adoption*, 100.

23. Vardalos, *Instant Mom*, 218.

24. Keck and Kupecky, *Adopting the Hurt Child*, 32.

25. Keck and Kupecky, *Adopting the Hurt Child*, 182–91.

26. National Institute of Mental Health, "Attention Deficit/Hyperactivity Disorder."

27. Keck and Kupecky, *Adopting the Hurt Child*, 169.

28. Child Welfare Information Gateway, "Selecting and Working with a Therapist Skilled in Adoption," US Department of Health & Human Services, accessed March 2017, https://www.childwelfare.gov/pubs/f-therapist/.

29. Jayne E. Schooler, Betsy Keefer, and Timothy J. Callahan, *Wounded Children, Healing Homes* (Colorado Springs, CO: NavPress, 2009), 24.

30. Keefer and Schooler, *Telling the Truth*, 66.

31. Bosco-Ruggiero, Wassell, and Groza, *Adopting Older Children*, 185.

32. Keck and Kupecky, *Adopting the Hurt Child*, 74.

33. Eldridge, *Twenty Things*, 159.

34. Bosco-Ruggiero, Wassell, and Groza, *Adopting Older Children*, 192.

35. "Understanding IEPs," Understood, https://www.understood.org/en/school-learning/special-services/ieps/understanding-individualized-education-programs: "A federal law called the Individuals with Disabilities Education Act (IDEA) requires that public schools create an IEP for every child receiving special education services. Kids from age 3 through high school graduation or a maximum age of 22 (whichever comes first) may be eligible for an IEP."

36. Beasley, *Successful Foster Care Adoption*, 69.

37. Keck and Kupecky, *Adopting the Hurt Child*, 211.

CHAPTER 13: UNEXPECTED BLESSING: THE WALTERS FAMILY

1. Prior to taking away a biological parent's rights and making a child available for adoption, a court will often require that the child and biological parents have the opportunity to visit with each other.

CHAPTER 15: RELATIONSHIPS BETWEEN ADOPTIVE AND BIRTH FAMILIES

1. Ann Fessler, *The Girls Who Went Away* (New York: Penguin Books, 2006).

2. Bosco-Ruggiero, Wassell, and Groza, *Adopting Older Children*, 95.

3. Krementz, *How It Feels*, 28–29.

4. Brodzinsky, "Children's Understanding of Adoption."

5. Pertman, *Adoption Nation*, 128–29.

6. Pertman, *Adoption Nation*, 128.

7. Eldridge, *Twenty Things*, 92.

8. Garlinghouse, *Come Rain or Come Shine*, 107.

9. Bosco-Ruggiero, Wassell, and Groza, *Adopting Older Children*, 98.

10. Carolyn Nash, *Raising Abel* (Carolyn Nash, 2011), 43.

11. Lois Ruskai Melina and Sharon Kaplan Roszia, *The Open Adoption Experience* (New York: William Morrow Paperbacks, 1993), 308.

12. Ibid., 423–25.

13. Ibid.

14. David Brodzinsky, "Children's Understanding of Adoption: Developmental and Clinical Implications," *Professional Psychology: Research and Practice* 42, no. 2 (April 2011): 200–207.

15. John, *Black Baby*, 331.

16. Hall and Steinberg, *Inside Transracial Adoption*, 123–24.

17. David Brodzinsky, "Children's Understanding of Adoption: Developmental and Clinical Implications," *Professional Psychology: Research and Practice* 42, no. 2 (April 2011): 200–207.

18. Eldridge, *Twenty Things*, 100.

19. Keefer and Schooler, *Telling the Truth*, 15–16.

20. Garlinghouse, *Come Rain or Come Shine*, 111.

21. Romesburg, "Where She Comes From," 17.

22. Melina and Roszia, *The Open Adoption Experience*, 426.

23. Bosco-Ruggiero, Wassell, and Groza, *Adopting Older Children*, 95.

24. Pertman, *Adoption Nation*, 144.

CONCLUSION

1. Keefer and Schooler, *Telling the Truth*, 78.

2. Pertman, *Adoption Nation*, 110.

3. Nash, *Raising Abel*, 25.

ACKNOWLEDGMENTS

···

To the families who so generously shared their stories with me: thank you for your courage, your honesty, and your candor.

To Eva, the very first person to read each draft of each chapter: You provided such valuable initial feedback. Thank you for being a wonderful friend and bedrock of support throughout the writing of this book.

Marcia, your encouragement is like none I've ever experienced. Thank you for taking the time to read and comment on each of the chapters as I wrote them.

Matthew, thank you for thinking to send that first chapter to Marcia, for your unwavering support, and for the many possibilities that lie ahead.

To my friends and family who read drafts and provided invaluable feedback on both early stages and final versions—Shannon, Vail, Nancy, Kerryann, Laurie, and Doni—thank you!

David, thank you for helping to create the opportunity for me to take on and finish this project.

Joshua, Rhonda, Adam, and Mark, I am grateful for your professional feedback and advice on both the process of writing the book and specific chapters.

To the many people who played a role in connecting me with families spanning multiple cities and multiple states: To help maintain the families' anonymity, I am not able to name you individually. Please know how much I appreciate you.

To Annie Tucker, a brilliant editor, who read every word multiple times and whose expertise guided what to keep and what to cut—thank you!

She Writes Press, thank you for shepherding me through the publishing process. SWP is a phenomenal company with a wonderful mission. I'm proud to be a part of it.

Finally, thanks to the families who care for foster children, the families who adopt children from foster care, and the many people—social workers, judges, county and agency teams, therapists, physicians, teachers, volunteers, and many more—who help create and support forever families. Together, you have positively impacted the lives of so many children.

ABOUT THE AUTHOR

Jean Minton witnessed many children lose their parents to AIDS in the early 2000s as a Peace Corps health volunteer in Malawi. This experience opened her eyes to the possibility of adopting. In San Francisco a decade later, she volunteered on the board of directors for Adopt A Special Kid (AASK), a foster-to-adopt agency. AASK's mission captured her heart and cemented her desire to create her own forever family with the help of the foster-to-adopt process. As she considered starting a family, she sought resources to help understand the foster-to-adopt process. She didn't find quite what she wanted so decided to write it herself. Minton earned a Bachelor of Science at Duke University and her MBA at UC Berkeley's Haas School of Business. She lives in Sacramento, California, works in healthcare administration, and is a Board Member for Lilliput Children's Services (a similar organization to AASK). She spends much of her time outdoors and with family and friends.

Author photo © Diana Miller Photography

SELECTED TITLES FROM SHE WRITES PRESS

She Writes Press is an independent publishing company founded to serve women writers everywhere. Visit us at www.shewritespress.com.

Filling Her Shoes: Memoir of an Inherited Family by Betsy Graziani Fasbinder. $16.95, 978-1-63152-198-0. A "sweet-bitter" story of how, with tenderness as their guide, a family formed in the wake of loss and learned that joy and grief can be entwined cohabitants in our lives.

A Leg to Stand On: An Amputee's Walk into Motherhood by Colleen Haggerty. $16.95, 978-1-63152-923-8. Haggerty's candid story of how she overcame the pain of losing a leg at seventeen— and of terminating two pregnancies as a young woman—and went on to become a mother, despite her fears.

Baffled by Love: Stories of the Lasting Impact of Childhood Trauma Inflicted by Loved Ones by Laurie Kahn. $16.95, 978-1631522260. For three decades, Laurie Kahn has treated clients who were abused as children—people who were injured by someone who professed to love them. Here, she shares stories from her own rocky childhood along with those of her clients, weaving a textured tale of the all-too-human search for the "good kind of love."

Blinded by Hope: One Mother's Journey Through Her Son's Bipolar Illness and Addiction by Meg McGuire. $16.95, 978-1-63152-125-6. A fiercely candid memoir about one mother's roller coaster ride through doubt and denial as she attempts to save her son from substance abuse and bipolar illness.

Breathe: A Memoir of Motherhood, Grief, and Family Conflict by Kelly Kittel. $16.95, 978-1-938314-78-0. A mother's heartbreaking account of losing two sons in the span of nine months—and learning, despite all the obstacles in her way, to find joy in life again.

The Great Healthy Yard Project: Our Yards, Our Children, Our Responsibility by Diane Lewis, MD. $24.95, 978-1-938314-86-5. A comprehensive look at the ways in which we are polluting our drinking water and how it's putting our children's future at risk— and what we can do to turn things around.